Questions Along the Way

Conversations With a Quantum Shaman™

by

Della Van Hise

Eye Scry Publications

Questions Along the Way
(Conversations With a Quantum Shaman)
by Della Van Hise

Copyright © 2016
by Della Van Hise and Quantum Shaman™

ISBN: 978-1-942415-09-1

Published by Eye Scry Publications
www.eyescrypublications.com

To visit the author's website, please go to:
www.quantumshaman.com

Address all inquiries to:
info@quantumshaman.com

Quantum Shaman™ is a registered trademark

For M
and for Wendy

Love is the reason.

TABLE OF CONTENTS

PART FOUR
QUESTIONS FOR THE INFINITE

ALPHA AND OMEGA

INTRODUCTION
The 4-Letter Word Known as Life

Who am I?
Where am I going?
Is there a God?
Does an afterlife exist?
Do we create our own reality?
Does life have meaning or is it only random happenings?
Are our lives predestined?
How do I know if I'm on the right path?
What am I?
Why am I here?
Who *am* I?

The first and the last question are always the same. And somewhere in between lies the proving ground which we refer to with a simple 4-letter word known as 'Life.' Perhaps for many people these gnawing and persistent questions are nothing more than passing dalliances - stray thoughts entertained as teenagers at a slumber party, but seldom more than that. But to anyone on a serious path of spiritual evolution and personal growth, these questions and others like them form the basis for what many refer to as "the path with heart" - a term used by anthropologist Carlos Castaneda to describe the process of going from an ordinary human being to becoming a man or woman of Knowledge.

In essence, it is the journey from the finite to the infinite, from what is mortal to what is eternal. This path has nothing to do with religious beliefs or faith - and, in fact, it is a path that will require the seeker to deeply examine her beliefs and even question her faith - both of which are usually found to be only underlying programs running in the background of our comfort zones.

Over the course of my own journey, I've had the

opportunity to interact with thousands of seekers. And though the languages may be different, those universal questions are always the same. So it is my intent with this book to shed some light on the questions and maybe even take one tiny step closer to some answers - though ultimately, any answers I may provide are only guidelines for your own unique journey, and any *real* answers you discover will be entirely your own, and always subject to scrutiny. Question everything.

I'm often asked when my own path began. Interestingly enough, I cannot recall a time when I *wasn't* on the path. As far back as early childhood, I was drawn to the mysterious and the mystical, not just to the shadows or what might be casting them, but to thoughts that asked, "What must my shadow be *thinking*?"

As I've grown older, I've found that the answers we gather along the way shift and grow as we ourselves come to a deeper understanding - and, to me, this is validation that the path is one of true evolution as opposed to simply becoming comfortable with a pat set of beliefs. My mentor once said, "You have come to a point where I can teach you nothing more until you are willing to release what you *think* you know so as to make room for the infinite knowledge that remains currently *un*known." Quite often, releasing those belief systems is not only difficult, but can be exquisitely painful, particularly when one's beliefs form the foundation for their personal identity.

I have told the story of my own struggle with the first question (Who are you?) in Quantum Shaman (Diary of a Nagual Woman), and for those who have read it, you may recall that it was neither easy to release what I believed, nor was it in the least bit pleasant. Yes, the journey was worth it in the end, though the trip up the mountain had its ups and downs, its wonder and, yes, its fair share of tumbles over various cliffs into a myriad dark nights of the soul.

Within the pages that follow, I have attempted to compile

some of the most pertinent (and potentially disturbing) questions asked by seekers over the years, as well as some of the questions I myself have wrestled with. Some of the answers presented are the result of my own assimilation, while others come directly from my mentor and double, who answers to the name Orlando, and who has been with me in one form or another since childhood. The questions and answers here span a period of approximately 20 years, coming from my online endeavors with forums, groups and the like, as well as personal one-on-one interaction with warriors and seekers from all over the world.

From a shamanic perspective, Orlando is my double - essentially the quantum energetic vessel which contains the totality of oneself; i.e., all past and future lives, all experiences the seeker has endured, both in her human form as well as through the mystery which is the double itself[1]. The purpose here isn't to provide you with a comfortable set of easy answers - ultimately, that's been the flaw of religion and politics from the dawn of time. The purpose here is to encourage you to always be asking the next question.

Della Van Hise - January, 2016

———

GLOSSARY
If you find a word or term with which you are not familiar, we invite you to use the glossary located at the end of this book.

---

[1] I've written much about the double in my first two books, *Quantum Shaman* and *Scrawls On the Walls of the Soul*, as well as on my website. In particular, if you would like to know more about my history with Orlando, please visit http://www.quantumshaman.com and go to the page entitled "Meeting the Mirror.

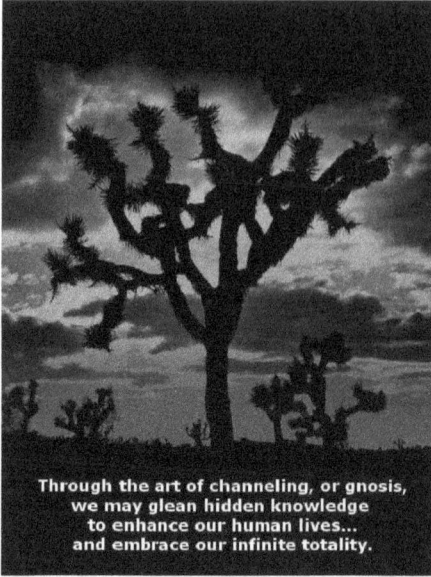

Through the art of channeling, or gnosis, we may glean hidden knowledge to enhance our human lives... and embrace our infinite totality.

PREFACE

Perhaps the most common question I am asked is this one. I've formulated my own answers over the years, but I still consider this one from Orlando to be the most accurate, and the one that is closest to my own heart. So before we begin talking about the path, let's take a moment to ask...

What <u>Is</u> the Warrior's Path?[2]
A Commentary From the Shaman's Quantum Double

Of all the questions I am ever asked from the beginning of time until the end of infinity (which is, of course, the return loop to the beginning of time), this is perhaps the hardest, for the answer can only be expressed in words when what is Intended is an expression of the heart. And so I would begin by saying that the warrior's path is the path of the heart, and if it could be defined without words, it is a path that is neither Toltec nor Buddhist nor Christian nor even a path at all, and only may be seen as a path in hindsight, when one stands on the far side of the bridge and looks back to see how the bridge was built.

Some would say that it is the path to ultimate freedom, but as you expressed in your question (where all answers are found), it is neither possible nor perhaps desirable to attempt

---

[2] If you'd like to watch a video on this topic, please visit
https://www.youtube.com/watch?v=W2EXzoFDg24 and
https://www.youtube.com/watch?v=0OSgoRViwY8

to define what is meant by "ultimate freedom" within the matrix of each individual. For myself and for Della, ultimate freedom may be defined at this moment as the assimilation of our cohesion into a state which has been expressed as "a singularity of consciousness" - a single point of awareness which is singular, but also infinite and ubiquitous. From such a state, The One may focus awareness at any finite point within the realm of all possibility, or may *not*-focus within the whole on all points, simultaneously. Intent would determine; and will would manifest.

And yet, I say this is how we may define ultimate freedom at this moment - allowing for the inevitability that as Knowledge and experience increase, definitions change and eventually become the silence of Knowing itself.

The warrior's path is a dance with no specific steps, enacted between the mortal self and the immortal double.

While one might learn certain steps of the dance through reading or instruction, the dance itself cannot be taught, for it is your dance, and if it does not come from *your* heart, it is someone else's dance. To some, therefore, the warrior's path is a waltz and a gentle entwining of self and double. To others, it is a seductive tango, fraught with dark turns and hot passions which weave the dancers through intrigues and eventually bring them together in a fierce embrace. To others, it is a chaotic, frenzied stomp through the jungle and may appear violent or even conflicted on the surface, but when viewed from the far side of the bridge, may be seen to be simply the steps of that warrior's dance enacted from that warrior's heart.

Some dances are more efficient than others, telling a cohesive story, and not all dances end with the dancers coming together in the final steps, and so it becomes a matter of choosing the steps wisely and falling in love with both dancers, allowing each a freedom of movement and expression which may be seen in hindsight to be guided by impeccability, intent and the moving force of Will, unrestricted.

What is most important to remember is that the steps cannot really be taught, but must be experienced by each warrior in her own manner. There are those who might follow certain steps outlined by other warriors or Naguals, and while that may be effective in the early stages for learning to dismantle programs, dependencies and attachments, it is in learning the art of improvisation that the warrior begins to leave any path and create his own steps which are uniquely effective for himself. And while that may seem like chaos, it isn't, for as long as impeccability guides the warrior's movements through what can only be expressed as "the right way to live."

Throw all these words away. Remember only this, and only for as long as it may take you to integrate it into your own heart: To fall in love with the infinite is the warrior's path, for it is that intense affair with the ineffable that will guide an advanced warrior far more efficiently than any words ever whispered into the night. When you follow the muse of your own heart, you create the steps of the dance in the process, and whenever the muse allows you to catch glimpses of her, you will find yourself gazing into your own infinite eyes.

PART ONE

NAVIGATING THE WORLD
OF MATTER AND MEN
(The Tonal)

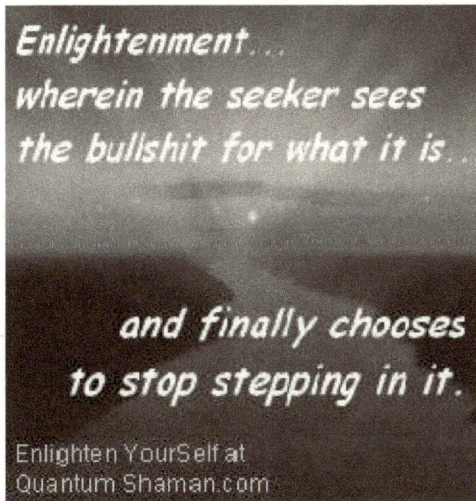

Enlightenment...
wherein the seeker sees
the bullshit for what it is...

and finally chooses
to stop stepping in it.

Enlighten YourSelf at
QuantumShaman.com

Questions concerning a warrior-seeker's path through the
matrix of muggles, phantoms and sleepwalkers in the day-to-
day world.

Quantum Zen Toltec Shamanism

How would you define your own foundation of Knowledge? I've heard you talk about Carlos Castaneda, Zen and even chaos magick. It would help my understanding of your teachings to know where you're coming from.

I would consider my own path to be "quantum shamanism" - a field that I pioneered myself, because absolutely *none* of the traditional paths seemed to encompass all the elements of what it means to create our reality and evolve into our singularity. To me, being able to take a foundation of Toltec shamanism and expand it with quantum comprehension has led to a system whereby I can actually use logic to understand magic, or use magic to bypass logic when necessary.

In basic shamanism, the double is *seen*, but not necessarily understood. In Carlos Castaneda's book, *Tales of Power*, don Juan makes the statement, "It is impossible to reason out the double." In quantum shamanism, it is not only possible to reason out the double, it is *essential*. When we actually understand more of our path rather than relying on faith - which is seemingly a requirement of certain branches of traditional shamanism - we have a far greater chance of success, because that understanding gives us a foundation upon which we may then begin to build upon what many spiritual practices have called "a separate reality".

That reality is made of energy and upheld by the structure of awareness. And we live in it right Now. That Now becomes an eternal Now through the two-part migration of the soul - the double becomes the vessel into which the mortal self uploads her life experience and Knowledge. In quantum shamanism, it is possible to actually comprehend how this process occurs; and in understanding the process, we are better able to participate actively in our own evolution.

A Look at the word 'Shaman'

Della, <u>are</u> you a shaman in the standard definition as shamans are defined?

Not in any traditional or Native American manner - definitely not. The name "quantum shaman" was given to me by Orlando many years ago - and that is a title I do accept as a transient but accurate definition of who I am. I prefer the word 'warrior' or 'seeker', because the word shaman can come with a lot of baggage and expectations and inaccurate definitions.

Ultimately, the word seems to come from the Siberian culture, and translates literally to "self-healed madman". The gist of it is that a shaman was someone who was often fragmented early in life, quite often different from his/her peers, and someone who may even appear to have had direct contact with the world of the dead or the otherworld. What made them a shaman was when they could heal the rifts and tears in their spirit and become Whole - at which point they usually became a teacher or even a spiritual leader or healer.

The problem was that they were attempting to teach people who had little to no experience with the concept of folly - which is dead-bang clear to shamans, warriors and seekers. The ordinary person thinks the world of illusions is real, and therefore also believes that all the roles and masks they wear throughout the course of their lives are real as well. In short, they do not know who they are. The shaman may assist others in learning to *see*, but it's always going to be up to each individual to take responsibility for her own fate.

Arnold Mindell gives some pretty good definitions of a shamanic personality in *The Shaman's Body* - and it's a book I would definitely recommend to anyone on a serious spiritual journey. By *his* definitions, yes, I'm a shaman. And so are most people who have what is commonly called a shamanic personality.

It's not about traditions and rituals and belief systems or creation myths. It's about the connection to Spirit and how one walks through this life as a result of that connection. I would simply add to his conclusions that far too many people who call themselves shamans are still at the level of madman alone. They can intuit the path and maybe even *see* it, but until they do the work of self-healing the fragments that divide the heart and split the soul, they remain at the level of believer or "the faithful" rather than Man or woman of Knowledge.

————

When they say "Get real!" does it occur to you to say, "Define 'real'?

I've been told all my life that I should be more realistic. Is the path toward spiritual evolution realistic? Is it something we can really do, or only something we very much <u>want</u> to do?

As a practicing metaphysician and unrelenting believer in the power and potential of the human mind, perhaps the most frustrating words I hear (and all too often) are "But, Della... you need to have more *realistic* expectations!"

Hmmm. I do wonder about the kind of person who lives their life around only what is realistic. Must be a damn boring existence, if you ask me (and no one did, but I'm going to say it anyway). The whole purpose of any sort of spiritual pursuit, and most creative endeavors, is to get beyond what we think we know and plunge headlong into the icy depths of the unknown. In my own life, that has come to mean questioning reality at every turn, flipping over every rock, and digging under every crumbling tombstone to see what might really be buried there. In almost every case, what I find in the dusty corners of the real world are the stagnant and poisonous remnants of belief systems which people cling to out of some sense of obligation, habit, or simply out of fear.

When I was a little girl growing up in central Florida, my mother and Crazy Granny began to suspect they had a problem child on their hands when I wanted to frolic in the creepy church cemetery instead of sitting in a dusty Sunday School room with my hands properly folded in my lap like all the other good little girls. Their suspicions deepened when they realized I was far more interested in the "transparent man" who appeared in my bedroom twice in the summer of my 8th year, than I was in the cooking and baking lessons going on in the kitchen. They finally knew they were in real trouble when it came time for me to be baptized, and the question I chose to ask the hillbilly preacher was, "Why do adults believe in these fairy tales, but don't want us kids to believe in ghosts? Wasn't Jesus fathered by a ghost and born of a virgin? I mean - isn't that one helluva fairy tale?"

My questions were not popular. I was properly baptized, but never officially exorcised, even though I do believe Crazy Granny thought me to be possessed by Satan Himself. She once sat me down and said, "You have the devil in you, little girl."

Having been taught to never lie, I replied, "But *you're* the one who put him there!"

She looked at me as if I'd gone daft, and asked me to explain. What it really boiled down to was this: the whole idea of a devil was not something I ever would have come up with on my own, and in fact it was the red-faced preacher shouting hellfire and brimstone about a guy with horns and a tail that first gave me the idea that such a thing might exist. I considered the possibility for all of about five minutes, dismissed it with the same nonchalance I had experienced when dismissing God and the Easter bunny and Santa Claus, and went on with my life despite the obvious mental illnesses of the adults all around me.

The reality was that I became possessed by a relentless gram of reason at an early age - though that didn't stop me (and still doesn't) from believing in "magic" - which I have always considered to be only science not yet understood. And, for that matter, have you ever stopped to consider that otherwise reasonable people stumble off to church every Sunday morning, singing hymns to non-existent deities, but in the same breath they will condemn anyone who says vampires or unicorns or fairies or mermaids might possibly be real in some isolated corner of this vast and mysterious universe. Really - what's the difference? If you're going to believe in God, who is even less plausible than Lestat or Ariel, why ridicule your children for believing in other improbable realities?

What is *really* the difference? If the question strikes you as absurd and you find yourself sputtering like a faulty carburetor, it's most likely because you are already invested in the belief system that only *your* belief system is plausible. People I know who believe in God always say... "I just know." Well, what about the goth kid standing in the rain who says, "I just know," when referring to her belief in vampires or ghosts or things that go bump in the night? Why is a belief in God any more plausible than a belief in fairies? No right or wrong answer, really. Just something to think about when you feel yourself rankle at the question itself.

As I've gotten older and found my voice and lost my fear of looking like a complete fool (what others think of me is none of my business), I've been testing the foundation of this "reality" humans cling to so fiercely, and I'm finding that it's pretty flimsy and tends to fall apart when the least bit of pressure is applied to exactly the right places. And admittedly

I enjoy applying that pressure from time to time.

And there are those words again. "But Della, you need to have more *realistic* expectations."

And yet, I somehow doubt that those with "realistic expectations" ever get their dreams off the ground. At the time when the Wright brothers had the idea of flying, it was hardly a realistic expectation. When NASA made the commitment to putting men on the moon, that was not only an unrealistic expectation, it was tantamount to blasphemy to many, and there are still people who believe we never really went to the moon, and it was all just a cheap Hollywood set somewhere in Los Angeles.

So when someone tells me I need to have more realistic expectations, I more or less unfriend that person in my head because in so many ways, that person has become the character of Agent Smith from *The Matrix* - a living, breathing, speaking program desperate to uphold the most commonly held belief systems and protect the status quo at all costs. For those who have met Agent Smith, you already know he isn't really a character in a movie. He is your father, your mother-in-law, your best friend and the guy standing on the street corner every morning when you walk by on your way to work. He is the one always looking at what you're doing and telling you why you shouldn't be doing it, or why you need to have your thinking adjusted, and - most of all - why you, too, should have more realistic expectations.

I recently read a quote from Lao Tzu which is at the base of this commentary. "At the center of your being, you have the answer. You know who you are and you know what you want."

It was such a simple statement, yet also one that echoed something my own mentor has said over the years. "Who are you, and what do you want?"

I sat in the morning light for over an hour, contemplating the quote while the new puppy rested in my lap - awake and aware, as if she, too, were meditating. I can say with complete honesty that I *do* know who I am. And I do know what I want. The problem - if it is one - is that what I want is often considered unrealistic by every other living soul on Planet Earth, and so I have stopped expressing it out loud except in the darkest hours of night, when it is 3:38 a.m. and the good girls and boys lie sleeping in the sanctuary of their warm and cozy beds, and time is going by. Tick tock. Tick tock.

"*The sun is the same in a relative way, but you're older. Shorter of breath and one day closer to death.*"[3] Pink Floyd sings in my head, reminding me of those unrealistic dreams of mine. But here's the thing...

The nature of dreams
is that they are seldom if ever realistic.

As children, perhaps we longed to fly or dreamt of finding ourselves on board the *Enterprise* - no, not the aircraft carrier, the real one, the one up there in orbit. As teenagers, perhaps we imagined going to the prom with the most handsome boy in school (even though we hated boys *and* insipid dance parties). As young adults, we dreamed of what our lives might be - James Bond in a high speed chase with the fate of the world hanging in the balance, or becoming a famous actress who would be the first woman to play the role of Bond. In our 20s and 30s maybe we began to lose sight of our dreams, trading those "unrealistic expectations" for more practical applications, and settled into a living death to which we committed ourselves with a genuine sense of duty, honor and obligation. But perhaps we also began to secretly resent some of those choices as time kept ticking by and the words of Pink Floyd started to sink deeper and deeper into that part of us which was moving further and further from our reach.

If we asked the mirror, "Who are you and what do you

---

[3] Pink Floyd, "Dark Side of the Moon" - Lyrics by Roger Waters

want?" perhaps we even learned to tell ourselves the convenient lies most normal people tell themselves. *I want to have a normal life. I want to raise a family and be a good mother and a good secretary at the office and just be happy.* That's what most people tell themselves, if they dare to ask the mirror-mirror-on-the-wall at all. And that's okay - *if it's real*. If it's really what we want, then it is something to be embraced and nurtured and treasured for the time it will last. I want to be clear that I'm not advocating turning one's back on what one truly wants - whether family and friends, or a life of reckless adventuring. Whatever it is that forms the foundation of one's dreams.

And yet, there are those who do not and seemingly *cannot* embrace that so-called normal life, those realistic expectations which comfort so many but are spiritual poison to quite a few. What does the human organism do when it realizes that what it truly desires is not only beyond its reach but - seemingly - not even within the realm of what the consensual reality would consider possible? What does one do when one truly desires the impossible and refuses to believe it *is* impossible?

When I was 11 years old and first encountered *Star Trek* on a blurry black and white television in the year 1966, I fell instantly in love with that world - which was neither real nor possible according to all conventional and rational thinking. Having already been bitten by that bug of reason mentioned previously, I certainly knew that, yet I could not stop dreaming about a day when it would be real. I talked of nothing else. I used my allowance money to buy an old manual typewriter (for those under 40, look it up), and began writing fan fiction until late into the night. My mother thought I had gone insane. Most of my friends agreed. But there were those shining few who actually saw what I saw, and somewhere along the road between then and now, we almost *do* live in that *Star Trek* world with flip phones and smart phones and computers that fit in the palm of our hand and so many other technological advancements which all would have been considered impossible before a few visionaries set out to make real that which had always been considered unreal.

> By believing passionately in something
> that still does not exist, we create it.
> The nonexistent is whatever
> we have not sufficiently desired.
>
> -Nikos Kazantzakis

So what's the point to all of this rambling? Maybe none at all. Whatever you want to take away from it to fuel your own journey. Ultimately, even if what we truly desire may seem to others to be impossible, I've found that the disbelief and cynicism of others is no reason to abandon my own crazy desires. I will believe in immortality and fairies and mermaids if it pleases me. And if they do not yet exist, I will desire them enough to create them. I will long for the impossible because I have lived long enough to know that what is impossible now will be commonplace tomorrow.

I will continue to dream. And one of those dreams will be of a world where imagination is alive and well and people may awaken to their own power and their own impossible dreams.

You are the most powerful being in the universe. Prove it... even if only to yourself.

The Path Thru "The Real World"

It's easy enough to be a warrior and practice the right way to live in the serenity of my own home, but what about at work or when I'm forced to engage with my family and friends? Can we really be cohesive and whole and walk the path through the real world?

To me, that's what the path *is* - because, as Orlando pointed out years ago: "There is only one world, divided infinitely by perception." If we're one person at work and another at home and still another at grandma's house for the holidays, we are fragmented and unwhole. And yet, as another seeker said...

It's easy enough to be a monk in a monastery, but how does that same monk fare in a whorehouse?

As I awoke from a nap one afternoon, it was to the sound of fierce winds hammering at the house, rushing through the trees with such force that even a huge desert pine was threatening to snap, and slamming sand and debris against the window with such fury that it seemed the glass would surely shatter. It occurred to me that I *should* be worried, or I *should* be unhappy that a storm was blowing in, or I *should* get up and go see what needed to be secured. It was deep into dusk, and if I didn't act quickly, darkness would soon obscure my way. "Be alarmed!" the voice of reason seemed to shout.

Instead, I simply lay there feeling exhilarated by the whole thing, listening to the voice of gnosis which whispered, *Eternity is in that wind. It is not the wind nor the objects blown by the wind. It is the force behind the wind that is both calm and fierce, dark and light, life and death and everything in between. Yet it is none of those things - and therein lies its nature and its power.*

Impossible to describe the mindset I had awakened into - but suffice to say it was where I most want to be in life - a state of ecstasy and detachment all at once. In that manifestation of the crack between the worlds - the perpetual dusk that must certainly reside at the end of all things - there were no worries, no concerns, no agendas. Dinner would wait. There were no wars to be fought, no disasters to divert, no immediate demands. My weenie dog was sleeping soundly at my side. Orlando was with me in a way that is impossible to describe - a tangible presence in the room, an essence of Spirit blown in on that magical wind.

For several minutes, I simply lay there absorbing it all - the actuality of silent knowing, the visceral reality of the crack between the worlds, and the serenity that came with simply Being a being who could perceive and experience the magnificence of it all - the violence of the wind, the eerie gold-grey light that hangs in the air after a sandstorm, the perfection of a single moment in all of time.

But eventually time drags us forward again, and even though a woman of Knowledge takes those perfected moments with her into the world, there is nonetheless an undeniable speed bump that delineates the passage from one world to the other.

As I got up and peered out the window toward the west, it was easy to see the damage. A large lantern in our yard was blown over and shattered; trash littered the Joshua trees; and one of the light-up Christmas trees had been dislodged from its stakes and was rolling down the driveway like some runaway toy afraid of being shoved back in the closet to endure a long season of darkness before it would be in good favor with the human consensus again.

Minor inconveniences, of course. Just things I noted during this passage between the worlds on a New Year's Eve of no particular significance.

So I cooked dinner, brought in some firewood, picked up the shattered lantern, and generally began going through the machinations of real life - and even though I was still pondering that profound state of mind I had awakened into, I was left with a sense of wanting to return to the monastery of my silence rather than putting myself through these strange actions which have no meaning whatsoever.

The world is a nuthouse and the lunatics are running the asylum, Orlando reminded me as I stood looking out the kitchen window to where the winds were causing even the stalwart Joshua trees to shiver like cold, brittle children.

I sighed softly, for even though I have uttered those words countless times as a source of amusement, I cannot deny that they are also terribly true. As I stood there in my silence, I could literally feel the other humans gearing up en masse for drunken parties, excursions to various clubs where they would engage in The Mating Dance, and all manner of debauchery assigned the label of "fun", and all of it occurring only because it was the night on which we throw away last year's "Puppies" calendar and replace it with this year's "Kittens". Arbitrary demarcations of time.

Some of those humans would even die as a result of their revelries - and though some might argue that it is better to have been puking drunk than never to have partied at all, I'm not the least bit sure that is a sentiment with which I could agree.

It is madness when viewed from outside the container of its own agreement.

The winds have gone still on the first day of the new year, and as I gaze out my window toward the west, it is to see a new snowfall on the top of Mt. San Gorgonio. The silence there must be phenomenal.

———

The Door

*I was at a talk you gave at your store not long ago, and was
drawn to the parallels in our early upbringing. Do you think how we
are raised determines whether we become warriors or just slump into
a life of boredom? I never wanted to be normal, but I fear that's what
I've become. I never really traveled and at the age of 50, I'm starting
to think any possibility for adventure has long since passed me by.
No regrets - just not sure where things went wrong.*

The fact that you came to a talk on the subject of
metaphysics pretty much refutes the idea that you settled into
a "normal life." Sometimes we're just too close to ourselves to
really *see* our lives with any sense of accuracy. As for things
going wrong, my feeling here is that *nothing* went wrong. Life
goes where we allow it to go, and where it allows us to go.
And it's never too late to chase the muse, if that's what you
find yourself wanting to do.

As a little girl growing up in the geographical center of
nowhere in a tiny town outside of Tampa, Florida, I had
plenty of opportunity for high adventure in my own back
yard, which consisted of five acres of swamp land, orange
groves and a distant shore across the black lake which was so
overgrown with cypress trees and brambles that no child had
ever dared to venture in. It was called, simply, The Thicket,
and stood as an unspoiled mystery and muse at a time when I
was involved in daily battles with a tyrannical father, a
mother who was absent at work most of the time, and a Crazy
Granny who did her best to raise me, but was seriously out of
her league. I was a wild child, though not a bad one,
completely impervious to the attempts to program me into
being normal. When Crazy Granny once suggested that I
should go pick a switch for her to use on my bottom, I could
only laugh at her wild eyes and red face and bad blue perm,
and wonder if anyone in history had ever fallen for *that*. What
kind of meek imbecile would do that, and why? Sorry, but I'm

not into the whole drama of the subservient child bringing the instrument of her punishment to her executioner. Wanna switch me? Gotta catch me. Granny didn't run very fast, and so the plants were allowed to keep their branches and I was allowed to keep my hide.

So when you ask if it was a matter of how we were raised that might determine whether we choose the warrior's path or not, I can say in my own experience, that didn't appear to be the case.

Despite the best efforts of my handlers to bring me up as a reasonable child, there was always something *out there* in the orange groves or down one of those long, lonely dirt roads that held far more interest to me than Mrs. Petty's Sunday School Class or Old Lady Crawford's long and boring dissertations on American History. Even sitting in that old faded green classroom where the windows were propped up on sticks and the scent of stale vomit seemed to permeate the unmoving, hot Florida air, sometimes I could just look outside and see it, *sense* it. Sometimes I could almost touch it.

The door.

Far more real than any ant farm science project, it was this mysterious anomaly that seemed to hang in the *out there* like a mote in the corner of one's eye. Sometimes I thought the door might lead to the world of dreams, where I would create other children to serve as playmates and companions. Growing up as an only child was both lonely and yet utterly empowering. Other times, it seemed the door might open into some Martian landscape where Ray Bradbury's voice would be forever reading, "There will come soft rains." And still other times, it seemed that surely this door would open onto the bridge of the *Enterprise* (or Spock's private quarters, depending on my mood).

As I moved into my high school years, I would often spend the entire day in those sticky-hot orange groves, chasing the door on the tip of my pen - all of which seemed to be a better use of my time than yet one more repetition of what I'd already learned in first grade math. It wasn't difficult to ditch class in those days. Duck behind a tree when the bus was approaching, disappear into the grove after it was gone, then magically reappear behind the Hiding Tree when the bus came lumbering back in the late afternoon. I was The Master. And the door was my witness and my ally. Together the two of us frolicked at the edge of the unknown for years. A glimpse here and there. A shimmer in the fabric of the space-time continuum that could not be explained away as a heat monkey dancing on melted asphalt or steam-ghosts rising off the bottomless black lake.

The door was both friend and foe, some days seeming to say, *Come ahead, I'm waiting for you, my love*, then just as quickly, like a fickle paramour, saying, *Go away, little girl. You aren't ready for me. Forget you ever saw me.*

But I never forgot. And over time, the door evolved. Like some mystical, magical portal. The Guardian of Forever in that old *Star Trek* episode, *City on the Edge of Forever.* No doubt Gene Roddenberry and Harlan Ellison saw that door in their dreamings, too.

As I grew into an adult, I honestly believed these childhood fantasies would fall away like baby fat, but instead, the door simply mutated, transformed. It still led to the same mystical worlds - or so I imagined - but now with an adult's perspective, an adult's desires, an adult's power, and an adult's blindness. But nonetheless, the door remained there in the darkest corner of the infinite. Waiting. Like the poet's muse, beckoning and then darting away whenever approached. A shy kitten with fierce fangs. A shape shifter. A sorcerer unto itself.

Sometimes, the door opened and allowed things to escape. Or, more precisely, it opened and set its denizens loose. There were times of high adventure, when it seemed I would be consumed by some of those strange anomalies who came from behind that door. Car chases in the middle of the night, only to discover that the license plate was unregistered. Telephone calls from people who knew a great deal about me, but would tell me nothing about themselves. If I didn't have witnesses to these events, I would have questioned my sanity.

In fact, even with witnesses, I turned toward the door and said, "Are you kidding me? Am I crazy? How can this *be*?"

The only answer made little sense. *Crazy is as crazy does.* So, for a time, I actually thought Forest Gump lived there, even though the door went on to say, *What is real is where I lead. Where I lead is the source of the source and the end of time. Come, take a closer look...*

And then it would vanish again.

Perhaps it came as no great surprise when I was reading the Carlos Castaneda books that don Juan and Silvio Manuel were also searching for this mystical door. To them, it was a very real construct - or at least it seemed so in the writings. I'm not sure what don Juan himself would have to say on the subject, but there were several mentions of this peculiar door and speculations as to where it might lead. At one point, it even seemed to suggest that this was the doorway to freedom - the secret exit from the stage of Life that did not involve an encounter with Death.

The funny thing is that I also perceive that I found that door and walked through it several years ago - on the night I sat down with Orlando for the first time and he changed my world forever. I walked through it again on the night I experienced my shamanic initiation, and again when I finally began to see that this mysterious being known as Orlando was actually my own double, my own higher self, the structure of my own singularity of consciousness.

And yet, is it at all surprising that the door is still out there, and that it continues to whisper of otherworlds and netherrealms and the source of the river where the light and the dark bubble up out of the nothing for no other reason than to provide a juxtaposition and a milieu in which we experience the door itself?

At times I have felt what is described as a warrior's melancholy - and when I dig deep into the source of it, I find that familiar but elusive door standing at the edge of the infinite, slightly ajar, with a yin/yang burst of enlightenment and oblivion shining through in exactly equal proportions.

Perhaps it is enough to simply Know and to *see* that it exists at all. What does it mean and where does it lead and why does it retreat whenever I move toward it? I know the answers to all those questions, but the questions remain as answers unto themselves.

That would seem to be the nature of the door, and the purpose.

It's been my experience that all true seekers of knowledge have *seen* or sensed this mystical door at one time or another - whether they call it by that name or some other - and that it is through the act of pursuing the door that our own awareness evolves and grows. As to what lies behind the door? The only way Know is to open it.

So in returning to your question, I have to say that the most fascinating travels I've ever undertaken are those that occur between the brows and in Dreaming. Only there can we truly go *where no one has gone before*.

———

Of Genies and Fallen Trees

What are your thoughts on the holidays? I've read that warriors probably shouldn't even celebrate things like Christmas, but isn't that just another program? I know none of it is real, but sometimes I feel like I need to pretend. Is that wrong?

First, there are no *shoulds* in the warrior's world. Anyone who starts telling you what you should or shouldn't do is operating under their own agenda. Personally, I'm not a fan of the holidays, mainly because the programs you referred to drive people almost literally insane, and insane humans are dangerous humans.

Ultimately, it's up to you to decide what's real or not-real about the holidays. If you enjoy the food and drink, enjoy it with awareness. If you love the music and the lights, focus your energy there. If you don't want to go to family gatherings, find a reason to not go, or go with full awareness of what you're walking into. The holidays can be a great time for what the Toltec practices call "stalking yourself," and I have certainly found that to be true. Here's an example of what I'm talking about...

––––

I found myself in the Wal-Mart garden shop, surrounded by the slaughtered bodies of spruce and pine, Douglas fir and balsam. The scent was magnificent - and transported me immediately on the wings of the ghost of Christmas past to all those years before when I would rush out on the day after Thanksgiving, find the perfect tree and drag it home to be adored for the duration of the season, until such time as it would eventually become a fire hazard around mid-March, and have to be dismantled with considerably less affection than was experienced at the time of its initial erection.

For a few moments though, it was interesting just watching my awareness move back and forth between The

Phantom Self of the Past, and The Warrior in the Now. Over the past several years, Christmas has become far more of a burden from the phantom world as opposed to any real and sincere joy. I don't feel a single shred of guilt over that, nor offer any apologies for my lack of Christmas spirit. It is simply what-is. But as fate would have it, Wendy rather likes the season for its pretty lights and garish decorations, and so I had toyed with the idea of getting a big tree again, if for no other reason than to drag out all those old ornaments from the basement to see what the mice have eaten and what might still be hung from some drooping branch in an attempt to elicit some emotion of nostalgia or whatever it is one is expected to feel at this particular time of the year.

And yet, standing there amongst all those trees, inhaling their scent and breathing in their history, there was a moment when I found myself thinking, *I wish it could be real*. The fact that it never *was* had no bearing on the idle thought whatsoever. Even as a child, there was never a moment when I believed in Santa Claus, so there was never any great grief when I found out he was no more real than the Easter bunny or God or the tooth fairy.

What surprised me was that feeling of simply wishing it *could* be real. What "it" might be, I cannot say. To the phantom world, perhaps "it" represents some season of brotherly love among families who may want to kill one another the other 364 days a year. Or perhaps it represents to some the birth of an idea of their own salvation - yet an idea that has no more power to save them than the pretty ribbons with which all those gift boxes are tied together. Tinsel and garland. Snow in a can and twinkling lights that all too often burn down houses where real people lie sleeping.

Whatever "it" is, I know it isn't real except as how it may be real within the Self. And that, alas, is not something that can be wrapped up and shoved under a tree, nor proclaimed by angels on high. "It" is simply the silence in the snow, the magic in the desert, the synapse between heart and beat where the infinite lies like a vast sea of eternal mystery and never-ending awareness.

And yet, for that one moment, I so much wanted that phantom "it" to be real. I sighed heavily, and although I had been poised on the brink of putting one of those dead green bodies into my cart so as to celebrate its beauty, I left it there in the garden shop and returned to my car.

For a few minutes, I simply sat there gazing at the store and the people going through the motions of all that hustle and bustle. Rosy-cheeked children clung to the bright red skirts of their mothers, granny emerged carrying a pile of wrapping paper more than adequate to wrap a dozen mummies; and it all had the appearance of actually being real. It left me momentarily sad, and at the same time, detached.

You can't put the genie back in the bottle, I heard Orlando's voice murmur close to my ear. *You can't go home again.*

And then there was just the silence and the wind and the blowing sand. Even the sadness had left me. Only when the genie is free is the warrior free, and "home" has very little to do with any location on a map. Ixtlan[4] is a beautifully-adorned illusion this time of year. But it is still, and always has been, an unsustainable fantasy.

The warrior's gift is the ability to see that, without sadness, without regret.

———

---

[4] *Journey to Ixtlan,* by Carlos Castaneda. What is Ixtlan? In this book, it is represented as an *idea* of a place that exists only in our minds. When we think of going "home," the reality is never the same as how we remember it. The problem the warrior-seeker faces is that there are always "phantoms on the road to Ixtlan" - those well-meaning souls who want us to join them in their illusory beliefs. Many times, those phantoms come out in force during the holidays.

Searching for Happiness

On one of the online forums I frequent, the subject was raised, *"What makes people happy?"* An article from the *New York Times* was cited, which begins with the opening paragraph:

> *A team of psychologists and economists is reporting today what many Americans know but don't always admit, especially to social scientists: that watching TV is a very enjoyable way to pass the time, and that taking care of children - bless their young hearts - is often about as much fun as housework.*

Regarding happiness, Orlando once said that he does not seek to be happy because in so many ways what we humans call happiness may actually be a dangerous form of complacency. I found that to be especially true in the opening paragraph of the article where the writer says that watching television may be "a pleasant way to pass the time." That turn of phrase really made me think - *Is that all we're here for*? To pass the time? And even if that were to be the case, would we choose to do it sitting zombie-eyed in front of a metal and plastic box while life passes us by?

I am not a big fan of television even though I used to be adamantly in love with it. But since giving it up, I've discovered that I'm far more happy in the sense that I get more done, have more time for spiritual pursuits, and I don't feel so programmed into asking my doctor about Viagra, Botox, or whatever the latest craze may be. It's

amazing to someone who doesn't watch television to really observe a random sampling of those who are essentially addicted to it - without even realizing it, they speak tv-speak, follow the fashions set forth by the latest popular shows, and take all the right drugs for PAD, SAD, BAD, RAD, DAD, and BEENHAD.

So I'm a radical where that's concerned. If I could give the world one free gift, it would be to turn off all the televisions for the period of one week. Those who didn't go stark raving mad might actually emerge from the experience far more awake. Don't get me wrong - tv can be a wonderful tool, but the problem is that the tool has become a substitute for living for a lot of people. May not be the fault of the tv, but sometimes one has to remove the drug in order to cure the addiction.

As for happiness beyond the box? What I've found in my own life is that I am usually happy at the core. Even at the worst of times, there is a quiet core of serenity and well-being which seems to sit somewhere in the vicinity of the solar plexus. It hasn't always been that way, and seemed to come about as a result of my own spirit-quest, which has been ongoing since 1988, though in hindsight I have been on that journey all my life. So, to me, happiness seems to be a matter of finding the alignment to life within myself, and moving forward with purpose from there. Not usually a happy-happy-joy-joy rushing river bliss-ninny type of manifestation, just a quiet little stream.

Deep Inner Meaning (DIM)

I realized recently that so much of what we believe is just the byproduct of what we've been <u>told</u> to believe. That being the case, how do we know what's real beyond all the lies?

As one advances on the path of knowledge, one resists assigning meaning to most things entirely - because it becomes clear over time that it's the conclusions we draw that are often in error, while the experience itself remains just what it is, whether it can be understood or not. For example, I'm always amused by websites offering to sell certain crystals with this or that "special properties." *Quartz for clarity! Amethyst for healing! Aventurine for fertility!*

They're just rocks. All of these meanings are only random assignations by humans, but the thing-itself is just the thing-itself. We might *decide* that quartz resonates and pulsates at the vibrational frequency of clarity, but that's just a lot of yada – words wrapped around the rock to make it more appealing and, let's face it, more saleable. Words meaning nothing.

With that said, a seeker might decide to assign meaning to a stone as a tool of "fake it till you make it", but ultimately a woman of Knowledge *sees* the underlying truth: it's still just a rock. The fact that it is a pretty rock or a different kind of rock doesn't alter the fact that it's still a rock. And, of course, "pretty" and "different" are also just random assignations.

The only thing that makes gold so valuable is our belief. The only thing that has kept the economy functioning for so long is our belief that there is gold behind all that paper. As the mass beliefs start to disintegrate, as the conclusions we have drawn cease to have meaning, the thing itself reverts to just what-it-is...

No-thing.

In the human world, it seems there is virtually no way to have a society that doesn't depend on conclusions and illusions, agreements and consensuses. If our economy weren't based on gold and paper, it would be based on beans and bones, or trains and taters. Point being: it seems our survival as organic beings depends on certain assignations of meaning, but at the same time our inorganic freedom depends on seeing beyond those things upon which our organic survival depends.

It's no coincidence that this is somewhat of a flawless trap - a basic construct of the consensual agreement which some have referred to as the foreign installation - a set of beliefs which amount to a false program that permeates the entire human race.

———

Gurus, Liars, Truthsayers & Shamans

When working with metaphysics, it can't be denied that a lot of what seems true to the practitioner will seem like outright lies and fakery to onlookers. Just because I've seen spirits or talked to a brujo doesn't mean anyone else has had that experience, and most wouldn't even believe me. How do you think that affects you in the long run? Can we straddle the fence between two worlds, or does it eventually cut us in two and kill the authentic self?

With regard to my own metaphysical experiences, I try to take them as objectively as possible. Beyond that, there are patterns of experience - when the same non-ordinary thing happens more than once or twice, it becomes possible to observe how those patterns may relate to our ordinary lives.

Which brings me to Carlos Castaneda's books. As I have said over the years, Castaneda's writings were largely corroboration for me. I don't necessarily agree with all of his conclusions, but I don't doubt most of his experiences. I've been there, done that, and therein lies the pattern. This isn't just some isolated, subjective experience. It can be repeated, so in that regard it is at least somewhat quantifiable. It happened to me. It happened Carlos. And I'm sure it's happened to thousands of others who have actually sought out the experience rather than just reading about it in a book.

It's when people treat their experiences as a religion that the trouble begins. For example, yoga is a practice, not a religion. Toltec nagualism is also a practice - not a belief system. So when someone gets up in arms because "Castaneda lied," I can only liken it to a religious man suffering what's commonly called a loss of faith. Having found out that the guru lied, the apprentice goes into anger-denial-bargaining-depression-acceptance and blames everyone but himself. Common pattern.

Some academicians use the argument that if Castaneda lied about one thing, he probably lied about all of it. Let's examine that premise just briefly. Assuming anyone studies martial arts or yoga, how would it affect your experience if you found out that your teacher lied about something? It's the old cliché of shooting the messenger. We can blame Carlos all day long for being a liar, but does lying about the characters invalidate the message for those who have actually experienced it?

The messenger may have lied about how he got the information, but does that invalidate the information itself?

One thing about shamanism that many do not know or choose to ignore is that most shamans are bona-fide liars - not by choice but by design. A large part of spiritual healing is often accomplished by what might be labeled by staunch critics as deceit on the part of the shaman. Shamans may pretend to suck out a deadly serpent from a patient suffering from pneumonia, when the reality was that the tiny garden snake was concealed in the shaman's pocket all along. But the patient gets better because he *believes* the shaman cured him (when the reality is that he cured himself) and isn't all that really matters? And doesn't it somewhat alter one's idea of truth? *If the patient was dying of pneumonia but can be cured by a lie, is the cure itself not then Truth?*

Expecting a real shaman to be an upstanding truthsayer is ludicrous, because the shaman's primary objective revolves around getting folks to let go of their consensual programming. And the only way to do that is to simply grab them by the scruff of the neck and drag them - kicking and screaming, if necessary - out of the matrix and into the world, which is not at all what most think it is.

Shamans lie because the world itself is a lie which must be unraveled to reveal the truth underneath. Get over it. If your teacher hasn't lied to you to get you to change your thinking, he's probably not a very effective teacher

Everything you need to know can be *seen* in *Star Trek*.

> Captain Kirk: *Harry lied to you, Norman. Everything Harry says is a lie. Remember that, Norman. Everything he says is a lie.*
>
> Harcourt Fenton Mudd: *Now I want you to listen to me very carefully, Norman. I'm... lying.*
>
> Norman: *You say you are lying, but if everything you say is a lie, then you are telling the truth, but you cannot tell the truth because you always lie... illogical! Illogical! Please explain! You are human; only humans can explain!*
>
> And this being done, the robot fizzled, his programming undone. Any questions?

As for magical abilities and such... Magic is only science not yet understood. We live in a quantum universe, where it may well turn out that everything is created by thought, intent and will. At the very least, we already know the universe is directly affected by our observations of it – in other words, we are inexorably connected. That being the case...

There are more things in heaven and earth, Horatio,
Than are dreamt of in your philosophy.
- Big Bill Shakespeare

Which brings me back to the beginning. The experience is simply what it is. The fact that we cannot wrap our minds around it doesn't invalidate the experience itself. And the conclusions we draw are not necessarily truth.

For as long as we are prisoners of our beliefs and our social and cultural programming, we are little more than extensions of our programmers (parents, teachers, governments, religious leaders). It is only as we begin to shake off the stupor (or have it ripped from us by our teachers, mentors and guides) that we find ourselves face to face with the realization that the world is nothing like we have been taught to believe, and we ourselves are perhaps more mysterious than anything we can begin to imagine.

That's where the real quest begins.

————

Truthsayer or Soothsayer?
Does It Really Matter?

I keep reading that Carlos Castaneda was a fraud and that he probably made the whole thing up - all of it. I've always believed the old saying that only the truth can set us free. What do you think?

As for whether or not Castaneda fabricated the whole thing, it really doesn't matter in the least for one simple reason. Whether or not don Juan existed, the truths being explored in the books stand up. My personal suspicion is that Castaneda probably did indeed invent don Juan as a vehicle through which to dispense the Knowledge he himself had discovered through whatever method. In other words, Castaneda *was* don Juan - whether consciously, unconsciously, or even if don Juan may indeed have been Carlos's double. If that's the case, then we have merely shifted the identity of don Juan from that of a Yaqui sorcerer to that of a UCLA anthropologist. Don Juan still exists, just not exactly as we might have envisioned him. But what matters in the big picture is whether or not the *teachings* of don Juan hold up.

For myself, after many years of experimentation and exploration, the Knowledge reported in Castaneda's books still holds up, and, indeed, I have been able to take most of it one-step-further - which means it is a valid foundation that can be built upon by those with Intent.

So, in response to your statement that "only the truth can set us free" - absolutely, 100% true. That's why I am a seeker of Truth and not a blind follower of Castaneda, who himself admitted to being a trickster. So the question then becomes - what *is* truth? Seems to me don Juan exists as a living construct of energy and Knowledge, regardless of who breathed him into life. What is... simply *is*.

During the course of a recent discussion, the comment was made, "Truth matters! If it's not true, how can it have any real power?" Hmmm. I know a lot of people who have had life-altering awakenings as a result of a movie - I'm thinking in particular of *Avatar*. At least two people I know were profoundly changed after seeing the film, and in essence it led them onto the path because there are elements of truth woven into the "fiction."

Writers often call this technique "fact-ion." Part fact, part fiction. Obviously *Avatar* wasn't a true story, and don Juan may not be pure truth either. But if the truths contained *within* the fiction are sufficiently powerful to shake someone out of their human stupor, that's good enough (for a start). Truth is

41

subjective. Everything begins with a thought, and in quantum perspective, anything that can be imagined also exists. It's how reality is created.

Ultimately, it comes down to this: we can hear the message or shoot the messengers. Most true shamans are not always saints and priests by human standards. Visionaries are not necessarily visions of virtue. This seems to be part of the riddle - that nature selects what some would call "frauds" to deliver the message about the path toward freedom (which may vary from culture to culture, but which is always the same at its core). Maybe it's because it's our various cultures are the real lie, and the so-called liars are the real truthsayers. The universe seems to appreciate irony like that.

———

Why Am I Angry All the Time?

I was recently asked by an advanced warrior, *"Why am I angry all the time?"* At first, I had to laugh - for it was a question I've asked myself a time or two. But even more than my own resonance with the inquiry, this is a question I have heard *many* times from *many* warriors, and so it seemed appropriate to take a closer look at the machinations of anger, clarity and the warrior's path.

What immediately comes to me is that warriors are, by nature, passionate people. Though a warrior may recognize that the world is full of folly, they tend to live by don Juan's admonition to "Play the game as if it matters." And, at times, it has been my observation that this can have the effect of creating a dichotomy of sorts in the mind/body/spirit of the warrior herself. If we *know* it is all folly, but we play the game *as if* it matters, there is a human tendency to get involved in the machinations of our own lives - whether job, family, friends, or entertainment. We can momentarily forget that it's all folly, and suddenly we find ourselves in the middle of an emotional reaction that seems real even though it has already been acknowledged as folly.

What to do?

The key to coping with anger is awareness - not just the awareness of folly, but the awareness of my own relationship *to* that folly. Put another way, I stop and ask myself, "Why would this matter enough to waste energy getting pissed off?" Usually, it matters not in the least and then it's just a case of releasing and reversing the automatic anger-response that kicks in when we momentarily forget that the nature of folly is simply to *be* folly.

But on a darker note, I have also concluded that clarity is the second enemy of a man of knowledge with good reason. The more clarity I have gained, the more disappointed I am in the world - or, more precisely, the humans. And yet, there is the simultaneous urge to just laugh at the abject madness of it all. It has been said (though it may be just a program) that it is human nature to desire some sense of order. Maybe when I was a child, that sense of order seemed more cohesive than it does nowadays, but I am also inclined to think that the world has gotten worse, and that it is a trend that is not going to reverse itself anytime soon.

Everywhere we turn, we are inundated with folly at its highest manifestation. We talk to robots on cell phones and wait on hold for hours while internet idjits stay up late figuring out ever-more-clever ways of stealing our identity or infecting our computers with some cyber virus that has the potential to destroy years of work.

A warrior with awareness *sees* the world as it is and as it could be, perhaps even as it "should" be on a certain level of spiritual well-being, and the gap between what is and what might be is so severe that sometimes an anger response is normal, all things considered. When we see that the world really is a nuthouse and the lunatics are running the asylum, it's sometimes difficult *not* to feel anger toward... *what*? The phantoms? The culture in which we live? All the blind, mad fools rushing headlong toward chaos?

I know from my own experience that I have already attained one of the highest possible goals of a warrior: I have dreamed my double and now he is dreaming me. So what does it matter if some turkey cuts me off in traffic or I am misdiagnosed yet again by the medical profession or the roof leaks or the dog took a dump on the rug? It becomes a matter of looking at myself in relation to the folly and coming to see that it really can't touch me on anything more than a surface level. Sure, it might destroy my world, kill everyone I love, even take my own life from me, but in the bigger picture, even that is only the dark manifestation of folly.

EVER BEEN SO ANGRY THAT YOU SKIPPED ANGER AND WENT STRAIGHT TO LAUGHING LIKE A LUNATIC?

When it is impossible for whatever reason to release our anger, the best thing we can do (both emotionally and spiritually) is channel it into something that does advance our path. I have a friend who does her best writing when she's angry at the world, and another who says she has the cleanest house on the block when her anger gets the better of her. So in addition to having awareness of the folly, learning to redirect can be a powerful tool for also letting it all go.

In the final analysis, it's all a choice. We can choose to be angry or we can chose to laugh at ourselves for the funny, naked monkeys we really are.

44

The Art of Communication

Is part of our progress on the path an ability to be straightforward with everybody, or does my handling of folly lack some skills as to how to manage tone, expression, timing, choice of the words being said? Maybe I don't appear to be an angry person, but I certainly do read the reactions of the people, that they dislike what and how I say it. Some see it as an insensitivity, some see it as anger.

Despite our best intentions, it is not always possible to be straightforward with everyone and still be accepted polite social circles. In Toltec terminology, a stalker's trick is to know when one is dealing with a warrior and when one is dealing with phantoms. There are some who do not like the drawing of such lines, but it is what it is, and painting the white wolf blue will not alter the fact that, underneath, he is a white wolf.

I base the level of my straightforwardness on what I perceive to be the other person's ability to accept it. When dealing with straight-up warriors, I tend to be 100% honest, but tempering it with an *attempt* to be sensitive to their feelings as well. I don't like the games some warriors of pointing the finger and saying, "You're being a self-important asshole." Even if it's true, that kind of straightforwardness only tends to make the other person shut down or become defensive and any forward motion is halted in the finger-pointing and tirades that inevitably ensue.

Communication itself is an art form. When dealing with phantoms, I have found that the best approach is often to just leave them in their comfort zones unless they demonstrate some evidence of spiritual awakening. It really isn't up to us to change their ways, or even to point out to them they their ways may be damaging their spirit and leaving debris in the path of others. Phantoms are phantoms because they *choose* to be, not because they are born that way.

Every human being has the opportunity to become enlightened and awakened. Most simply don't make that choice.

In regard to the other aspect of the question, I do find that *how* we say things dramatically affects how the other person receives it. One thing I have learned from Orlando is what he refers to as the art of non-violent communication. Even the words we choose *may* be perceived by others as a form of attack or accusation even when that isn't our intent. It's why it's often wise to phrase things in a manner more impersonal. Instead of saying to someone, "Your self importance has stopped you in your tracks," I might re-think my wording and say, "We need to ask ourselves when our self-importance might be getting in the way of our own progress." In general, I've found that any sentence that starts with "*You*" and is followed up by an observation about the person may need to be re-thought with regard to *how* it is expressed. A good teacher reveals the mirror to someone without breaking it over their head.

Isn't it amusing how we have to walk on eggshells around other people? If we could all just *be* honest and not take everything so personally, we might live in a better world. Sensitivity comes into the equation when recognizing another's foibles without having to point it out to them - "You're fat! You're stupid! You're being self-important!" - but at the same time using the reflection of those foibles to examine our own shortcomings. I've found that it's possible to be direct without being hurtful - at least 95% of the time. The other 5%, well... some people *choose* to be hurt or have a drama, and that's just their little quirk. Whenever possible, I just don't get caught up in someone else's movie.

46

Benefactors, Teachers and the Shaman's Double

Is it necessary to have a spiritual teacher? How can I be following my own path if I'm sitting at the feet of some guru?

Our greatest teachers and our greatest fears are reflection of the Self - the ability to create ourselves Whole, or the ability to destroy ourselves completely. "Look within," as the old saying goes.

If one happens upon a teacher or benefactor with whom one can personally connect, then they might consider themselves truly fortunate. But I do not for a moment think an extant teacher is necessary, for the simple reason that the first knowledge had to come from somewhere.

Who was the first Zen master?

Who was the first Toltec benefactor?

Who is The One?

It is always and only the Self - connecting with the infinite through gnosis (silent knowing). I did not gain my experiences sitting at the feet of any guru, nor uploading the belief systems of any religion, nor analyzing my reflexive behaviors through the prodding of any human being with letters after their name.

Human beings have agendas. There can be no exceptions, for that is the nature of being in human form. Psychiatrists have a vested interest in keeping their patients coming back, so they aren't going to offer a cure right away unless they themselves are truly evolved, and most simply aren't. The same is true for spiritual teachers, psychics and the like. Unless they are spiritually evolved themselves (and most aren't), they have a powerful interest in keeping the hook in the student, and so even if they have their finger on the pulse of All Knowledge, they aren't going to reveal it in a single setting because it isn't profitable to do so (nor is it possible). Even those who offer their services and advice for free are often feeding on the adulation and dependencies of their apprentices, so there is *always* an agenda from *anyone* in human form.

Not all agendas are bad, but to think they don't exist is foolhardy. What matters is having sufficient awareness to *see* this. In so many ways, *everything* we do is self-centered to one degree or another. Even if we give money to a homeless guy with no strings attached, somewhere inside ourselves our agenda involves making ourselves feel better - not just about the homeless man, but most of all, about the self.

Each of us has to do the work of our own evolution, and it's always the self-double at the helm. A good extant benefactor can point out our weaknesses and strengths and maybe even provide advice or working with both, but all too often the student gets ensnared in the process to the point that the *process* can take the place of actual evolution. The double will not allow this to happen, because it isn't in his/her own best interest, and so it's like a constant push once we set our intent and begin opening to our own gnosis - which really is the only guide we ever need, because it is the direct interface between the Self and the infinite.

Any warrior who has come far enough on the path to recognize the need for a benefactor is rather like Dorothy in Oz. The ruby slippers were right there all along, but Dorothy had externalized her salvation to the wizard, who, in the end, couldn't save her at all.

Click your heels together. Meet your double in the mirror. Take back your own power. Within that equation lies the single centimeter of chance that leads to Freedom.

———

Your Person Must Die

What about my family and friends? I've found myself being very secretive about what I believe because they are mostly conservative Christian Republicans and I'm about as far from that as anyone can get. Not meaning to sound cultish, but does there come a point when a seeker needs to disconnect from his past entirely?

This is a topic that's been discussed at length over the years, and while there's no definitive conclusion, here are some of the observations and ideas that have shaped my own life.

I think everything boils down to one act: you must leave your friends. You must say good-bye to them, for good. It's not possible for you to continue on the warrior's path carrying your personal history with you, and unless you discontinue your way of life, I won't be able to go ahead with my instruction.

Your friends are your family, they are your points of reference. Therefore, they have to go. Sorcerers have only one point of reference: infinity.

You must simply leave, leave any way you can.

You have never been alone in your life. This is the time to do it. I don't want your body to die physically. I want your person to die. The two are very different affairs. In essence, your person has very little to do with your body. Your person is your mind, and believe you me, your mind is not yours.

I'll tell you about that subject someday, but not while you're cushioned by your friends.

The criteria that indicates that a sorcerer is dead is when it makes no difference to him whether he has company or whether he is alone. The day you don't covet the company of your friends, whom you use as shields, that's the day that your person has died.

-Don Juan (to Carlos Castaneda)
THE ACTIVE SIDE OF INFINITY

49

The Toltec goal isn't to become one with the all, as it is widely understood in a lot of new age teachings. Instead, the Toltec goal of freedom is to enter infinity as a Whole being - a singularity in a sea of madness, as I have referred to it in the past. To become "one with the all" really doesn't work for me, nor for a lot of others on this path, because within the "all" is also contained all of the "ills" of the universe, and I do not believe a true evolution of consciousness would seek to become one with that. Granted, there is an interconnectedness, but part of the process of evolution is learning to differentiate between the aspects of being-ness that enrich us, and those that keep us from achieving our highest potential.

As far as cutting oneself off from family and friends, I realize this is *not* a popular opinion, and it is certainly up to each person to make their own choices, but in hindsight, I wholly realize I could not have done this journey had I remained in alignment with former friends and family members. Why? Simply because the hive mind is far more powerful than we realize, and once it is recognized by the consensus that someone has embarked on the warrior path, every possible attempt is made to bring the warrior back to a more "reasonable" worldview. That "reasonable" worldview, in most cases, is the mindset of the phantom.

Do I realize how paranoid that sounds? Of course I do. But I've lived it, and so has every other legitimate warrior I have ever known. Eventually, one has to choose between one's path of heart or go on feeding the phantoms. Perhaps it will be different for you, but I must report with absolute honesty that there could be no middle ground for me.

And while I've found that it may be possible to maintain a marginal contact with former friends and family members, the minute I begin to allow myself to care what they think or how they perceive me is the minute I lapse back into phantomhood. For example, phantoms exist within their nature to *be* phantoms - and that means embracing all those programs which try to tell us that the Norman Rockwell

50

painting is real and we're all going to go to heaven when we die. My mother was a born-again Christian - and though I had feelings and concerns for her well-being, it cannot be denied that whenever we got together, her primary agenda became one of attempting to either 1) save my poor lost soul; or 2) understand where she went wrong (thereby manipulating through guilt, whether intentional or not).

We can try to pretend these things don't exist, but ultimately they *do* exist, and so the warrior proceeds with utmost awareness and absolute caution whenever dealing with any phantom - whether a stranger on the street, or a beloved friend or family member. Ultimately, most of the hardcore warriors I have known usually end up as loners on a lonely path - much maligned by proper ladies and gentlemen, and much misunderstood even by those who once professed to love them most.

> *Is it your fault if you remind others of dreams they do not want? And who can blame the group, either for resistance to you or for the life-and-death struggle that ensues? These people are fighting for their lives, equilibrium, homeostasis - indeed, for the perpetuation of history. "Do not disturb us more than we can take," they say.*
>
> *From a global viewpoint, you disturb your organizational system, and history must fight for continuity. In this universal and fated interaction, the warrior's friends become the voices of the web. Their warmth turns to ice. They accuse you of unjustifiable behavior, egotism, and criminality as they become possessed by their lawmaker role in this eternal drama of human history.*
>
> *The collective you live in must pursue you for what it experiences as criminal acts and bring you to trial, just as you have challenged other rule breakers in the past. Now it is you who enters into a life-and-death struggle with the universe..."*
>
> -Arnold Mindell - The Shaman's Body

The mere idea that we can help others really is nothing but our own self-importance. At first, it is difficult to believe that, for we like to think we are beings full of love and light and wisdom - but the bottom line is that our desire to help others often stems from our need for validation, recognition, applause and kudos. Again - nothing wrong with that - and it's a difficult concept to really internalize unless and until the warrior has had a lot of heart-to-heart talks with her mirror in the dead of night.

If someone comes to me for spiritual advice I'm just as likely to chase them off into the wilderness as not - because it would be the absolute height of arrogance for me to think that anything I could tell them would be of any value whatsoever. The reason I do my website and my counselings certainly isn't with any idea that I'm going to help anyone. I do it for myself, for my own assimilation. If someone else benefits from it, that's grand. But if not, I don't have my energy tied up in their expectations - i.e., hooks, dependencies and self-indulgences are avoided simply by keeping it straight in my own head that the minute I set out to help others is the minute I have placed myself above them - and that is another definition of self-importance.

———

A Lonely Path?

I've heard a lot of advanced warriors say this is a lonely path. Does it have to be?

Prior to becoming a warrior, I tended to define myself by my romantic relationships (whether male or female), and - especially - by my relationships with friends. I think that's why don Juan stressed the "friends" aspect so strongly in his admonition to Carlos that Carlos must "leave - leave any way you can." Our friends, in many cases, have even more influence over us than our family - because in so many ways, friends are the family we choose instead of the one we're born with. Conscious of it or not, we want to please them and may actually be intimidated on a certain level to go against a peer group.

I'm lucky in that, being a Type A personality (whatever *that* means), and so I always tended to be more in the role of leader instead of follower - but in many ways, that was just as bad if not worse, because it meant I would often turn around to find a group of friends looking to me for guidance, support, validation, redemption from this or that - and so on. So when I did begin to shed those relationships, it was a lot harder on them than it was on me.

Getting rid of the labels turned out to be paramount in my own life. I found that I couldn't play the expected role of leader, entertainer, hostess, etc., because even if *I* knew it was all just a role, the expectations being put onto me by my friends were such that it was a very real struggle not to fall into that role by default. And once one falls in, it becomes more and more difficult to climb out, because the role has a tendency to become all too real if we're not careful, and we begin to depend on those external definitions and might even mistake them for who we really are. In some weird way, I suspect that my decision to move on in many cases has actually been beneficial for the others as well (though not my concern one way or the other). I say that because - as Orlando constantly reminds me - "We program others how to program us."

If I accept the role of the leader, it was programming my friends to play the roles of followers. If I play the role of den mother and spiritual advisor, it was programming them to expect answers from me instead of looking for their own. If I play the role of problem solver, it was enabling my friends to live in the shadows of their own weaknesses. They were good people who deserved better. Walking away was the best thing I could have done - for them and for myself.

———

Through Vulnerability We Become Invulnerable

I'm fairly new to the path and I'm finding that I'm more afraid than ever. I know Castaneda says the four enemies of a man of knowledge are fear, clarity, power and old age, so where do we start with overcoming fear? Everything I find out about reality, the more it just reinforces that everything I ever believed is a lie. Is anything real?

For starters, a sense of humor is a powerful tool in the warrior's arsenal - and it's why don Juan and don Genaro were always laughing. One of the primary things I do when working privately with newbie warriors is try to bring them face to face with the "recovery process" - essentially a phase in a warrior's life where she has to recover from the shock and disappointment that comes with discovering that the world is nothing like we've been taught to believe, and that we are beings who are going to die.

Let's take an imaginary newbie warrior and call him Joe. Joe has realized there's more to life than his nine to five job, his wife and kids, and his friends - so he's done the

54

rudimentary work of asking the first question: "Who am I?" He's at the first gate of learning to *see*. He's seen through the illusions of the consensual agreement, but he finds himself torn between what he calls "the real world" and "the warrior's way." He stumbles around in this milieu for some time (months or even a few years), but finally realizes that he has not yet made any real connection to his own double, and he seems to be losing energy and impetus on the path.

This is usually the stage newbies are at when they begin engaging with a Nagual or any manner of spiritual teacher - their Intent is in the right place, but their lives are largely rooted in what I call "the 3 Ds" - distraction, diversion and dissipation. They have come face to face with their own programming, have the ability to *see* that, but lack the tools with which to deal with it.

The first thing I tell Joe is that he's going to have to let go of the roles he plays in his day to day life which serve as reference points for friends, family and even for himself. He cannot play the role of businessman at the office, hop into the role of father when picking up the kids from school, then slide gracefully (or not so gracefully) into the role of loving husband when meeting his wife for dinner. This is the height of dissipation - like an actor spreading himself too thin.

The funny thing is that - every time - Joe will begin to argue. Not with me, but with himself. "But it's different for me," is how that argument usually begins. "My wife is this way and my kids are that way and my boss is something else entirely, so I have to be different with all of them if I want to keep my world intact."

And somewhere right about there, he hits the nail on the head. The warrior's world really does go through a process of destruction. That does not mean we have to jump out of bed one morning and break all ties with family and friends - in fact, doing so would be foolhardy, because at that phase, Joe has neither the personal power nor the wisdom, Knowledge or experience necessary to be alone in the world. He has defined himself utterly by those around him, and to remove all those reference points in one fell swoop could be potentially disastrous.

"When I said I would destroy your world I meant it literally, but the truth is that I'm slipping you the tools with which to cut the bars of the prison yourself. Ah, but the darker secret is this: the prison is a living entity as much as a cage and because it is such an interwoven part of you, the cutting away of the consensual disease must be performed simultaneously with the transplantation of superior replacements lest the cure destroy the patient altogether, yes?"

-Orlando - January, 1999

Part of the recovery process is learning to dis-integrate the personality from the roles and expectations put onto Joe by others, while at the same time, developing a foundation of Knowledge (what we *know*, not what we believe) which supports Joe's weight and sustains him during the destruction phase. Without that foundation, Joe will plunge head-first into the abyss. And quite often, he does just that - which is one primary function of a benefactor or mentor. As long as Joe doesn't choose to wallow in the abyss, the benefactor can throw down a rope which can be used to climb back out.

The other thing about this recovery process is that it really does involve having the courage to surrender to the destruction of our world. Meaning: as long as Joe is clinging to what he *thinks* about the world, he is following the human tendency to seek validation for what he already believes, and will actually begin to defend those illusions with great anger, vehemence and histrionics if left to his own devices. So one of the hardest parts of the journey is learning to let go. A good friend once used the approach: "Through vulnerability, we become invulnerable."

This made a world of sense to me, for it is only when we can lay down our weapons and be without fear of annihilation that we have truly become a person of Knowledge. It is only when we can let go of our existing worldview without fear that releasing it will destroy us, that we have found the Self as an identity existing as a singularity of consciousness.

I realize this is a difficult concept for some, so allow me to use an example in my own life. I had come to a crossroads where I knew Orlando was very real, but I was truly afraid to face the possibility that he was my double. My fears kept telling me that if he was myself, then everything I had learned from him was an illusion, worthless drivel, because it had come only from a lowly human - *myself*. Obviously, this is a dangerous program of self-denigration, fueled largely by organized religion and disorganized society - we are programmed to disempower ourselves in order to sustain the power of the powers that be.

Fear also whispered in my ear that it was madness - true schizophrenia, split personality, MPD and the padded room. And because one of my inherent "Della-fears" had always been a fear of losing my mind, this one took root. I would not allow myself to even consider for many years that Orlando was my higher self, until I encountered the concept of "through vulnerability we become invulnerable."

I had to be willing to risk it all before I could embrace any of it. I had to be willing to look into the mirror, and stare myself in the eye before I could ever hope to embody the power, knowledge and wisdom of the double. I had to be willing to accept the possibility that Orlando was nothing, and at the same time to accept the possibility that he was everything. Had to be willing to face the possibility that he was a hoax I had played on myself, a joke the universe had played on me, or the vessel of unconditional love which I would inhabit into eternity.

Nothing much. Just all or nothing. So after having tested the validity of vulnerability = invulnerability on a few lesser demons, one night I finally turned full perception onto Orlando, let go of what I wanted to believe or had to believe, and simply experienced him as a totality. It was a journey of consciousness that lasted over twelve hours, and was simultaneously the most enlightening experience of my life, and the most terrifying. But the bottom line is that once I could release the fear and the expectations, I was able to experience myself in eternity, from the perceptions of an eternal being - and that was the day I learned to laugh again. To laugh at my fears which had held me back from this, to laugh at the pathetic human drama that keeps us isolated from the higher Self, and to laugh at the "Joe" in myself who had been trying so hard to hold the world together with string and glue that he was failing to perceive the infinite power of his own potentially cohesive awareness.

It was only when I was willing to let go, to become vulnerable to the ravaging forces of the infinite, that I was able to embrace the totality of myself, only when I was willing to face the possibility that I could be dead wrong about everything, that I finally learned to use the gift of gnosis as an extension of human awareness into the infinite. I had to release it all in order to have it all.

It's an ongoing journey, of course. It didn't end that night. That's when it began - and it was the milestone in my own recovery process. Only after my world was destroyed could I see that wasn't really the case at all. What was destroyed was the eggshell as the inner being hatched into a much larger universe. The problem is, most people are simply comfortable in the shell and will fight to the death (literally) to stay in the cocoon. Their choice, of course, but I'd rather have wings.

———

The Long and Winding Path of Joe Blow

It is widely recognized that many folks with a shamanic personality may succumb to a variety of distractions, dissipations and diversions: alcohol, drugs, gambling, sexual addiction, or anything that can be used as a mind-numbing distraction between Joe Blow and what-drives-Joe Blow. That's where the words "self-healed madman" come into play. Joe either gives in to his vices and addictions (even if they are "harmless" addictions such as television, workaholism, or other more socially-acceptable diversions), or he pushes himself past those addictions through the force of his own Intent and the application of his will. It isn't easy, but neither is the idea of dying into the abyss for all of eternity, losing the Self, and becoming nothing more than a transitory gnat on the ass of a universal yak.

If Joe is defined as the newbie warrior-seeker, he may have enough personal power to connect with a facilitator - someone who is a *seer* and has already walked the path for many years. So in that regard, Joe avails himself of a roadmap of sorts - or at least a tour guide who may be able to keep him from sticking his head in the lion's mouth. What pushes Joe? Again, if we're saying Joe is the newbie warrior, what pushes him is his own Intent to *be* a warrior. He can see it, smell it, taste it, touch it... all he has to do is manifest it. Rather like Orlando's statement: "You have to *be* immortal before you will know how to *become* immortal." What pushes Joe is that taste of the infinite, that brush with the unknowable that sent him on the path in the first place.

What is the outcome for Joe? It depends entirely on his actions and his choices. The roadmap - whether an extant teacher or the voice of his own double -would reveal to him that he is no longer at the mercy of a random universe. He is in charge of his own fate, at least with regard to whether he will gather the cohesion of his spirit into Wholeness so as to experience eternity as a singularity of consciousness; or whether he will lose his cohesion, and go back to gnat-on-yak's-ass phantomhood. It would be politically correct of me to say, "One isn't better than the other," but obviously that would also be an untrue statement. Don't know about anyone else, but I don't think being a gnat on a yak's ass is particularly satisfying for the yak or the gnat, despite what well-meaning gnats might try to have us believe. *We are here to evolve* - for that is the nature of all living things. But we are given free will (through nature) to make whatever choices we desire. We don't have to evolve. But there are consequences if we don't.

A good friend recently said to me: "There has to be something within Joe that is receptive to Spirit, or he is lost."

That something which is receptive to Spirit is Spirit itself - the unknowable aspects of ourselves that often seem to stand to the side, whispering in our ear, telling us what we already know but are afraid to face: *The world is not at all what you think it is.* Often, what pushes Joe is the first birth cry of his own double - and that is a cry which is often heard outside of time, when we ourselves are still children, long "before" (linearly speaking) we even gave thought to creating the double. This is because the double is the higher self which finds a way to trick time, to stand apart from it, to exist before its own creation. To some, the idea of the double "existing before its own creation" leads to a misshapen belief that the double is eternal by default. I often hear the argument, "My spirit has always been here and always will be." Followed inevitably by, "So even if I don't get it right in this lifetime, I am already eternal."

Not in my experience. But that's part of the trick of the shaman's path - learning to see beyond what we believe, what seems obvious, but may only be a trick of the light. There is certainly the spark of Spirit which is eternal (just as the matter-energy of our bodies is eternal), but that's a far cry from being born with an immortal soul, as a lot of organized religions like to preach. Why are we taught this? Because then we are justified in doing little or nothing - when the reality of it is that Spirit is like any other aspect of the self. If it isn't nourished, developed and expanded, it tends to wither and die on the vine - like a flower without water. This is the unpopular aspect of this path: people need to believe they are born perfect - because then, in many ways, they think they are free to just live like a sprite in the woods for the duration of their lives.

What pushes Joe is the intuitive Knowing that this is not so. What pushes him beyond the 3 Ds (diversion, dissipation, distraction) is the commitment of Intent to take this rare and beautiful opportunity known as Life, and create and unearth his potential as a Whole being - which is essentially a full conjoining-integration with the double.

"What is the double?" Joe asks at some point along the way. The double is the self in eternity.

The double is the limitless eternal vessel into which the mortal self uploads the totality of experience - a singularity of consciousness which is held cohesive by the unique, individuated spark of *I-Am*.

As to why Joe reaches out into the infinite to embrace that while others end up on the shrink's couch? It boils down to Joe taking responsibility for his own path, while many others need someone else to take responsibility for them - either with a pill or a prognosis. Joe is driven by the need for freedom, whereas most are driven by a need for security within an existing set of pre-established belief systems which, nonetheless, do not feel real at the deeper levels of awareness. So, in many cases, shrinks, pills and the like are used to kill the little voices inside of ourselves that cry out for freedom. And - most definitely - it's a huge industry in service to the consensual agreement.

Chasing the Muse

I want to kick myself for feeling this way, but sometimes I'm like that character in The Matrix who just wanted to go back to a normal life with a juicy steak. I don't like what that says about me.

Orlando recently asked me, "Do you regret coming on this path? Do you ever miss something from your past, and if so, what?" After thinking about it, I replied that I have no regrets whatsoever. As to the second part of the question, I miss the high adventure of a certain part of my life, right about my early 30s. Though I didn't know it consciously at the time, it was as if everything had just come together. My relationship was at an incredible peak of discovery and expression on all levels; I was writing heavily for an underground press I owned at the time, and making a fair amount of money doing it; we had bought a house next door to a good friend; and there was a constant sense of flutter-in-the-tummy due to a lot of inexplicable but fascinating occurrences in our lives. Mysterious strangers came and went. The door to the infinite wasn't just open a crack, it was standing wide open and a stiff wind was blowing in my face like the sweet scent of a lover.

I had not yet officially embarked on this journey, but I was almost deliriously happy in so many ways, yet spiritually unsettled in so many other ways. In short, I had taken life by the balls and it had embraced me in return.

And yet, there was a sense of restlessness that could not be assuaged. In hindsight, I can only call it a sense of pseudo-sexual tension and anticipation that comes when one has met the object of their deepest desire, but hasn't yet fully realized it. There was an aching, hurting, wanting needing deep inside me that was like a feeling of needing to consummate my affair with the universe, with life, with the infinite. Like living on the constant edge of never-ending tantric foreplay.

Though I had no language for it, I used that energy in magical ways as a force of creation. I dreamt of "the perfect man." I called him to me, summoned him from the Nothing, extracted him one molecule at a time from the heart of the nagual. I had no clue what I was doing - nor did Wendy, who shared my crazy passion and joined in the fray with great enthusiasm. But in hindsight, it is plain to see that the magic worked, for it was actually a function of Intent, a manifestation of Will which is at the core of creating the double through dreaming.

And so it stands to reason that it was at the absolute peak of this magical madness, I went to the post office one ordinary morning to see Orlando standing there as if he had just fallen out of the sky. For those who don't know the story, it is presented in its entirety on my website, or in my first book, Quantum Shaman (Diary of a Nagual Woman[5].

Since that day, my life has never been the same. Literally. And though it has unfolded in such a manner as to bring me to this point and I wouldn't change a thing even if I could, I must say that my sense of wild and adventurous happiness is the thing that was sacrificed when Orlando came into my life that day. Not in the sense that he has made me unhappy - far from it! - but in the sense that nothing is ever as it seems, and magic seldom if ever manifests as one might have imagined. I had created and summoned to me my immortal creator, and what had to be sacrificed, of course, was the illusion that I was already happy.

Despite my best efforts (and I was pretty adept), the bastard never allowed me to seduce him (and that was as it *must* be). Despite my best efforts (and I was pretty clever), he never let me get inside his head (though he got inside mine in major ways). In short, he intentionally remained always in the distance - the mystery to be sought, but never captured; the muse always running one step ahead.

---

[5] Quantum Shaman (Diary of a Nagual Woman) is available on Amazon or through the Quantum Shaman website. For those with a keen interest in the double, it is a must-read.

So when I gave him my answer and told him I have no regrets, only a few nostalgic moments of happiness that occasionally haunt me, perhaps it makes sense that he responded with the following:

"If I had not manifested myself out of the shadow of your spell when I did, you would have drowned in your own bliss, believing it to be real rather than only the driving force to <u>seek</u> what is real. I could not allow that, of course, and so I have stolen your happiness and spirited it away to the seventh sense, so you will be forever chasing it... and me, see?"

Back to the chase.

———

Role Reversal

I come from a weird family and had a lot of negative stuff put onto me as a kid. I want to embrace this path fully, but every time I think I'm done with my past, it creeps up to bite me on the ass. How can I be in the Now when I'm stuck back then?

I myself came from a past that included an abusive father, but once he was out of the picture - he died when I was 17 - it never occurred to me to go on defining myself by whatever had happened in my past. In fact, it wasn't even an issue at all until later in life, when I casually mentioned to a good friend that my father was abusive, and she started going through all the machinations of, "Oh my! How are you dealing with it? Are you in therapy? What does your doctor say about your prognosis for maintaining healthy relationships as a survivor of abuse?"

Eh?

To me, *that* was the madness, even more than my father had ever been - some notion that I must be scarred for life just by virtue of these things having happened years and years in the past. Made about as much sense as the notion that my arm would fall off entirely because I once scratched it on a tree as a kid. Psychologists will wail and disagree. Psychiatrists will make me the poster child for their definition of denial. So be it. But experience has shown that we do not have to be the victims of our personal history unless we *choose* to, unless we buy into the program that puts money in the pockets of doctors and pharmaceutical companies - the only ones who profit from such an epidemic dispensation of anti-depressants and feel-good pills.

If left to our own devices, we normally heal from almost anything. There are obviously exceptions, but for the most part, it is only when we cling to the identity of ourselves as a victim that we enact the role of a victim. Or, as I'm fond of saying, "That was then, this is now." The things that occurred in my childhood shaped the woman I became, but they do not define the person *I-Am*.

There's a term in Toltec shamanism - recapitulation. Basically, it refers to re-visiting certain events in our personal history so as to recapture energy trapped in the past. I have mixed feelings about recapitulation, since my own nature has always been one of recapitulating as I go - which is where the term "teflon warrior" came from. If nothing sticks in the first place, there can be no attachments to the past. That is my way, quite by nature. Others find it necessary to spend years (literally) releasing the energy hooks one by one, but to me, that can become not much better than living in the past unless one is *really* aware and conscious of what they are doing.

It's releasing the energetic attachments to the past which is the key to allowing the warrior to move forward. When we discover sore spots involving past relationships is when recapitulation can become a powerful tool for releasing our own energetic attachments to the event so that our energy remains focused in the Now rather than being trapped via a long and tangled umbilical cord to the past.

Cronehood

If this question is too personal, I understand. But I'm just turning 45 and my body is approaching that unmentionable state known as menopause or "The Change" (sounds ominous!). Since you've referred to yourself as a crone, I'm assuming you've been there, done that. What can you say about it as it relates to female warriors?

I was recently asked by a friend what I know about menopause. Probably not much from a medical standpoint, but from personal experience, I've learned a few things that may be of value to others, particularly from a shamanic perspective, so I'm going to focus on those angles most of all.

First, I should point out that my own onset of menopause was perhaps not entirely normal. I was barely 38 when I first missed a moon cycle, and after that, the cycle became more sporadic until, by the time I was turning 39, I had become a crone. By traditional standards, this is a very early onset, but I must say that it felt entirely natural to me. I had never been comfortable with the whole moon cycle anyway - just felt like a tremendous waste of time, energy and blood, since I had known since age 5 that I would never have children. So, it has been suggested that perhaps my own Intent was at least somewhat responsible for this early onset. I simply had no use for the cycle on a physical level.

It is also not lost on me that my most intense interaction with Orlando began just shortly before I was entering menopause. It was during that time that we began receiving his letters, and also during that time that I entered into my most profound peak of my shamanic awakening. During the previous part of my life, I had always been extremely sexually awake and aware - and so when I became aware that I was losing my desirability and could no longer turn heads just by virtue of entering a room, I went through a phase of depression that lasted for about as long as it took me to figure out that I could no longer define myself by my sexuality or my desirability or even by my pheromones. In short, menopause seemed to open that door and that awareness - so in that way, it was a very good thing that it came early in my life, when I still had the time, energy and motivation to look inside myself for the power which had always been just a given part of my sexuality in the past. In short, menopause forced me to find something else of value in myself, or risk sinking into a deep dark depression based on the fact that I was no longer desirable. Ho hum. In hindsight, seems obvious. At the time, it was definitely an issue.

Another thing about menopause is that once I was freed from the biological need-to-breed, it's as if a film was stripped away from my eyes, and I began *seeing* the world clearly for the first time. Some of it is downright funny - most of all the machinations of our fellow human beings, who seem to live in pursuit of the dictates of their gonads. As a crone, it becomes so obvious that the mating dance is, in so many ways, the dance of madness. Every movie we see, every tv show on the airwaves, every song on the radio is about getting laid. Hell, even the drug companies are getting involved! Aside from all the jokes about Viagra (prescription: mydixadroopin, mycoxafloppin), there's that one that always makes me howl with laughter - where a bunch of women are in search of their lost libido through some concoction designed to reawaken their lost passion.

Life is cyclical and we are part of life. Trying to hold on to some definition of the self based solely on libido or sexual prowess is rather like trying to hold on to the bone structure of a 12 year old girl when one is a 50 year old crone. Doesn't work, and can lead to all sorts of emotional and spiritual imbalances if one isn't careful. I see a lot of women in Palm Springs (the cosmetic surgery capital of the world) still trying to recapture their lost youth - and if it weren't so sad, it would be downright comical. They all have that perpetually frightened look from too many face-stretching surgeries, not to mention the permanently tattooed eyeliner and rouge - which, more often than not, makes one look more like a circus clown than any refined lady of some illusory high society.

It's in our heads - this idea that we must be thin and blonde and perpetually horny. The reality is altogether different - but in our attempts to live up to society's expectations, we can end up trapped behind the programs designed to disguise what-is behind a mask of if-onlys. We can end up trying to satisfy everyone else or define ourselves by some Hollywoodized idea of who we're programmed to think we should be, instead of simply learning to listen to the body's rhythms and finding a natural harmony on the inside which may or may not be reflected on the outside.

So, in a lot of ways, I would say that menopause opened my eyes - and my third eye in particular. I found that so much of what I accepted as a younger woman was only beliefs and not truths at all - but instead of railing against the lies, I am grateful for the veil having finally been lifted.

In conclusion, one thing I've also observed which may or may not be directly related to menopause is that my focus on the world (and beyond) is altogether different. Whereas in the past I might focus on a task to the point of obsession, it seems my assemblage point has shifted much further into the realms of Spirit. To some, this may translate as perceiving me as more scatter-brained, but I prefer to think of it as a shifting of focus from the world of matter-and-men to the world of self-and-spirit. As we shed some of the biological demands of youth, we are given the opportunity to open the third eye onto ever-increasing vistas of awareness which go far beyond any previous definition of Self we may have held previously.

———

A Secure Foundation

As someone who's followed your forums and blogs for years, I'm curious about some of the turmoil and controversy that seems to have erupted around you from time to time. How does that kind of thing affect your mindset, and does it ever really get to you?

WARNING

TROLL
BRIDGE
AHEAD

DO NOT FEED
THE TROLLS

Trolls are a dime a dozen, especially on the internet. They make a decent pudding if you grind them fine enough and add enough sugar to disguise the inherently bitter flavor. Other than that, they are little more than a nuisance - though they *do* excel at being precisely that from time to time.

It has come to my attention that the closer one gets to "the truth" (whatever that may be for each individual), the more the trolls come out of the woodwork in a grand effort to distract, divert and dissipate the energy of one's discoveries. For what it's worth, this is not just my paranoia speaking - I laid that demon to rest years ago, right next to the demon of self-importance that might try to tell me that anything I had to say would ever be important enough for anyone else to attack. So what I'm talking about here is actually an extant, quantifiable phenomenon which seems to have its roots in a certain branch of consensual programming, and can be observed throughout history, in both small and large manifestations.

A lot of turmoil erupted within 24 hours of my announcement on my website that my first book, *Quantum Shaman (Diary of a Nagual Woman)*, was completed and would be published later that year. The book had been in the works for over four years, may have absolutely no relevance to anyone other than myself; and so to my way of thinking, there was no difference between before book announcement and after book announcement.

And yet...

After book announcement, I was literally besieged with a long and distinguished list of detractors who wrote to tell me just how full of shit I am - not to mention what amounts to several hate-based discussions taking place on online forums; a very public and unexpected betrayal by a long-time friend; and another long list of paranoid schizophrenics who believe they are being stalked by demons (of which I have become the patron nether-saint). If it wasn't so sad, it might be comical, but since I am a being of no-pity, can't help myself for laughing at some of the shenanigans.

But the bottom line is that all of this came at a time in my life when I was being guided by spirit and my own higher self to take it to the next level - which really does involve working with warriors at an advanced level, seekers who have learned to *see* beyond their own paranoid delusions, people who are attempting to evolve as individuals rather than remaining stuck at the level of trying to detract, divert and destroy anyone else on a path which in any manner disagrees with their own narrow and limited visions of what a warrior *should* be.

There are no *shoulds*. There are no rules. There are no gurus. There is only the Self and the infinite and the five elements of Creation - Earth, Air, Fire, Water and Spirit. What we do with them determines the answer to the first question: *Who am I?* We can use those elements to create the double and inhabit that assemblage point as a singularity of consciousness into infinity; or we can abuse those five elements of creation by warping them into weapons to use against others. It's a choice. But there is only one impeccable choice - and that choice is obvious to anyone who sees.

Over the years, I've had people tell me, "I disagree with you about Orlando!" Or "You're wrong about reincarnation." Or "You're self-important because you have a website." The list is endless. But it really doesn't matter if someone disagrees with me. I'm not here to get anyone to believe as I do or follow me as their guru. I'm here for my own assimilation and my own education. If anyone else benefits from it, great. If not, no matter.

What I find amusing is the degree of anger, paranoia and violence-of-word people will sink to in some strange attempt to prove to me I am wrong and they are right. It really makes no difference whatsoever if anyone else believes in Orlando or not. I've met him, touched him in the flesh, saw him burn with the fire from within, and continue my relationship with him through direct gnosis - some of which has been published on my website and other places on the web. I don't need belief for that, because my experience has become my Knowledge, and Knowledge is unshakable.

There are people in this world who have experienced something called the stigmata - the wounds of Christ. I'm not Christian, so this means very little to me, except that it is a fascinating mystery. But even as a non-believer in Christianity, it would never occur to me to go to someone who has had this experience and say to them, "You are wrong. It's all in your head. And you should believe instead in Be-al-pha-zohr of the 9th Dimension because that is *my* interpretation of *your* experience."

Reminds me of all those government documents stating that all UFOs are swamp gas just because that is the explanation that suits their agenda. To the person who has had the experience, particularly when that person has done the long and arduous journey of assimilating the experience into a workable foundation of Knowledge, how self-important would it be for me to attempt to tell them they are wrong, or that I disagree with them? Disagree with... *what*? I might not share their conclusions, but how can one even begin to disagree with their direct and personal experience?

What does tend to become tedious is when people take their disagreement into the realm of the weird and the hateful - because that's when it becomes obvious that their own foundation is not secure; and like mad dogs traveling in a pack, they tend to attack anything that moves just in case it is somehow a threat to their status quo. In reality, of course, the attack itself creates the reality in which the paranoid fears become manifest. What might have been a potential friend becomes an enemy when attacked, manifesting the self-fulfilling prophecy. I've seen it play out too many times not to acknowledge the reality of it.

A few years back, as I was sitting underneath a massive live oak, I turned to face the infinite universe and asked it quite simply to reveal the truth to me with regard to my own path. *Am I deluding myself?* I asked, thinking about all these recent attacks and detractors and betrayals. *Is Orlando nothing more than a tulpa from my own yearnings, dreamed into being just so that he would be? Am I a fool to publish my books at all because they might reveal my vulnerabilities to a predatory universe, a savage garden? What is the meaning of life? Why am I sitting underneath this tree at this moment asking these questions? And, once and for all, is Jim Morrison dead or alive?*

The answers were not at all what I expected. Nothing came at first. Nothing at all. The new leaves on a sycamore tree shivered in the cold morning breeze. My toes ached from the chill. And the universe was altogether devoid of answers or truth or even meaning...

...until something inside myself said, quite simply but with ruthless Intent, "I will not accept Nothing."

At that moment, I heard a raucous laughter somewhere in the distance, and someone started playing, *Light My Fire* on the bagpipes at 7 a.m. A leaf fell from the live oak to land in my lap, and Orlando's voice whispered in my ear, like a lover, *I'm right here in this leaf and in the current on which it drifts to you from above; and you are sitting here at this precise moment so that this leaf might fall from the tree of all Knowledge. I'm the thought you were thinking that made the bagpiper choose that song above all the others he might have chosen on this chilly spring morning of no special significance. And as for the meaning of life? The meaning is that there is no meaning other than what you assign to it, what you weave into being with the five elements of creation. For now, you have woven me and so I am weaving you in return, for that is the sorcerer's trick. So this is what I am - the weaver and the weaving, the dreamer and the dreaming, the unending search and the meaning at the end of the rainbow which always lies in the distance, yet begins in your own heart.*

The rest is just window dressing, distraction and diversion.

The path is clear because the foundation is secure. Trolls need not apply pressure to that which cannot be shaken - though I am certain they will always try.

———

Joiners Need Not Apply

A seeker recently asked whether or not he should join a particular organization. He went on to say that the founder of the organization seemed to advocate raping and eating children. Whether this was a misconception on the part of the seeker or a legitimate nest of crazies, who's to say? On the internet, one can never really be certain. But the fact that anyone would even *consider* aligning themselves with such an organization prompted the following response.

———

If someone is seriously talking about raping and eating children, why in all the collective cosmic hells would you even *think* of joining them? And for that matter, why would you want or need to *join* anything at all? In almost all of the esoteric teachings, joining is a fast track to mental and spiritual enslavement, and potentially a whole lot worse. You won't get super powers or immortality through *any* form of ritual or from any community. You will get it through *doing the work* for yourself. What does that look like, you may ask?

1. Define your intent. What do you really *want*? And what could you want so much that you would consider joining a group that rapes and eats children? Ask yourself this question - *"Am I right in the head?"*

2. While some groups will claim that "Evil is in the eye of the beholder," consider that it is also in the *heart* of the do-er. There is a concept which Carlos Castaneda calls "the right way to live" - an intrinsic knowing that tells us right from wrong. In order to attain even simple enlightenment, you really do *need* to make contact with that aspect of yourself. That is where you will find the assemblage point of unconditional love - which is not some ooey-gooey lovey-dovey sweetness-

and-light crap. It is the seat of your existence and the source of the power of your own self-creation. *Find it!* And if you can't, go to the bother of creating it.

3. Identify and thoroughly examine all your belief systems - including and especially any beliefs that are telling you there is a short cut to power. Look not only at *what* you believe, but ask yourself *why* you believe it. Begin with the things that may seem trivial. You probably believe the sun will rise tomorrow morning. Maybe the belief is true, maybe it is false. Either way - *why* do you believe it? Who told you? Upon what evidence do you base your belief? In this case, you probably base it on the fact that the sun has always risen every morning since you were born - so you base it on subjective experience. But when you start looking at the bigger belief systems (god, religion, good, evil) you may find that most if not *all* of what you currently believe is based on nothing more than what you have been told you *should* believe.

Start with a simple question in each case - "Does this thing even *exist* apart from my belief in it?" If you are at all honest with yourself, you'll find that most of these esoteric beliefs are nothing more than fairy tales. Here's a head start for you to think about - good and evil don't really exist as extant elementals. They are extensions of Man's doings, but even more than that, they are extensions and *creations* of Man's beliefs. In and of themselves, there is no difference between good and evil. What *you* believe is good, I may perceive as evil. We are both wrong. And once again, I direct you to "the right way to live" - which is really the only guide we have to tell us right from wrong.

4. Release your belief systems altogether (this will take time and actual work), until you become a *Seer* - basically someone who is able to *see* the world as it is, without the distortions created by false beliefs. This is a stage where you may experience great joy or great anger, and/or extreme

ecstasy, and/or extreme depression. Reason being - all those feelings are just the death throes of your false beliefs. We want-to-believe there is goodness in the world. We want-to-believe that the things we do somehow *matter*. When you become a *Seer*, you see equally the beauty and the futility in all things. This is where you graduate to controlled folly.

5. Controlled folly - instead of deteriorating into the state of deep depression because you finally *see* the futility of existence (but also the potential for doing the impossible, equally), is when you begin to live your life in a way different from how you've always lived it. Knowing nothing matters, you nonetheless start to live your life *as if* it matters. You learn to pick your battles. You don't waste time chasing after political causes or religious fanaticism, you don't involve yourself in causes that are ultimately futile, but you do decide what you are going to do *as if* it matters.

To some people, maybe that's raising a family - though that comes with a whole load of programs and issues that I've never personally wanted to undertake, so that was not a battle I chose. To other people, maybe it is a stand of action for animal rights - not in any political arena, but in direct experience. If you're going to get involved in something, you do so with the knowledge that in the end, it won't matter one wit. But maybe for one individual (yourself), it will make a difference in the direction of the building of your Will and the manifestation of it. If some temporary "good" comes of your actions, so much the better - but if you engage your controlled folly with that *expectation*, then you have missed the point altogether.

6. Controlled folly will also require the art of detachment - which involves getting away from the indulgences in all those comforting belief systems. As long as someone believes in God, just for example, there is always the underlying implication that "God will take care of it." When you release

that belief, you begin to come into your own personal power. As long as there is *any* hope of salvation or divine intervention, you have defeated your own power and settled for a role of passive observer rather than the creator of singularities.

There is also a mantra that comes with any doings of metaphysics. "As it harms none, do as you Will." This does not mean to do as you *please*. It means to do what your Will is capable of doing - what you yourself are capable of bringing into manifestation. "As it harms none..." Think about that before you would even consider joining any group, particularly a group that clearly intends to use "evil" as a means to an end (and an end that will never manifest). Anytime you join anything, you have given away your power to the group. Is that really what you want to do? I don't think so.

Thou art god. Create yourself accordingly.

———

Brainwashing

I read a lot of spiritual self-help books, and after awhile I can't help but think I'm being brainwashed! What do you think about that?

In the course of talking to spiritually-minded people I meet every day, I encounter a lot who are afraid of "brainwashing" who never stop to consider the fact that they have been brainwashed, programmed and duped since they first poked their head out of their mother's womb and took their first screaming breath. That's one of the things shamanism is all about - undoing all of those programs which really are the brainwashing put onto us by a society that wants our cooperation and servitude, and cares very little for our well-being as individuals. Like it or not, we are the batteries that run the government, church and society - and it is only when we can deprogram ourselves that we finally start to see that only when we help ourselves can others actually benefit from our actions.

I do agree that cults and gurus are a potential problem. But if you're awake and aware, you simply cannot be brainwashed by any cult leader. And to worry about it is rather ludicrous. Yes, there are bad people out there - but you're far more likely to get hit on the head by a random meteorite than to get snagged by some wild-eyed cult-leader, because in the big picture, cult leaders have plenty of followers without ever needing to go out and look for recruits. So if you're not a follower, you have nothing to worry about.

The person who benefits from cutting ties to family and friends is the person who does it - not because someone else tells you to, and not because you read it in a book, but because after awhile, it may (or may not) become obvious to the warrior that it is one's closest friends and relatives who fight the hardest to maintain the status quo by keeping the warrior brainwashed into the standard rhetoric of the consensual reality.

Don't get me wrong - I have no use for cult leaders, but I can recognize why they may choose some of their methods. Perhaps, in the beginning, even with good intentions, their motive really isn't to isolate someone, but to give them the space away from the status quo so as to allow for the apprentice's suppressed Self to peek out. I would certainly have welcomed a place where I could retreat from family and friends for a short time to hear my own inner voice in the absence of their yammering. Hard to hear the voice of the double when your friends are telling you it's Satan and your mother is telling you it's a delusional fantasy and your father is just telling you to bend over. Where is the reason in any of that? Where is the sanity?

If a person is serious about being a warrior, there may

come a time (as there did with myself) when it simply becomes reasonable to turn and see that the real brainwashing is coming from those who benefit the most from keeping those old programs uploaded. "Forgive and forget." (Says the abusive husband as he beats his wife and then demands her loving forgiveness.) "Family is everything." (Says the out-of-work brother who expects to be fed and sheltered for years while living on the couch.) "Love conquers all." (Says the self-pitying but well-meaning old woman who has given up her life to care for a bunch of lazy schmucks with a sense of entitlement.)

Those who uphold the existing programs are those who benefit most from their existence. You would do far better to see the "cult leader" in the Pope or the president than in any so-called religious fanatic I've ever encountered. Why? Because the consensual agreement stands behind those cult leaders, telling us it's okay to be Catholic, and patriotic to condone the actions of a war-mongering madman.

The question isn't that we are brainwashed. We very much are, unless we have gone through the process of un-doing the programming which has been uploaded all our lives. All those huggy-lovey feel-good programs are the bread and butter of those who benefit from them. There is no reality to them beyond what significance we give (or fail to give) to them as warriors. Just because we've heard the old clichés all our lives doesn't make them real.

So it's not a matter of arbitrarily cutting all ties with our past just because some book somewhere said we should. It's a matter of awareness and honesty with ourselves. And, for some of us, it has been a matter of coming to *see* in hindsight that some of that "radical" stuff we read in some of those books just happens to hold a great deal of truth. I'm not telling you to do anything, not even suggesting it. I'm certainly not into either/or propositions - but I have learned after a great deal of experience that if we don't take out the trash, flies will come.

HEALING

Meditation for Molecular Reorganization

I realize we're all made of energy, but whether we like it or not we're apparently stuck in these organic meat suits that are subject to deterioration and decay. What has been your experience with healing? When I get the flu, I get the flu. To what extent are we organic as opposed to energy?

This is something I discovered several years ago when I woke in the middle of the night to discover that I was coming down with the flu - rapidly, severely, no doubt about it. The problem was, there was something I absolutely *had* to do the following day that could not be postponed, nor could it be done if I were ill. So, I *literally* had no alternative but to be well. So I sat there in a lazy lotus position in my bed, staring out into the darkness for a few minutes, until I began to receive instruction from Orlando, which amounted to this: *The flu virus is an invading organism. It is not part of you at the molecular level of the organic self. Knowing that gives you power - not only the power to heal, but the power to be not-sick in the first place. Reorganize the molecular arrangement of your organic self, and you have the power to recreate yourself here and now, but in doing so, what you are recreating is your Self without the invading virus. At this level of reorganization, the virus does not exist because it has no place to be. It is not part of you at the energetic core.*

It took me several hours of meditation that night to fully internalize this, but it was in the process of coming to understand it that I actually *did* what was being suggested. It is a powerful technique for healing, which is dependent on the awareness that the things that happen *to* our bodies are not part *of* our bodies, so when we can invoke the will to molecularly reorganize our structural vessels (not as difficult as it may sound), we give ourselves the power to essentially banish dis-ease by the awareness that "it" is not a natural part of "us" in the first place.

What is the proper attitude for healing?

Depends on you. For myself, I find that healing I work on myself is best when I inhabit the assemblage point of self love, unconditional love, and the awareness that, simply, "Today is not my day to die." Translated, this becomes a statement of intent and an invocation of Will. It becomes a mindset which is unbending and ruthless, yet at the same time nurturing and loving.

I've worked with others who say they have better luck with healing when they come at it from the perspective of a battle - visualizations wherein the dis-ease is an invading enemy which must be slain with sword or martial arts or whatever method of combat one might prefer. If that works for you, go for it. I find that a more quantum comprehension of the nature of dis-ease at the energetic level enables me to combat it more easily than engaging it in battle. When I engage something in battle, I am giving it power. When I engage myself at the level of molecular reorganization, I am taking back my *own* power, and the dis-ease is simply eliminated.

Does it work every time? With yourself or someone else you are trying to heal?

Unfortunately, no. Regarding the molecular reorganization technique, I would say that it works for me approximately 85% of the time. I really can't say why it works sometimes and not others, but such is the mystery of ourselves as humans.

———

Soul Retrieval and the Quantum Shaman

Have you had any experience with soul retrieval? How does that work, and is it something best performed by myself or with an experienced healer?

There are many different methods of soul retrieval. Some require the intervention of a shaman or natural healer, while others may be performed by the patient themselves. I would add with regard to the latter, that if someone intends to attempt their own soul-retrieval, the idea is that you would be working directly with your own double to facilitate the task, and so it would be something I would only recommend for those who have a strong connection to their double already. But remember - anything is possible. Knowing that is the seat of power for healing or anything else in life.

If a shaman or healer is going to perform a soul retrieval, the mindset of the person being healed should ideally be one of openness, self-love and relaxation - essentially giving the shaman access to the levels of spirit which lie beyond even the awareness of the Self. The theory behind a soul retrieval is that when we are sick, it is because the spirit has wandered away from the body for whatever reason. Sometimes it may be the result of some trauma in your life (emotional, spiritual, physical), but other times it is a disconnection that has occurred over a long period of time due to circumstances in your life: depression, fear, stress, anxiety. Whatever the reason, the body becomes dis-eased, and in order to remedy the dis-ease, the shaman journeys into the underworld to find the wandering spirit and attempt to determine if it can be convinced to return to the body.

What occurs in the underworld is a negotiation between the shaman and the wandering spirit. There are some shamanic practitioners who will attempt to literally wrestle the spirit back into the body, but I have never found that to be effective. In fact, I would not attempt it except under the most dire of circumstances, because if it is the will of the spirit not to return, chances are high that it will not yield to being forcefully brought back to the body, and the condition could be worsened rather than healed. In the soul retrievals I have done personally, I locate the spirit in the underworld and begin a dialog with it which will usually reveal the core reason for its departure from the body.

One young man I worked with had terminal liver cancer, and when I found his spirit in the underworld, what it revealed to me was that both spirit and man were simply at a point in their journey where it was time to let go. He had accomplished the creative work he had set out to do. He had provided a home for his wife, whom he loved dearly. And he had found the spirit road between himself and his double. His work on Earth was finished.

I negotiated with the spirit for a long time, but could not convince it to return to the body. When I spoke with Keith afterward, he just smiled and validated that everything I had learned was true - though he asked me not to reveal it to his wife until after his passing. In essence, he was done with the world, and even though he said he would just as soon go on living, he acknowledged in total awareness that he knew his spirit had already set off on its infinite journey.

I've had other shamanic practitioners tell me that sometimes a spirit may be held by a demon - literally imprisoned in the underworld by some other spirit - but when I have done my own journeys to look at this, what I've discovered is that the "demon" is not usually an extant spirit. For example: certain fierce addictions may have the outward manifestation of holding the spirit trapped. Heroin, for example. Or meth. Every drug or addiction has a personality - but the bottom line is that it is not an extant spirit, but some aspect of the patient's own psyche. And that, again, brings the power right back to the *self*. Take. Back. Your. Power.

The other aspect of soul retrieval would be when the warrior uses her own double to make the journey into the underworld. This can be a bit more tricky depending on one's personal beliefs or experiences with their double, but it can also work very well. For me, I do not see Orlando as my "spirit", and so I would have no problems with contradictions or conundrums if I needed to send him into the underworld to do a soul retrieval. Other warriors have reported that they cannot see the difference between their double and their spirit, and so that may stop them from performing a soul retrieval of this nature.

For me, the double is an energetic vessel which the warrior projects, and which eventually takes on a life of its own. The double becomes greater than the sum of its parts, and in doing so becomes what I have come to literally see as the vessel of awareness which stands entirely outside the box, beyond the eagle's reach. Spirit, on the other hand, is what might be visualized as the lifeforce or cohesion which connects the mortal self to the immortal double. Spirit is the glue, and it is when that glue is no longer present in the body that the body becomes dis-eased.

So if I were to send Orlando into the underworld to perform a soul retrieval for myself, I would be relying on the connection of gnosis to reveal whatever he might discover on his journey. If the warrior has a good connection of gnosis with her double, then it is always desirable to participate as much as humanly possible in your own healing in this, using your own double as the go-between. If the warrior does not have a reliable gnosis connection with the double, there can still be results, though it may be more difficult for the warrior in the world of ordinary awareness to interpret what occurs in the underworld.

Ideally, whenever possible, I recommend both methods for warriors who are sufficiently advanced to have that kind of communication with their double: an extant shamanic practitioner and working with one's own double. The stakes are life and death in some cases, and using every bit of awareness and resource at your disposal is what will manifest the power of your own Intent.

In the big picture, I can only say that the attitude of healing is an attitude of taking back our own power - remembering that you are the most powerful being in the universe, who can recreate yourself through Intent and the application of Will.

When you take back your power...

There is no limit to what you can do.

THE ENIGMA OF FAITH, RELIGION AND GODS

The Destruction of Faith
Awareness 101

What about faith? Is faith a matter of religion or a matter of simple self-confidence?

What would you lose if you let go of your beliefs and lived your life from a somewhat opposite perspective? I've done this as a matter of self-awareness from time to time - walked through the world with the belief that I am a 90 year old black woman (one experiment), or that I am invisible (another experiment), or that I am scheduled to be executed at midnight this very night.

The results are that when I shift my awareness into an entirely different position, I actually *see* the world quite differently - and that enables new windows to open, new cracks in the cosmic egg to become visible.

When I begin stalking myself and asking where my opinions come from, I usually find that if they are only opinions, they do not come from my own life-experience, but from either book learning or second hand information. Not of much value in the nagual, nor even in the tonal, actually. We can't truly *know* anything until we let go of what we *believe* - even if the letting go is painful and shatters our (false) identity altogether. That shattering of the self is the real crack between the worlds.

What about the idea of forgiveness? Is forgiveness something we give to someone, or something we do to release the hooks someone might have in us?

A lot of people do a lot of talking about forgiveness, but I don't think that word means what people think it does. Forgiveness isn't about giving someone a second or third or tenth chance to go on being an asshat. It isn't about saying, "They're sick or troubled or just can't help themselves." The reality is that everything is a choice, and even though we are all human and make mistakes, to go *on* making the same mistakes over and over (such as emotional or physical abuse, for example), is just a series of bad choices repeated ad nauseam because others put up with you.

Expecting someone to forgive you for being crazy when crazy is a choice... is just... well... *crazy!* Forgiveness, therefore, isn't about turning the other cheek. It's about giving *yourself* permission to move on and move away from those who otherwise drag you down into their misery and then ask for forgiveness. It's about giving yourself permission to *not* let the other person's craziness become *your* downfall.

So I'm re-examining the idea of forgiveness and coming to *see* that it isn't something we hand out freely to the murderers and rapists and First Class Assholes. It's what we do for our own survival and sanity. I've learned to forgive *myself* for pulling the plug on friendships and relationships that require constant and unending drama and daily forgiveness. Detachment and self-reliance are the warrior's best defense against the folly and madness of the world. I may often walk alone, but I am never lonely - and I ask no forgiveness for that.

———

"Of course I want religion to go away"

I don't deny you your right to believe whatever you'd like; but I have the right to point out it's ignorant and dangerous for as long as your baseless supersitions keep killing people.

ANTI-THEISM:

The conscientious objection to religion.

ATHEISM 411

Do you believe in God? Do you even think God exists or ever did?

Someone on my Facebook group was dismayed by "so many anti-theism posts lately." And yet, it's not hard to guess why we're starting to see more people demanding not just freedom *of* religion, but freedom *from* religion. So many radical acts have religion at their core and those who are not at all religious can't help but see it as a bit whacko - slaughtering people in the name of some god who may not even exist, and who certainly wouldn't condone their actions if he did. Additionally, religion has been at the heart of persecution since the dawn of time. The Crusades. The witch hunts. Every holy war ever fought.

"Holy war." When I think about that, my brain just wants

to twist. What is the purpose of murdering people because they don't share one's belief systems? If that isn't the definition of insanity, I don't know what would qualify.

When I was growing up in central Florida, everybody I knew was a Christian (or claimed to be out of fear). Even the kids in my class all went to church. I couldn't fathom it. Even though I was raised in a *very* religious environment (Southern Baptist), none of it ever made one lick of sense. I thought something was wrong with the adults who gathered in a hot building every Sunday morning to sing hymns to a ghost when they could have been at the beach or in the forest or anything more pleasant and more in tune with spirit. It wasn't that I was bored. I was actually fascinated - but not in the way the church ladies might have wished. Kinda like watching a train wreck - it's a horror of epic proportions, but sometimes you just can't look away.

My deeper disgust with "the church" (aka organized religion) came when my mother, who was 85 at the time and living on a fixed income of less than $700/month, told me she had just been visited by the pastor of her church. His sole reason for the visit? To encourage her to fill out a "Pledge to Tithe." In other words, give 10% of her very meager income to "god." At that point, I saw the true evil of that which claims to be good.

God doesn't need an old woman's money.

Most religions rob people of their personal power - not by accident, but with deliberate and malicious Intent to control. By always telling true believers to "let go and let God", organized religion takes control of free thinking. People find themselves shoved into all sorts of beliefs, many of which are designed to be self-perpetuating. "If you don't believe this, you're going to hell!" "If you don't give God your money, you are giving it to Satan." The list is long. The manipulation is right up there with original sin - and in this way the church has become the very devil it so vilifies.

If someone wants to believe in God, that's all fine and

good, so long as they aren't being coerced or threatened into believing it because they are told they should... or else. Of course, these are just my beliefs. I don't expect anyone to follow them, because that's just another manifestation of religion.

––––––

Freeing the Sheeple

In a discussion with a member of the Baha'i faith, we began to touch on the idea that organized religion may indeed actually disempower the individual rather than providing any real sense of truth or any real tools of spiritual development.

I do think part of the challenge we face on the philosophical and spiritual levels has to do with the limitations of language. The words faith, belief, truth, religion, spirit, god, just for starters, are going to mean something entirely different to all of us, even within our collective agreement.

"Although a person of good deeds is acceptable at the Threshold of the Almighty, yet it is first 'to know,' and then 'to do.' ('Abdu'l-Baha, Tablets of 'Abdu'l-Baha v3, p549)

Knowing very little about the Baha'i faith, I can only respond to the words here, out of context. It is the words "at the threshold of the Almighty" which give me pause, because the implication is that "the Almighty" is an entity separate from the self, and therefore someone or something his followers must adhere to in order to receive his favor. If I'm wrong about this with regard to the Baha'i faith, my apologies, but this is getting toward the crux of what I see to be a major issue with most organized religions, where the entire doctrine is written around an extant manifestation of Spirit.

When Spirit is externalized, followers are created. It can't be any other way, because whenever Spirit is turned into an entity (such as the Christian god), a series of rules and regulations for pleasing this entity are automatically generated (What shall we do to be saved, oh lord?), followed closely by a series of taboos and boundaries which the entity's followers are cautioned against crossing, lest they suffer this or that ill fate (whether going to hell or being reincarnated as a dung beetle).

In short, it is within the limitations of those rules and regulations, taboos and thou-shalt-nots, that the Self begins to be pigeon-holed into what is acceptable or unacceptable - and most times, the results are like a program of behavior and belief which the follower uploads almost unknowingly at first. And once the program is uploaded and becomes a belief system, it is the reality of the follower, regardless of what basis it may or may not have in any sense of truth and reality.

The individual becomes disempowered at a spiritual level when programmed to believe that the real power lies outside of herself.

And so the journey I have undertaken, both as practitioner and counselor, involves removing all those old belief systems in order to bring the individual into contact with the godforce within themselves. God can still exist, but the *individual* is god, and so the relationship becomes intimate, personal, and ultimately self-empowering - because the boundaries between self and god are removed, the rules and regulations and taboos fall aside, and what occurs is a spiritual awakening, in which the individual embraces "god" within herself, *as* herself, and begins to take responsibility for her actions in every aspect of her life.

BLIND FAITH
Because thinking is hard.

I feel this was the original goal of most of the original teachers - Christ, Buddha, Mohammed, and many others - but the problem is that the organized aspect of religion cannot help but create boundaries and limitations which ultimately impact the spiritual potential of its followers.

In seeking to form an agreement (a religion is a collective agreement), the original Intent of the teachings becomes watered down, rendered down into shoulds and shouldn'ts, and the vast majority of that religion's followers are sheep - and, in fact, many even refer to themselves in such a manner in Christianity. Granted, perhaps that is an extreme, but the general point I'm trying to make can't be denied.

Jesus himself would be the first to cast the church as it stands today asunder - because in so many ways it goes against everything he was attempting to teach.

Near as I can determine through vision quests, meditations and truth-seeking, Jesus was a shaman who figured things out for himself, did the long and difficult task of stripping away the programs put onto him by his society, and emerged in the aftermath of it all as an enlightened spirit. He tried teaching this to a few select disciples, and maybe at that one-on-one level of instruction, some of them actually grasped it and went on to achieve their own enlightenment. But what has followed since has been, simply, followers. For centuries.

Now, instead of being told to "Do and you may be able to save yourself from the obliteration of Self at death," followers are simply told, "Believe and you will be saved from hell." The Intent has been lost, replaced with a much watered-down, more palatable version of "Salvation in 5 minutes – just believe!" It doesn't work that way. Jesus knew it. Buddha knew it. And at some level, we all know it – but the problem is that too many people are too afraid of finding out that they've been wrong all their lives, so they would rather go right on being wrong, because at least they're comfortable in the familiar territory of long-held beliefs. The earth was once flat, too. The moon was made of green cheese. Epilepsy was a sign of possession by the devil.

Do you follow the religious path you are on through blind faith - that is, in spite of no evidence for it or, worse, in spite of evidence against it? (I'll be pretty shocked if you say yes to that!) Neither do I, nor does any Christian I've ever met.

I do not follow any traditional path. I forge my own, based on truths I have found to be universal or higher truths, (no matter what the source - Buddhist, Christian, Toltec, *Star Trek*), but I always pause to reflect on the validity of whatever truth I am practicing. A lot of people I work with in the capacity of spiritual counselor are actually afraid of their own abilities because of the programs put onto them by their religion - so in that regard, I have to say that most of the Christians I have met really *do* follow their religion based largely on blind faith. Perhaps they felt some spark of spirit in the initial stage of their journey, but by the time I make their acquaintance, that spark has been rendered down into "Thou shalt not" fill in the blank. Many have lived their lives believing that if they work hard enough in the church or pray hard enough or tithe more, their god will favor them with a better life, and when it doesn't happen, all too often the church leaders either place the blame on them. "You didn't pray hard enough." Or respond with the typical rhetoric, "God moves in mysterious ways and ours is not to question why."

That's where I have a major problem with organized religion - because in the organization of what the congregation should or shouldn't believe, the individual gets swept under the rug and herded into the pew like one more sheep in the fold. Most simply do not have the tools (emotional, spiritual, rational) for seeing beyond the belief system and into the core of whatever truth may or may not lie beyond the organized belief system itself.

Without the inner spark of religion, I doubt that most people would bother with the rest.

A lot of people start off with that inner spark, but instead of leading them on a journey of self-exploration, it leads them in search of an agreement. And that's the danger of organized religion, in my opinion. The reason there are so many religions, ultimately, is because none of them can really agree on what is truth. That is where the individual's own sense of spiritual responsibility must come in to play. We learn and grow by Do-ing, not by believing.

"The destruction of faith
is the beginning of evolution."

PART TWO

BEYOND THE EDGE OF THE WORLD
(The Nagual)

Sailing off the edge of the known world, we find ourselves in the uncharted territory of the unknown, and sometimes the unknowable.

Inquiries from warrior-seekers who cross the threshold between the mundane consensus and ever-changing path to the Infinite.

Enlightenment, Young Grasshopper!

In a recent discussion the question was asked, *What is enlightenment?* During the course of the ensuing conversation, it was stated by one seeker that "There is the old anecdote that the rivers and the mountains are the same before and after enlightenment."

Among other things, being enlightened really means living in a mental state of awareness and responsibility to the self as an infinite and eternal being. And, of course, when we are responsible to the self, we usually end up engaging "the right way to live" somewhat by natural instinct.

I like the analogy of the rivers and the mountains being the same before and after enlightenment. The only difference, perhaps, is that the Self actually *sees* the river and the mountains somewhat differently after achieving a state of sufficient awareness. Before becoming a person of knowledge, perhaps we tend to see the rivers and mountains as separate manifestations of nature - biological accidents of a sort. After becoming a woman of knowledge, there is more of a tendency to *see* the energetic matrix of the rivers and mountains as interconnected components of what Philip K. Dick once called VALIS - a vast, active living intelligence system. Through seamless and infinite awareness, we *are* the river, the mountain, and the space in between.

Another interesting byproduct is that this kind of awareness tends to create a state of being in which we *do* become responsible to the Knowledge and even to the rivers and the mountains. When we *see* ourselves reflected in them, it changes *us,* and that is part of the state of being I would call enlightenment.

The atoms of our physical self have always been here, going through a series of evolutions, changes, births and deaths. So, in that regard, some particle of some former manifestation has certainly nurtured the Joshua trees or fell as rain into the oceans or burned to ash that has been carried on the wind to the farthest reaches of this physical earth. In that way, I am literally a physical part of the All. I'm just re-using the molecules shed by Goethe or an apple tree in the first garden, or a mushroom ingested by don Juan.

More importantly, as a result of creating my double and recognition of the fact that the double is a non-local singularity of awareness, it stands to reason that my awareness also exists within *literally* every atom of the All as well. Therefore, it is a statement of both fact and philosophy to say *I-Am* the rivers and the mountains, etc. The VALIS (vast, active living intelligence system) that Philip K. Dick and others have been searching for eludes them because it *is* them.

If taken further, it becomes obvious that this is not a closed cycle of life and death, but an actual process of evolution, through which some beings will achieve enlightenment and reach their wholeness within the VALIS. At that point, it could be said that one has achieved the status of a singularity of consciousness - existing everywhere, yet entirely non-local unless one might Will oneself into some form of molecular manifestation.

Having a quantum comprehension of this cycle of evolution is just one of the things that gives it "permission" to exist in the world I share with others. This is just one way in which I create reality - by having a better understanding of its machinations and its possibilities. That isn't to say it wouldn't go right on existing *without* my understanding, but at least *with* my understanding, I give myself a broader foundation upon which to stand, and that as my world grows, so does my Knowledge.

The things we allow to exist in our awareness expand the universe both physically and spiritually. It's how reality is created and how it is expanded. It's actually a process of removing the limitations we have placed on ourselves, so that we may begin to experience (directly and literally) our Self as all manner of creation - river, mountain, snow, star, tonal and Nagual.

The Warrior's Party - Reality or Myth?

Is there really such a thing as the warrior's party as it was discussed in Carlos Castaneda's book, The Eagle's Gift? Or is it only a metaphor or even a myth?

> The average man is hooked to his fellow men, while the warrior is hooked only to infinity.
>
> *Carlos Castaneda*

From my own experience and Knowledge, I'd have to say that the idea of a warrior's party as it was described by Carlos is probably not as viable in today's world as it was when Carlos was roaming the desert with Don Juan Matus (and that's *if* those events really happened as they are described, vs. whether they may be at least somewhat allegorical). Though they are valid either way, it is my opinion that *if* the events as described are accurate, what Carlos left us with is what amounts to a road map to freedom. Both Carlos and don Juan made comments that the old lineages were ending. That being the case, it is also my contention that Carlos was selected (whether by Don Juan or by Spirit) to chronicle some of the Toltec wisdom and the ways of nagualism - not just as field notes for an anthropology thesis, but for future generations.

If read as a whole unit, Castaneda's books (as well as the writings of many other Toltec/nagualism authors) provide the seeker with various techniques, as well as with the suggestion that any *real* change has to come from the Self. No teacher, no other warriors, no Nagual man or Nagual woman is going to take you to Freedom. If you're going there, it's a one-way trip and a one-person ticket. The idea of a warrior's party (in my opinion) is more of an allegory than a fact - so for those who are actually looking for a warrior's party, you may have better luck looking for leprechauns or Lilliputians.

This isn't to say that warrior's parties don't exist. They probably do. But I'm not sure they are what a lot of seekers imagine them to be. So many seekers I've worked with over the years have an idea in their head that a warrior's party means gathering in the desert to participate in mitotes, to argue vehemently with other warriors, and to sit at the feet of some don Juan character who exists solely in their own head.

The path *must* evolve - and I feel that it has since Carlos wrote his books, and it will continue to evolve and adapt because that is simply the way of Spirit. It approaches us on the level where we presently exist, and encourages us to advance, grow and evolve. *Take it further*, the voice of gnosis instructs. And how could it be any other way?

I'm sure there was a time when actual warrior parties were the way of things. But that is no longer the world in which most of us live, and yet I know from direct experience that Spirit still calls to us and gives us the means whereby to reach Freedom. No warrior's party necessary. What is necessary is "The Work", but also the willingness to let go of the ideas in our head which try to tell us - "It can only be this way and no other way." As long as seekers cling to such fixed and inflexible ideas, they are probably not in service to themselves, but to the Program, and to the Eagle.

The idea of a warrior's party is extremely appealing, even spiritually romantic in many ways. And yet, I don't perceive it to be a practical goal in the context of the world we live in today. Most of all, a warrior-seeker has to be adaptable and forward-thinking at all times (fluid, in other words). Spirit and the nagual are all around us, and when we learn to connect to them through the power of silence, we have the library of the Infinite at our fingertips. The warrior's party is inside each and every one of us. Learning to recognize and identify the various "characters" within our own skin is just part of the journey. You are already don Juan, don Genaro, doña Soledad, La Gorda, the witches, Silvio Manuel, and all the rest.

Do you want to be hooked to your fellow men, or to infinity? Take back your power - that's where you'll find the warrior's party.

———

Retroactive Enchantment

What is retroactive enchantment? How would it apply to a seeker's path - particularly a path of Toltec sorcery?

As defined by Peter J. Carroll...

It is worth noting that the paradigm predicts the possibility of several magical effects that have often eluded notice or been misinterpreted in the history of magic. Most magicians are comfortable with the idea that it is possible to divine for events hidden in the past or in the future. CMT (chaos magick theory) allows this but states that any such information found represents, at best, the highest probability events that were likely to have occurred or that might occur, for the magician can only look through shadow time, as the ordinary pseudo past and future have no existence.
Most magicians are also comfortable with the idea that enchantments can be cast to force, or at least nudge, the hand of chance as far as the future is concerned. However, CMT asserts that the opposite effect, namely retroactive enchantment, is possible. In fact, many of the bizarre and anomalous results recorded in the annals of magic can only have been due to retroactive enchantment. In practice what happens is that a spell is cast and some time later a result is recorded which strongly implies that an alteration has occurred to events that probably occurred prior to the spell being cast.
Once it is remembered that the past and future in ordinary pseudo time do not exist except in terms of memory

and expectation, then the conceptual difficulties with retroactive enchantment disappear.

As to how this would apply to Toltec sorcery, I have found through experimentation and validation from others on a similar path that we may have the potential as seekers in the Now to actually influence our Self (or selves) in the past - in particular, we seemingly have the ability to seduce the senses of our childhood selves to insure that they wake up to the realization that the world is nothing like we have been taught to believe. Since it seems so many of us on a spiritual path came from difficult childhood situations, I am finding this to be a fascinating area of exploration, since it would appear to have quantifiable results - at least on the level of one's individual life and how our past can be contrasted against our "Now" to see where we came from with regard to our spiritual and mental evolution.

For me, it's become a matter of revealing to my childhood self - through my Intent and application of Will in the now - that there is more to life than boys or drugs or mindless adherence to religion. There is, simply, the unknown, the unknowable, the infinite, what Toltec calls the nagual. *There is more.* It is virtually impossible to describe the techniques I have used. Often nothing more than reaching backward in time with my awareness, finding the child self sitting alone underneath a tree, for example, and causing some anomaly to occur that will catch her attention and simply cause her to wonder.

Since this is new territory, I am admittedly rambling in the dark, but often that's where assimilation of new knowledge begins. We learn by do-ing, even when that would appear to be doing something traditionally believed impossible. *You can't reach back in time,* we're told. *All things die,* we hear. *There's no such thing as a ghost,* the consensual reality informs us.

If we believe these things blindly, they become programs.

But if we can step outside the box of belief and begin to question through the *active* do-ing of personal experimentation with consciousness, the world often expands beyond the confines of the programs which are attempting to hold it together, and most people cannot stand that kind of rattling to the foundation of their status quo.

The best advice I can give is to be gentle and loving with yourself when moving in the direction of intentional retroactive enchantment. Even if you happen to see your past childhood self as stubborn or irredeemable or simply boring, it is unconditional love that has the power to bring her into the Now and assist in healing whatever made her the way she was as a child. There are aspects of my child self that I don't like either, but I tend to focus on some aspect I *do* like and make my journeys from that mindset. I'm not really trying to fix anything in these journeys. Far more, I'm trying to prove to this very reasonable child (who is also totally wild) that the world is nothing like she is being programmed to believe.

Once when I was probably about 8-10 years old, I was lying on the old metal slide attached to my swing set in the back yard (5 acres of swamp land and orange grove), staring up into the most perfect blue sky with light puffy clouds anyone has ever imagined. All of a sudden, I felt my consciousness elongate and stretch up and out into the void, like a beam of light shot out of a high-powered laser. I suddenly knew the definition of infinity and eternity - and both of those words flashed through my mind, which is odd, to say the least, for a pre-adolescent young girl in the early 1960s. These were not topics on my mind. I just suddenly understood the concept of infinity in all directions - the juncture of the space-time continuum being the meeting point between eternity and infinity as each infuses the other.

My mind could barely wrap around it. And in hindsight, I'm pretty sure that was what amounts to a full-on psychic download from Orlando - a gift of Knowledge that gave that little girl a strong sense of the infinite at a very early age.

None of these excursions (either as me in the Now *do-ing* it, or as the little girl in the past *receiving* it) have had anything to do with directly attempting to heal anything. I'm not even sure anything was broken - in fact, I'm sure it *wasn't*. So perhaps it's more a matter of revealing the ineffable to the child self, giving her some mysteries to ponder, some unexplained happenings that fly in the face of reason. Rather like the time traveler from the future visiting himself in the past, and giving him a coin from the future to titillate the child's fantasies, keep his mind always wondering.

This is very difficult to put into words, so the words themselves may *not* make sense. In cases like that, Orlando usually tells me, "Read from the corner of the third eye in little glances - not to understand what is written, but to *see* the essence of what the words are attempting to describe."

———

Unbending Intent

What does unbending intent mean? What does it look like? How does one determine its presence? Is it a raging fire or a slow steady flame? Does it matter? Does it imply a kind of 'rigidity' of the path?

Unbending intent is fluid, first and foremost. I proved this to myself many years ago with my experiments regarding the creation of reality at a sub-atomic level. To use a silly example I've written about before, I once said to myself that I wanted to see a red hearse before I got home. In the middle of the desert, middle of summer, middle of nowhere, this seemed unlikely. But as I pulled up to a stop sign, there, facing me in the oncoming lane was a *white* hearse... but it bore the license plate: 1RED338. I had to laugh, of course - it was a hearse, but not a red one, yet the word "red" was there for all to see. Ditto for other experiments in the same vein. I once said I wanted to see a lion before we got home, and came around a bend in the freeway to see a sign in Hollywood in the shape of a lion's head, with a sign beneath advertising the play, *The Lion King.*

There have been other such manifestations as well, but what's interesting to me is that if I am rigid in my attempts, I will get nothing. The trick is to intend the thing clearly and then release it, so that the energy of intent may then find its path toward manifestation. All the intent in the world is useless if it is held too tight. So, when you ask what unbending intent looks like, I would say that it is an actual force of energy no different than wind or rain or nuclear power or what have you. It can literally manifest reality or change our personal world, but if it is not fluid (allowing for interpretation within the realm of all possibility), we may thwart ourselves with some vain effort to control what we hope to bring into manifestation. If I had insisted that *only* a real lion would suffice, I would have missed the magic and the humor inherent in the magic itself.

With regard to the bigger picture of freedom past the eagle, I once said to the universe, "I give you permission to be whatever you need to be in order to teach me." I had had certain expectations all my life, but only when I released those expectations and gave them over to Power did the path really begin to unfold for me. The result is that I've been truly blessed with manifestations from the infinite that have been nothing like I could have imagined or predicted. Intent has prevailed through its own force.

Looking for Mr. Right

Many people hold deep rooted ideas about what a Nagual or enlightened being should look or walk or sound like. For instance, what if they drink? smoke? gamble? have lots of sex? What if it's kinky sex? What if they do stumble, fall, bang into walls? Then what? What if there's nothing perfect or ideal about them?

If you find a perfect Nagual, I would strongly suggest running as fast as possible in the other direction. That's one of the common misconceptions - and one of the prevailing causes of the downfall of would-be apprentices.

Naguals are simply human beings with a connection to the infinite. Most of them are neither perfect nor anywhere close *because* they are human beings. Sure, many have lost their humanform, but that does *not* mean they are glowing beings of light who don't take a crap in the morning or don't bleed if you cut them. Through impeccability, a Nagual or a warrior does the best she can, but the bodies we inhabit are nonetheless organic constructs that have fatal flaws. Carlos allegedly died of liver cancer, and to those stuck in their rigid notion of what a nagual *should* be, that invalidates everything he ever said or did. In reality, that's just the way an apprentice chooses to disempower herself - by looking at the flaws of the messenger instead of the truths contained in the message.

———

Mortal Self, Immortal Other

Is it possible to achieve physical immortality?

On the way to Palm Springs, I enter a deep trance state as the car rolls thru the desert. Below the level of conscious awareness, I hear myself asking the question, *Is physical immortality possible?* Deep in this trance, a voice not my own answers, *Physical is the wrong word.* The All transmits the knowledge – whole and intact, a full concept – that once we pass thru this evolutionary transformation, we are no longer even physical in the sense most humans use the word.

When we achieve the ability to renew our bodies at will, to move in and out of the energy web of which all things are made at a subatomic level, we might appear physical, even to ourselves, but it seems that the achieving of immortality in this way will make us more energy that matter – self-renewing, a manifested consciousness, whole and alive, but not physical as we use the word. In this deep trance state, I hear my mind rephrase the question, *Is it possible to achieve a continuation of consciousness in a form recognizable to self and others in the space-time continuum we call the present reality?* The All answers, *Of course.* It seemed to want me to realize the nature of what we are seeking. If it allowed me to think in purely physical terms, the seeking itself would perhaps take a different form. Only by understanding as much as we can of the nature of the thing we seek can we ever hope to Realize it.

Whereas the human enters life and breaks off from the energy web by essentially pulling up his roots, the eternal being moves in and out of the web naturally and at will, continually self-renewing, manifesting or remaining unmanifest, entirely at will. The goal, it seems, is for us as humans to learn how to reinsert ourselves into the web through conscious intent – rather than looking at this as a quest for continuity of this body, it might help to see it as an attempt to renew and regenerate the lifeforce by becoming one with the energy web and learning to manipulate it into and out of manifestation, as a matter of will.

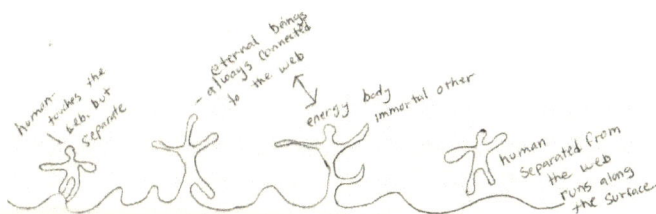

Unconditional Love and the Warrior

I hear a lot of new age jibber jabber about unconditional love, but in the immortal words of Inigo Montoya, "You keep using that word. I do not think it means what you think it means." So I'd like to hear your take on it. What is unconditional love?

Perhaps the greatest thing I have ever learned is the concept of unconditional love. When I first encountered the term mixed in with a lot of new age mumbo jumbo, I didn't comprehend it for what it really is, but over the course of the journey and working with Orlando, I've come to really *see* that the one thing a warrior needs first and foremost is unconditional love.

Even warriors at an advanced level sometimes have a serious misconception about what is meant by that term, so allow me to give my own definition. Unconditional love is about being able to love someone regardless of who they are, what they do, whether they agree or disagree with me, and so on. I can truthfully say I have unconditional love even for someone like David Westerfield (a notorious child-killer from San Diego), yet I would also have no qualms whatsoever if I were asked to administer the lethal injection. That would also be an act of unconditional love. Okay, that's the extreme. I've also used the example about sitting in my car at an intersection while an old man is trying to cross the road. I can feel absolute unconditional love and even empathy for him, but at the same time, I can feel frustration that I wish he would get his butt out of the road before I'm late for my movie.

Unconditional love, in my opinion, is very necessary for warriors. When people don't have it is when they lapse into fear, paranoia, anger, hatred and - worst of all - vengeance. That isn't to say warriors should be without emotion. I don't believe for a moment that someone is a better warrior just because they can suppress their emotions. No, they're just a better actor. If you're in human form, you *will* feel anger and pain and hurt and every other emotion humans are capable of, but what regulates those feelings and enables the warrior to use them to her advantage is the state of unconditional love - because that is the state that never wavers.

Even when I am angry at someone, I do not stop loving them. Even when I was betrayed very deeply by an old friend, I did not and cannot stop loving him. In fact, the love I feel for him is the only thing that makes what happened bearable, because it is the love that survives even when the friendship lies in ashes. This is why I've said in the past that love is the glue that holds it all together - and I don't mean that in any smarmy new-age way. I mean it literally. Love is a *force* which Orlando has called "the fifth element" - meaning that it is just as much a part of creation as earth, wind, fire and water. Love is the evolved sentience that seems to bind it all together and give it meaning. Love survives, and that is what I mean when I say Spirit is made of love.

So it seems to me that those who may play at being cold and hard probably don't get it. I know a lot of warriors who like to put on what I call their Vulcan-mask, and go around pretending to have no feelings. It's one thing to be detached as a warrior, but it's another matter altogether to squelch any feelings we may have so that we become nothing more than observers. At that point, might as well be a camera or a tv monitor, because that which cannot feel is not human.

Love is the reason and the cohesion.
Without it, the eagle has already won.

———

Unconditional Love (Part 2)

I have an asshole neighbor with a garage band who thinks nothing of pounding his drums at 4 a.m. or giving alcohol to underage teenage girls while they all run rampant and half-naked through the desert, screaming so loud the dead are complaining. I'm no prude. I've done it all and hold no judgments. But there comes a time when I have to accept that my actions affect other people, and if I cannot take responsibility for that, I have to accept that someone else will. My father was a tyrant who once shot a stray cat right in front of me – an image of horror I still carry with me to this day. Unconditional love for some people becomes a challenge.

The thing about unconditional love as it applies to assholes is that it really makes no difference if they are assholes or not. They are a lifeform on a journey, and while I may despise the things they do, I have an unconditional love that has to do with respecting their journey upstream. Even if they are just swimming in their own droppings, and I may feel nothing but loathing for them on a level of ordinary awareness, I have to *allow* myself to have unconditional love for them at the higher levels of awareness, or else I begin to limit myself by withholding the catalytic element of creation – the moving force of unconditional love. People with hatred in their hearts never really transcend, because ultimately it requires a lot more energy and effort to create the web of hatred than it does to simply allow the element of love to express itself through its natural manifestation. Without that force, it's all just random chaos that I might pick and sort through like discarded items at a thrift store.

So as for people like the Green River Killer and David Westerfield and all the "bad" people of the world, I mean what I say when I tell you I would be the first to administer their lethal injection, yet I also love them unconditionally because that love is the glue that holds my own cohesion together. It's not about them, but about my *self*. Without the ability to love unconditionally, I am less than a fragment.

There is a concept Orlando has talked about for years - duality. Not the dualism of black/white, good/evil or any of the traditional perception-by-juxtaposition. Rather, duality is what enables the warrior to "be immortal so you will know how to become immortal". It is what enables one to love unconditionally and at the same time feel absolute loathing for the actions of oneself or the actions of another. We don't have to choose one assemblage point over the other – love or disgust. Both can exist simultaneously if we are willing to allow that balance.

In the big picture, perhaps it doesn't matter, yet because I am human here in the now, I have to find the glue of love to maintain my cohesion even in the face of absolute madness.

Unconditional love is a force of creation. Remember - I'm speaking of the physics-quantum force. So, in that way, this force is like a natural stream that flows through us at all times unless we permit it to be dammed up by the actions of others, or even our own choices to hate or fear.

Our entire process of evolution is about learning to love ourselves and let go of that which impedes us, so that we may create the Whole self as a singularity of consciousness capable of withstanding the forces of infinity.

———

Tools of Spirit

A question was recently posed about what kinds of tools people might use in their quest for an evolution of consciousness. For myself, I started out ages ago using the traditional tools of "magic" - Tarot cards, tea leaves, palmistry, Ouija board (if anyone cringes or feels a twinge of fear, good time to check your attachments to programs). What I found was that the tools were effective to a point, but it didn't take long to realize I was beyond the tools even as I was using them, and they were actually limiting.

Of all the tools I used in that early phase, the Ouija board was actually most effective - not as a method of contacting the dead, but as a tool for getting in touch with one's own higher self. It's unfortunate that all the Hollywood hype has turned one of the few readily-available tools for spiritual self-development into a much maligned and feared "instrument of the devil." If people are getting demonic messages on a Ouija board it's either some dark fragment of one of the participants coming through loud and clear, or one of the participants attempting to create drama by buying into the fears and superstitions surrounding the tool itself. But if used properly and with respect (like any other tool), a Ouija board can provide a remarkable instrument of communication between the mortal self and the eternal Other - one's own double, or even the sentient universe at large.

Other tools have been the mushroom ally - which is in a class by itself. I have used that tool no more than a handful of times throughout the course of my journey, because its effects are so profound and all-encompassing that it is literally like an immersion into Knowledge itself. Once the assemblage point of the ally was learned and integrated, there has been no further need for the tool itself. Should the need arise, however, it is a tool I would not hesitate to use again, except for the fact that it is literally the most frightening experience of a lifetime, as well as the most enlightening. And under no circumstances would I recommend the use of this ally or any other of the power plant allies without the supervision of a master shaman.

Awareness itself could be called a tool, but in such a different way that I don't really think of it as such. I was recently sitting in a restaurant with Wendy, talking about a prominent news story involving a man who had been cheating on his wife. Just as I was saying, "He's guilty as a fat cat in front of an empty bird cage," the canned music cut into my awareness with the lyrics of an old Billy Joel song, *An Innocent Man*. Of course, one could write such things off as coincidence, but to anyone with awareness, what is being put forth is the suggestion to at least take another look at the equation. The man may or may not be truly innocent, but the portend was showing me that there were other aspects to be considered.

Quite often when we are on the road, I've found I can predict how things will go by the movement of certain birds, and in particular, observing the shadows of ravens on the ground. Quite often, a raven will fly over the car just as we are leaving the desert, casting his shadow either directly on us, or just in front of us - always a good portend. Why? Who's to say? But awareness of these events over a long period of time has shown a pattern and it is in observing patterns that we are able to make certain predictions.

Ultimately, my connection to the infinite nowadays is simply through silent knowing. No other tools required, though it could be observed that it was through the use of certain tools that I came to have the ability to access gnosis directly. As children, we use our fingers to count. Hopefully as adults, we grow beyond that and into a more conceptual forward thinking. I see this journey in much the same way - we begin with tools, and come eventually to a place where any tools we might ever need are completely contained within the Self.

You are the universe incarnate. What other tools would you need?

———

THE ENEMIES OF A MAN OF KNOWLEDGE

Clarity

When I first read the books of Carlos Castaneda, I remember encountering the section where don Juan explains that there are four enemies of a man of knowledge. Fear. Clarity. Power. And old age. I understand why fear, old age and power are enemies. But why is clarity?

Perhaps the best way to answer that question is through a personal anecdote which occurred in February of 2004...

Strange day yesterday. Got up around 7 with the intention of going into Los Angeles on one of our buying expeditions for the business, but decided to turn on the tube to see what the weather was doing. As if by magic, the weatherman was standing there in his slick new suit and funny bow tie, informing all the world that the storm had passed at long last, and a day of intermittent clouds and sparsely scattered showers should on the SoCal menu.

Knowing the relationship I have with the television, I

should have turned it off the instant I got the information I was looking for. But instead, distracted for a moment, I turned back to catch a glimpse of a huge Siberian tiger - clearly dead - being airlifted by a helicopter, in a net, and unceremoniously dumped into the back of a pick-up, amidst a hubbub of male onlookers who poked and prodded the poor beast like a bunch of would-be hunters in some primitive tribal ritual.

As these images flooded the screen, the over-zealous newscaster spoke in grandiose terms about how "the big cat" had been tracked and hunted for five days in an LA suburb, and was finally shot and killed mere feet from an elementary school. All the world was a safer place, and the jesters cheered and there was much feasting and rejoicing and the singing of minstrels.

I could only stand there in horror and disgust, for clearly the atmosphere was one of celebration, the triumph of the great white male hunter over the wild beast. Never once did the reporter give any indication as to why an endangered animal couldn't be tranquilized and taken to a zoo, or why it was reasonable to shoot off a bunch of guns in the vicinity of an elementary school in order to protect the little darlings from an animal that was clearly more afraid of them than they could ever be of it.

Would it perhaps have made more sense to keep the children indoors for a few hours, and use some of our alleged intelligence to capture the animal? Of course not. Would it have disrupted the daily schedule, the grind of the cogs in the machine? Would it have changed the rotation of the Earth to do the *right* thing instead of the easy thing?

After turning off the television, I stood in front of the window for a long time, watching the cold winter rain fall slowly, steadily over the desert. I wanted to weep, yet it would serve no purpose. I wanted to wail in despair at the poisonous, contagious, seething stupidity of the human race. It would change nothing.

So I got dressed and drove into the city, drifting in and

out of gnosis as I tend to do on long drives. Orlando pressed close, yet at the same time seemed to slip away, quicksilver evading capture. The restlessness I had been feeling for the past weeks had turned to irritability as I thought about the future, what it might hold, the potential changes to come as a result of the upcoming publication of my first book in the *Quantum Shaman*™ series.

Futility and clarity - strange bedfellows, to be sure. *Seeing* the madness with abject clarity could *only* result in a state of restless futility, and in that way there is no doubt that clarity can quickly become an enemy, for it opens one's eyes to the fact that there is very little even the most powerful warrior can do to change the world.

It was that odd realization which brought such a sense of despair at seeing the news report of the tiger. The world is mad and all the dancing phantoms just actors in some misshapen script of chaos and fragmentation, and absolutely *nothing* I can do will ever change that. Men will still hunt wild animals because it is written into their lizard-brain programming that this is somehow good, it will impress the females at the watering hole and result in increased mating rituals.

Politicians will start wars in the name of God and dupe the masses into believing it is a just war, a good war, a holy war to protect the freedoms of their cell phones and their Play Stations and their gas-guzzling SUVs. The church will go on selling salvation to the highest bidder, while simultaneously condemning those who have found it for themselves. Storms will come and go. The Earth will one day roll on her side and cast off most of these mad lifeforms like the parasites they are.

And nothing – *absolutely nothing* – will have changed, except that it will be a new morning somewhere in the space-time continuum, and all of our folly will be at the bottom of a new sea where Los Angeles or New York used to stand.

Seeing this so clearly, I cannot help but wonder what the purpose might be. The warrior lives impeccably in the now, and plays the game as if it matters, knowing all the while that it is futile and altogether silly in the frame of the big picture. The galactic asylum is alive and well on Planet Earth.

Clarity is the second enemy of a man of Knowledge because it allows the warrior to *see* this, but offers no suggestions for any possible solution.

———

Old Age

From a warrior perspective, what does it mean when an otherwise impeccable warrior is diagnosed with some disease?

When I told a few select friends about being diagnosed with Type 2 Diabetes in 2008, the reactions ran the gamut from supportive to outright mean. One friend of long-standing actually said, "If you'd been more impeccable with your health, this wouldn't be happening to you."

While I am a major advocate of the Knowledge that we create our own reality, I am also sufficiently aware to *see* that no matter how impeccable we may be with our health, we are still in human bodies that age with the ravages of time. It's *why* old age is the fourth enemy of a woman of Knowledge, after all. In theory, we're all gonna die of somethin'. I just don't intend to do it anytime soon, nor do I intend to accept this label just because it has been offered.

What this has really brought home to me is the realization that a lot of warriors seem to have some bizarre notion that some high degree of discipline and impeccability will spare them from their own appointment with Death. The thing is, I'm somewhat divided on this issue, and will present both arguments just for laughs.

First, I will start by saying that everything we think we know about life, death and everything in between is part of an agreement known as the consensual reality. We have been so programmed to believe that "all things die" that maybe we have a tendency to stop looking for that "crack in the cosmic egg" written about so eloquently by Joseph Chilton Pearce. We live with the *belief* that "all things die", but we can only know what is revealed to our individual perceptions. Could it be that immortals walk among us? What of The Tenant[6]? As individuals on our path, we only truly *know* what we have experienced. The rest is only a belief system. We *see* death all around us, but perhaps we *fail* to *see* an immortal being simply because that being is a stranger on the street. How would we know if the man standing next to us on the corner is 30 years old, or 3,000 years old? We make assumptions, but we cannot really *know* anything other than what is in our own experience.

On the other hand, let's just say that it *appears* that "all things die", and it certainly appears that don Juan was correct in his statement that "Old age is the fourth enemy." Even after losing our humanform[7], we are still in human *bodies*. We are organic. But we are also organic form which is comprised of energy at its molecular level. The energy is eternal, but as it manifests as organic matter, it takes on the properties of mortality. In other words, no amount of grazing on fruits, berries and scattered nuts is going to make me immortal. No amount of jogging around the yard or sitting lotus position in front of the universe is going to spare me from disease eventually. But even *that* is just a belief system.

The funny thing about us is that we are human. Even the best warrior is still human. When I turn to Orlando and say -

---

[6] In the works of Carlos Castaneda, a being is encountered who is described as "the tenant" or "the death defier." Whatever label is assigned to it, she or he is an immortal who attained the immortal condition through her own efforts (in other words, s/he was not born that way. She is self-created... or so the story goes.
[7] Losing the humanform - The state of being that results when the human warrior sheds all belief systems and programs. It's a bit more complicated than that, but in the interest of brevity here, that's the simplified definition.

"Hey, fucker, why me?" his response is to put a loving arm around my shoulder, take me for a walk in the yard where a fine fat raven is strolling through the pet cemetery, and say to me, *I've lived ten thousand lives, and the only thing common to all of them is that they have all ended in death, and yet I am still here and nowhere and everywhere, because that is the Dream of your Intent. That is the nature of the infinite singularity.*

When I unravel what that might mean, I am left with the Knowledge that eternity is experienced through consciousness and awareness within the singularity - a singularity consisting of an infinite number of lives which are all only this one single breath in the Now that makes it all possible. The breath of living in a mortal body is the source of all possibility.

Trying to wrap words around the unknowable is rather like trying to eat broth with a fork. What it all boils down to is that we are human beings on a journey of evolution toward Wholeness. Whatever labels the consensual reality attaches to my body do not define my spirit nor bring my impeccability into question.

What does it mean when a warrior is diagnosed with some dis-ease? It means you are human. Nothing more. Nothing less.

———

Amendments to the Toltec Teachings
The Fifth Enemy

Fear is the first enemy of a man of Knowledge, but I would expand on that old adage to say fear is also the first *ally* of a man of Knowledge. Until we acknowledge that we are beings who are going to die - with all the heavyweight baggage that goes with that realization - we have no motivation to really *live* the path. Without that motivation, the path may be only words. So, as with anything else, it's a matter of walking the razor's edge. Have no fear at all and you will have no motivation. Have too much fear and it can cripple you. Yin and yang, each containing a bit of the other.

I'm going to amend the Toltec teachings here by adding a fifth enemy whose name is Anger. While some might say anger is a manifestation of fear, I don't think that's always the case. Many times, anger is a manifestation of self-importance in the face of personal inadequacy. Maybe that really *is* fear at some level, but it seems important to acknowledge anger as an enemy of a man of Knowledge as a force unto itself - one that must be dealt with utilizing the same ruthlessness and impeccability as with any of the other four enemies - fear, clarity, power, old age.

It is only in acknowledging the enemy and confronting it head on that we gain the power to overcome it.

———

The Sixth Enemy - End of the Road

I've gone so far down this path till there is no path. Now what?

The funny truth about paths is that they do end, and there is nothing you can do about it from this point forward except to forge your own way. When I talk about the path, it is seen on many different levels. There is what might be called a process in the beginning - some warriors connect with it through Castaneda, others through Zen, others through various manifestations of shamanism. But there comes a time when one runs out of road, and there is just the warrior and the worlds, with no real path left to follow. You have the Knowledge, but no clear indicator of where to take it, what to do with it, nothing at all. Just you and the end of the road – yet it seems that when we run out of road is when the journey really begins. And that's the part of the equation that is difficult, scary, and has caused more warriors to turn back than any encounter with allies or power plants.

When I think of the four enemies of a man of Knowledge, the way I see it is this: fear is obvious, and something we deal with as an ongoing enemy. Clarity comes and we revel in it - sometimes getting lost in it for years. But as we come to the end of the path, we see with clarity that there is just a vast, untouched universe waiting for the creator's hand. It's knowing that we *are* the creator that gives us pause and brings us face to face with Power. Usually, there is a relatively long period of time during which we simply don't know what to do with our Power, and it's at that point that a lot of warriors turn back - because they have become accustomed to being *followers* of a path rather than *forgers* of a path.

When we're following that initial path (whether Castaneda, Zen, or whatever), it could be said we're not really following, but learning from the experiences of others. But then comes that day when we have learned all our teachers can teach us, and we then have to go out and push the envelope of Knowledge "where no man has gone before." There's something to that old *Star Trek* cliché - because that is the warrior's ultimate journey. Where *no* man has gone before. You are the first, and so the path disappears from beneath your feet, leaving you only with Knowledge.

A few years back, I was playing with a concept which I called "beyond human comprehension"; and a related concept "beyond human experience." This is the territory of the unknown, which defies words almost entirely. But what it amounts to is that there is an almost physical pain/confusion/anguish which the warrior begins to experience when she comes up against this idea of "beyond human experience." There is much humans cannot comprehend, yet it is in the attempt to do so that we push the envelope "beyond human experience". That pushing is, in itself, part of our evolution.

Sadly, very few ever make it to the end of the path, because the sorcerer's secret is that the path itself is part of the tonal, and is comforting and alluring in so very many ways. To admit that the path *has* an end, and to find oneself facing only the vast unknown means evolving to a new level of thinking, a new level of responsibility, a new level of awareness - and *that* is far scarier than anything on the path the warrior has taken to get to this point.

———

LIFE, DEATH, LOVE, HATE, GRIEF, JOY... THE THINGS THAT MAKE US HUMAN

Love is the Reason

Where does love figure into the seeker's path?

"Love is the reason." Something Orlando has repeated often over the years, followed closely by, "Love isn't enough." Some believe this to be a contradiction, but I have found both statements to be equally true. When we really look at our lives, almost everything we do is done out of love - even the "dark" things. We bring a kitten home out of love, and we take an ailing elder pet to be euthanized out of love. The diabetic takes insulin because he loves to go on living, and the crack addict takes crack because he loves how it makes him feel, even if it kills him. Life and death dancing the infinite tango on the yin/yang of love.

So why isn't love enough? Why can't we just do the things we love because we love them, with no thought to the consequences of our actions?

Any real spiritual path is a journey of personal evolution - and evolution is a process of moving past our indulgences and dependencies. Love is the reason, but Intent and long-term commitment cannot be ignored if the seeker ever plans to inhabit the Totality of herself.

What is the Totality of Oneself?

Simply put, it is the higher self, the dreaming body which is infinite and eternal. It is the energetic vessel of the *I-Am* which holds all memory and knowledge of all you have been or ever will be. It doesn't exist just because we believe it does. It exists only when we create it and nurture it through the process of living - not just when it's fun, but especially when it's difficult or at times even seems impossible. It is the reason that love is the reason, and the reason love isn't enough.

Evolution isn't something you do for awhile and then stop because you think you've arrived at some profound pinnacle of knowledge. It is The Work of a lifetime - the work of an infinite number of lifetimes which are all happening right here, right now, within the mystery which is the double.

Quitters need not ever begin.

———

The Love Affair With the Unknown

While glancing over an old forum I moderated several years back, I came across this entry from 2007 - one year after the death of my mother. Since time marches by so quickly - well, not really *by* us as much as it marches *over* us - I had forgotten ever having written it. Upon reading it, I realized it still has relevance - perhaps not just to myself, but to anyone who has ever fallen in love with the unknown, to anyone who has ever taken time to reflect not only on where we have been, but where we are going.

Just a brief bit of background... My mother's name was Ruby, and she was considered by most to be a simple woman - generally happy and content, never complaining even when it might have been to her advantage to do so. She passed away on October 4, 2006, from colon cancer.

———

October 4, 2007

It was a year ago tonight that my mother died.

I look at those words hanging in cyberspace, and ask myself if it is possible to even wrap my mind around such a thing. And at the same time, I *see* that it is such a simple thing that no understanding is possible.

Death simply *is*.

So as I sit here at my desk in the early morning stillness, I am comparing what I know now to what I knew a year ago at this time, and I find that not a lot has changed, yet everything has changed. And again, there is a peculiar sense of juxtaposition. I ask myself questions which are nothing more than markers on the hem of time. Was I happier then or now? Have I accomplished my goals for the tonal in this past year? Have I moved forward in my love affair with the unknown? Do I know anymore about myself than I did a year ago? Do I know anymore about this thing called death?

Do any of us know anything about anything, or are we all just madly jabbering corpses who haven't yet fallen into our crypts?

Perhaps the most important thing about these time markers is that they compel us to reflect. And what I am *seeing* in my reflections is that I am essentially content, even happy with regard to my path. And yet, there's that juxtaposition again. At the same time, my eye is drawn to those areas where I see work being required, and to the changes I would hope to make. There are those who would say that I tend to focus on the negative - but I have never really seen it that way. To me, attempting to sweep the negative under the rug only makes for a lump in the rug. So when I see areas where improvement is needed, I take on a warrior-stalker's perspective and begin to examine what is perceived to be lacking so that I might have a better opportunity of making it whole.

Lest anyone think I'm talking about changing the world, curing cancer or solving terrorism and global hunger, allow me to assure you that I am talking only about matters of Spirit, for ultimately it is the assemblage point of the self which determines our experience of the world.

So is it, then, a matter of simply moving the assemblage point into some happy space, so as to perceive only the positive aspects of the world? Though there are many who might think so, that has not been my experience. To me, that only makes that lump under the rug grow larger and eventually one trips over it while ambling along skyclad with only rose-colored glasses for attire.

One thing Orlando has stressed emphatically over the years is the need to be *able* to ask the next question. Sounds simple. But something I have really observed over this past year is that most folks simply are not capable of thinking for themselves beyond the rudimentary levels of being able to feed themselves and tie their shoes in the morning. I've tested this with deliberate intent by asking questions which require not a recitation of some rote memorization, but would require actual forward-thinking - which, to me, is one of the major cornerstones for the foundation of any evolution of consciousness.

Ask the next question...
www.quantumshaman.com

When you find yourself at a crossroads in the jungle, the direction in which you proceed may not always be defined by the head, but far more often from the heart. What is your heart telling you now? What do you want to do? What would you change if you could? Orlando's words to me.

What's amusing is that the questions themselves usually reveal far more than we might realize at first glance. When my heart is telling me something, it is usually because I may not be particularly content with whatever is going on at the

126

moment. When I ask myself what I want to do, the question itself reveals to me that some sort of change is not only desirable, but may be required in order for me to move forward. When I ask myself what I would change if I could, the implication is that the status quo may not be satisfactory and so I must ask the next question.

What is the desired outcome and how might I best move toward that goal?

I look back on my mother's life. Simple things brought her the most pleasure. Raking leaves in her yard. Playing her organ for no one but herself and her dog. Savoring some chocolate thing. She once said that she never had any big dreams and so she never had any big disappointments.

When I think about that, I know it was her own philosophy of the right way to live. Whenever I would ask her about her philosophical beliefs, she would tell me that she placed her faith in God, and left the power-thinking to the pastors and priests and spiritual leaders of the world.

That, of course, is where we differed. And though we both came to be comfortable with that difference, I find that my own questions are not as easily answered. The only god I know is me, and the only faith I have ever known to be founded is the faith I place in myself. And as lonely as it may sound to some, I have truly found that it is a solitary path - a universe of one, yet a universe filled with all possibility, and that it is in asking the next question that we determine which of those possibilities we will force to go through the motions of actually occurring.

All things exist within the realm of possibility, but only some things will be forced to go through the motions of actually occurring.

- Quantum Theory

What do I want to do now? When I look at the question with the right eye of the consensual world, there is no single answer that resonates. Many things. No one thing. When I look at the question from the left eye of the Spirit, I am immediately filled with a sense of magnificent exhilaration - the way one typically feels when anticipating a long-awaited consummation of a grand love affair. *Tonight is the night*, the unseen muse whispers from the sharp edge of a shadow. *Tonight is the night when we will dance the stardust into manifestation and sing the spirit alive.*

What I have come to realize is that *every* night is the night. And though the muse can never be caught, the love affair is in the chase and the unwritten steps of the dance, and the barely heard music of the universe's one man band.

The magic is in the magician.

What do I want to do? Only that. Yet there is no defining "that". There is only the experience of it, the voice calling your name in a crowd, but when you turn to look, no one's there. The caress of a seductive hand at 3 am, but when you move to embrace your lover, you find he has taken a step sideways in space-time, and all that remains is the sensation of having been touched by something other, something beyond the realm of human understanding. The scent of cologne - fresh and clean - in a room that has been unoccupied for months. Footprints in desert sand that lead to the middle of nowhere, and then abruptly and inexplicably stop.

The love affair with the unknown. There is nothing else. I do not believe there ever was.

Looking back on the events since the death of my mother, I find that virtually everything we engage in is folly. Perhaps it's a bit amusing to discover that what is the most real to me is what would be considered the most *un*real by most sane and normal human beings. But that's okay, too. When sanity is measured by the average human being, I am delighted to be considered mad.

———

The Manifestation of Intent

I hear a lot of talk about Intent, but I'm not sure I'm getting it, since I don't seem to be able to manifest it in any noticeable way. What can you tell us about how Intent really works?

Even seekers who have been on the path for many years may be tending to view Intent as a wish or a desire - more of an intangible vision, or even an object of creative visualization. While those things may be part of Intent, they only touch the surface of what this *force* actually is.

Intent is the rearrangement
of energy at a sub-atomic level.

This is a statement which reinforces itself through gnosis time and time again. In other words, Intent is actually a moving *force* of energy. In the beginning, perhaps it is the thought or vision of something we need or desire, but as the advanced warrior begins pushing her unbending Intent against the infrastructure of the universe, what I am shown through gnosis is a process rather like silly putty being pressed against a comic strip to pick up the image - a transference of thought into substance which we tend to think of as magic or the power of prayer or may even dismiss as a convenient coincidence.

But the reality of Intent is that it does not work directly in accordance with our humanform desires - and so it may even seem at times that the path to getting what we want or need out of life may negatively impact others along the way. For what it's worth, that's the nature of energy, life and reality. It isn't always sweetness and light despite what a lot of new age books on the subject of manifesting your desires might have you believe.

The reality of Intent is that it is undoubtedly the most powerful force in the universe, because it functions at the level of pure energy. Just words. Something Mr. Spock might have said. But the actuality of it carries a lot of heavy gravity, and only when the warrior truly begins to internalize the nature of Intent does the warrior truly become enabled to engage with Power.

Trying to really define Intent is like trying to hold the wind in one's hand. The thing is this: Intent is neither good nor evil, it simply exists as energy and power. And, in fact, I might go so far as to say that even the warrior cannot intentionally direct Intent to be "good" or "evil". Power chooses the most energy-efficient path to bring itself into manifestation. For example, even if I were to envision my business competitor driving his truck off a cliff, the energy itself which might manifest that vision is neither good nor evil. It is simply energy. The energy itself would choose its own manifestation because that is its nature. We can choose the goal, but we can seldom select the method. And, for the record, I never wish ill on others, with Intent or otherwise, because my experience has shown that their own dark deeds usually lead them to a confrontation with power all by themselves. If my Intent were simply to be free of my competitor, it will usually manifest in such a way that he finds a better job, moves to the east coast; or I slide into another field of endeavor quite naturally and by choice. That is the path of energy efficiency.

With regard to Intent and how it manifests, Orlando once told me very sternly, *Get out of your own way. You're trying to control, trying to pick and choose, and in doing so you are limiting your own vision.* What he was referring to was the fact that even advanced warriors may have a tendency to try to direct the play, when what they really need to do is simply scribble a brief outline on the fabric of the space-time continuum, and then let it go. *Only when it is released does it have power.*

130

I used to have a tendency to try to select certain aspects of how I wanted my Intent to manifest. When I was into ritual many years ago, I was working a manifestation wherein I wanted my teacher to come to me in a dream. He was to have black hair, dark eyes, be of a certain height and stature and so on. My thinking was that this was how I would recognize him. But as Orlando pointed out, I was limiting the vision. What if the teacher showed up with grey hair and was a dwarf? Would I ignore him altogether because he wasn't what I had asked for? So I had to get out of my own way.

The warrior also has to learn not to limit the scope of her Intent. Where unbending Intent is concerned, what we are after is the goal - but where we have to come to grips with reality is in Knowing that the path Intent takes may not always be in accordance with our visions. Our teachers may come as coyotes or hummingbirds rather than tall, handsome strangers. And from time to time, it may appear that our Intent manifests in such a way as to bring misfortune to ourselves or others - thus the old adage, "Be careful what you wish for."

Perhaps one of the deepest programs imbedded into us is the idea that the things we do must "harm none". And while that is certainly a beneficial idea and in accordance with "the right way to live", it's important for the warrior working with Intent to realize that every living thing lives and survives at the expense of something else. Yes, even vegans. The seeds and berries are, after all, the living essence of a new plant, and so even the most gentle-minded thrive on life at some level. It cannot be avoided, and is simply part of the cycle of life.

I mention this because it's at this stage of the game that I begin to see a lot of warriors cringe in fear of their own power, their own Intent. I once had an apprentice say to me, "If I have to survive by harming something else, then I'm not sure I want to survive at all." Those are the eagle's words and nothing more.

That isn't to say we would go out and pillage and plunder

for our own gain, because for the warrior who examines her own heart, clearly that is not "the right way to live". So somewhere in the middle of it all lies a balance, and this again relates directly back to Intent, even though some of it may appear to have dark connotations at times.

What we have to know and accept about Intent is what I seem to keep repeating: it does not always manifest in accordance with our ideas because Intent is a *force* of energy that is going to choose the path of least resistance. Energy moves, and Intent rearranges reality at a sub-atomic level. The most energy-efficient path usually results in the creation of alternate pathways.

Intent is a small word, but carries with it an extremely powerful gravitational field which the warrior really must come to terms with at some point. While it is certainly possible and even desirable to have positive thoughts when working with Intent, it's equally as important to realize that Intent can be directed, but it cannot be directly *controlled* anymore than a rushing river can really be controlled except through damming it up and stopping its flow.

The warrior's trick is learning to hold our Intent in our mind/body/spirit, and release it at the same time - breathe in, breathe out. And, finally, the secret lies in getting out of her own way.

———

Life, Death and Freedom

Do you believe that if you do not have a shamanic death, you will not reach the Freedom which is the immortality of your awareness?

I think a lot of folks will make it past the eagle, into some form of immortality, but I've *seen* that there is "existence" (a form of awareness without much ability to do or to evolve beyond that point), or there is an actual *evolution* of consciousness into what many have called the "state of freedom".

The path of the warrior is largely about acquiring and developing the ability to evolve into that state of freedom where one would be not only aware, but also possessing sufficient power and individuality to maintain what we think of as an identity that is both a part of and yet distinguishable from All sentience.

My personal understanding of the state of freedom is that one would have seamless immortality (existing in all places and times simultaneously), but at the same time would maintain one's own individual cohesion. One would be *I-Am* rather than "it is" or "we are".

As for the idea of a shamanic death, I think all creatures have it within themselves to live a shamanic life, even if they have never heard the word 'shamanism'. At the core of every living thing, there is "the right way to live" - an instinct that brings us into alignment with the evolutionary mindset of the sentient All. In that regard, the old adage of "There are many pathways to the bardo" is very true. But at the core level, I think each individual either does the work of spiritual evolution, or doesn't do it. If it isn't done, then the individual is most likely discorporated after death. The energy would remain as part of the universal sentience, but the *I-Am* would most likely be lost, dissolved into information (impersonal) as opposed to Knowledge (Knowledge itself implying there is an

I-Am based in experience - in other words, by strict definition, there is "*one-who-knows*").

For obvious reasons, this isn't a particularly popular opinion, which is why most organized religions take the more palatable approach that the soul is immortal no matter what. While that is true at the level of energy, most shamanic cultures recognize that the individual's life and how it is lived have a direct influence on how one spends eternity. From personal vision quests, I have come to *see* that Christianity's concept of Hell undoubtedly originated from the same basic core realization that, without some form of "redemption", the soul is cast into limbo after death. Unfortunately, all too many religions seek to place the idea of redemption into the hands of an external deity, whereas shamanism (and nagualism in particular) recognizes that the evolution of the Self is the only possibility for redemption from that discorporate awareness-without-identity.

I've been to both places in vision quests - the place of sentient awareness without identity, and the state of ultimate freedom. While words cannot describe either one adequately, one thing I'm sure of is that without the *I-Am* there is only a sense of eternal limbo - awareness without cohesion. Personally, I found that discorporate state of passive observer to be deplorable because there was no sense of differentiation - and without that, all is virtually sameness, the universe looking at itself through its own eyes and finding nothing new under the suns. It is the *I-Am* which gives meaning and enables the love affair between Self and Spirit.

———

Animal Spirit

What about animal spirit? Can animals transcend death, or is the whole idea of the 'rainbow bridge' just wishful thinking? I lost my dog last year and it feels like a hole has been ripped in my own soul. Are ever reunited with the animals we meet during our lives?

Over the years, I've lost so many animals that at times it feels like I will be crushed under the weight of the grief, yet at the same time there is a warm and perfect Remembering that brings them back, even if for only a moment or two on an otherwise insignificant Saturday afternoon. The anecdote below is my experience of losing one who was close to me. In the interim since this piece was first written (2005), I have lost many more, including Zero and China, who are mentioned in the piece that follows. Some say love and hate are opposites. I've found it's love and grief that share space in the dark mirror of life. I was recently asked in regard to Zero - "If you could go back in time and never bring her home in order to avoid the grief, would you do it?" While I normally say there's no such thing as a stupid question, that one came close.

———

Life Goes On

I heard all the right words coming out of my mouth as I stood in the vet's office, yet it was as if I were off to the side of myself watching the play unfold yet again, time and again. My vet is a little person - I believe that's the correct term - but her heart is clearly infinite. So we stood there looking at one another across the exam table, while one of our eldest cats, TK ("Tiny Kitten") lay between us, his fate in our hands, his lifeforce ebbing.

For a moment, it was 13 years in the past. I had gone to the convenience store one night and heard a tiny kitten mewing, lost. Took some doing and chasing the little fellow around the parking lot which adjoined to a very busy road, but eventually he cornered himself, and I scooped him up and brought him home. Just a little runt of a thing. Eyes still blue. And pissed as hell to be caught, because obviously someone had failed to inform me he was the master of his fate, the guardian of his own destiny. So that night, I sat on the bathroom floor showing him his food, water and litter box (it offended him that I should think he would need to be shown at all), and I told him with a little chuckle that he had allowed me to catch him because it's his destiny to live with us. That seemed to calm him down. Even got him to purr just a little.

By the next morning, his eyes had turned green. Normally a gradual process in kittens, the change from newborn-blue to adult-green literally occurred over night - probably as a result of the trauma of being captured, a vet later postulated, even going so far as to say, "You brought him into this world kicking and screaming." Even then, it had seemed like something a sorcerer would have said, a reference to shifting the willful kitten's assemblage point.

Time went by, and TK integrated into the house with the other critters and became the comedian of the bunch. About 18 months ago, he was diagnosed with diabetes, but once we got his insulin stabilized, it didn't seem to bother him much. He could still sneak out the door between one's feet like an unseen ghost, but was content to spend most of his time sitting on the windowsill twitching his tail at jackrabbits and garden squirrels.

All of these memories played out like a flash fire on the hologram of my thoughts as I was standing in the vet's office, wondering how his life had come full circle so quickly. He had seemed quite his usual self when we went to bed last night, but this morning it was obvious something was seriously, fatally wrong. No point recounting the details, but suffice it to say the vet speculated a brain tumor or some type of severe trauma. Since trauma was virtually impossible, being an

136

indoor cat, the reality of a malignant brain tumor began to weave itself into the molecular structure of Existence as I stood off to the side in a state of emotional detachment, questioning how an animal who was healthy yesterday could be literally dying in my arms less than 24 hours later.

Life is fragile. And there are few answers as to the hows and whys of it all. Here today, gone tomorrow. No guarantees for any of us. You. Me. TK. Ask the dinosaurs.

By the time I got home from the vet, I was in a peculiar state. I could sit in the silence of my shady sanctuary and cry, but for whom? TK has gone to the garden beneath a pile of earth and stones, but that is no longer TK. I could hold my emotions in check, but for whom? No one around but me at that moment, plus the two weenie dogs and TK's daughter - my sweet China - who is almost a photocopy of her father. Like a ghost in the shade of a sapling poplar.

So I sat on the doorstep for awhile, gazing out at the huge cactus blossom which opened up overnight. It, too, is fragile, blooming for less than 24 hours. A transient thing of beauty to be appreciated and experienced for the time it is here. No different, really, than anything else, including TK. Bees buzzed at the flower's center, so heavily laden with pollen they were like heavy bombers hanging in the air. Zero was enthusiastically digging at a squirrel hole, giving me space to grieve.

And I felt a soft, gentle licking at my toes. Looked down to find Morgan (Wendy's Weenie) sitting at my feet, looking up at me with bright brown eyes that seemed quite wise in that moment. Without waiting to be asked, he simply climbed up into my lap and snuggled against my chest - a sun-warmed, fuzzy, living presence in my arms, such a contrast to the lifeless body I had just consigned to the dirt in the little pet cemetery. Though Morgan is normally off chasing squirrels and exploring with Zero, it was as if he paused in his journey to offer comfort and even amusement in the midst of so much pain. Like TK, he is a comedian most of the time, but for that moment, he had become a somber sorcerer, a wise old man who is frolicking in a weenie dog suit for the time being.

"Life goes on," he told me as surely as if he had spoken out loud. And for a timeless instant, the full meaning of those words stretched beyond the sphere of my being and into the infinite. Life goes on. Within the hologram, TK exists for all time. Beyond the hologram, we become as we *will*. Zero sleeps in my lap now, Morgan on the royal purple pillow on the couch, and TK dreams in the shadows of the chaparrals.

Life goes on.

Jackalope

Just a quiet Sunday morning around here - sky so blue it hurts the eyes to look upon, snow-capped mountains in the distance, still and calm. Even the hummingbirds are sitting in the Joshua trees instead of flitting to and fro as they normally do.

Upon first rising, I glanced out the window to the south and noticed a small cottontail hopping underneath one of the vehicles parked in the yard. Sitting in the shade, his ears splayed lazily to the side, an odd play of shadows gave him the appearance of antlers, and I had to smile to myself. *Jackalope*, I thought. Coyote's younger brother - no less the trickster.

So I smiled to myself and went on about my business. It was about half an hour later, as I was sitting at my desk writing an email, that I glanced out the window to the east, and saw a huge jackrabbit the size of a small pick-up standing on his hind legs, perhaps intentionally tormenting the weenie dogs who had gone out for their morning duties in the yard. What caught my eye was that the low-hanging branch of a chaparral bush had created the illusion of antlers on this giant hare, and so there I was face to face with the jackalope once again. He seemed to be almost laughing at me.

"What makes you so sure it's just shadows and branches, m'dear?" the jackalope inquired, licking at one large paw and then using it to smooth his handsome whiskers as he regarded me from a safe distance. Safe for which of us, I am not quite certain. "Why are you so quick to create explanations for the vision I have brought you instead of rejoicing in the vision itself?"

He had a point. So I smiled, bowed slightly from the waist to show proper respect, and met his eyes, which seemed to be kaleidoscopes of mischief and mystery, doorways to the nagual. "Old programs," I explained, though I knew he required no explanation. It was using the explanation to assimilate my own thoughts. "Guess I'd gone back for a moment to believing there's no such thing as a jackalope. Thanks for the reminder."

His nose twitched as he regarded me. I thought he might charge and run me through with those fierce antlers, for jackalopes are known to be aggressive and unpredictable, but instead the corners of his mouth formed a dangerous little smile. "Reality is what you make it, m'dear," he said. "See the shadows alone and I am naught but a simple hare. Allow me my antlers, and you begin to take back the power your day to day world leeches from you."

"You make it sound so simple."

He shrugged a furry shoulder. "Does it need to be complicated?" He glanced suspiciously from side to side, then

leaned forward in a conspiratorial manner. "Got any grass?"

The few sprigs of wild grass which had cropped up after the winter rains had all turned brown and dry. Not much for a wayward jackalope to eat. "I'll get you something from the house," I offered, but he had already started moving away, back into the shadows, underneath a flowering yellow senna bush at the edge of the desert.

So I came back inside and gathered up some celery, carrots and the last red apple, and left them at the opening of the rabbit hole which seems to go deeper and deeper into the infinite and mysterious unknown.

Still, couldn't help thinking as I looked back and saw that apple, that it was the jackalope who had once again given me the fruit of Knowledge and rekindled the fires of the infinite.

Does it need to be complicated?

———

THE GOD DILEMMA

The God Question

You seem to be saying that believing in God is wrong for anyone on a spirit quest, and that doesn't make sense to me. If beliefs are just intangible ideas, what difference does it make? And how could it hurt someone to believe in God, whether he or she is real or not?

I don't necessarily think believing in God is wrong for anyone on a spirit quest, for one simple reason. The idea of "wrong" is nothing more than a humanform assignation based on one's personal point of view. If someone wants to believe in God or the Easter bunny, it makes no difference to me. I don't think they're wrong, but as a *seer*, I also don't *see* that their beliefs are founded in anything more than fear-based hope - wishful thinking.

What I do believe based on a lifetime of seeking and a lot of direct experience is that when man puts God outside of himself, he is segregating himself from his own natural and innate abilities. As long as someone truly believes God is going to save him or grant him eternal life, that person has no real incentive to do the work of self-realization. I often hear the phrase, "We are saved by grace." To me, that's not only a dangerous assumption, but a sad bit of programming that keeps the individual always at the level of victim/slave/child. What saves us (if anything can) is our own efforts to evolve beyond the sum of our parts. It is a choice and that choice is based not only in free will, but the power of intent.

So, in a nutshell, the belief in the traditional version of God can hurt people by rendering them spiritually impotent and placing them in a position of servitude to an organization that has nothing at all to do with what God really is - the creative and omnipotent force within each and every living being. Even if organized religion was well-intentioned in the beginning, it has become its own definition of evil over a period of time. By disempowering its followers through subjugation of their own abilities, the church takes on the role of suppressor, whereby a man's "soul" may be sold back to him for those 20 pieces of silver in the collection plate every Sunday. In the quantum shaman's world, the only real "sin" is to keep another from flourishing in their journey - and the church as an organization is the master of that form of sin.

One reason I am so adamant about this is that I have witnessed up close and personal the damaging effects religion can have on the human spirit. My mother, who was in a long process of dying of colon cancer, had been an avid believer all her life. But as she faced the end of her days, it was clear to me that her faith was failing in light of the clarity impending Death can give us, and though she continued to say the right words, I could see in her heart that she was alone and terrified as she came to understand that the church really hadn't given her a foundation capable of supporting her in her final days.

In short, her belief in God (sold to her by the church) kept her from exploring her own abilities. I know now that she was a gifted *seer* in her own right, but because the church preaches that such things are "of the devil", she suppressed the ability and actually spent a lot of time feeling guilty because of it.

So, yes, what we believe that cannot be validated through experience into Knowledge can and does harm people's journey. I'm sure there are shades of gray, but for the most part, I see no advantage to believing in anything that would require me to worship it and pay 10% of my earnings to its earthly edifices. Does that make sense to *anybody?*

———

The God Question, Part Two

I believe that the entire length of the way humanity has evolved has been in God's plan... yet, simultaneously, humanity has been making many wrong choices as of late.

First, to assume there is a god or there is a plan is to place both power and creation outside of yourself, and that seems to be in contradiction with the very structure of reality as many of us on a spiritual journey have come to define it. To sum it up, I would simply say - Thou art God. We are the architects of reality - and I can assure you that the manner in which humanity has evolved as a whole would not be in accordance with any plan I might have envisioned. At that level, it's all based in individual free will - because, frankly, if there *were* a God, I can't help thinking s/he would have done a far better job.

Attempting to place god outside of ourselves or assume there is some plan has never worked for me. Perhaps you are intending these words in a different light, but as they are

142

written, they read to me more like a grasping at faith rather than an expression of personal experience. To believe there is a plan is to place ourselves in the automatic role of pawns - just pieces on a chessboard at someone else's whim.

Also, to say humanity has been making many "wrong choices" is also a bit tricky, since both right and wrong are human assignations. There is the idea (which I do personally agree with) of "the right way to live". Most people have no concept of "the right way to live" because of the programming that has been put onto them by religion, government, and society, so humanity can only make the choices that are in alignment with its programming. If the programming is flawed (which it is), then eventually the entire system will crash (which it will).

We must not lose faith when we look around and see the world as it is, for we must realize that everyone is innately enlightened yet most people are simply utterly ignorant of this fact. To try and save all of humanity is misguided. One can only hope to save their own self and as many other people as they can help.

This would imply a belief that other people even *want* to be helped. When you say "we must not lose faith", I have to ask, Faith in what? Faith in whom? Also, to say that "everyone is innately enlightened" is a rather bold assumption, and one I have not found to be in alignment with my observations of the world. The only way we become enlightened is by doing the work of self-realization that brings us out of our humanform programming and places us outside the box so that we may see ourselves through the eyes of detached clarity. If everyone were innately enlightened, we would live in a different world - because clearly no "innately enlightened" individual would choose to make war or perpetuate famine or subjugate other individuals in a manner that would keep them from thriving on their own path.

I do agree that trying to save all of humanity is

misguided, but I also think that trying to save *anyone* other than oneself is equally as misguided. If we help others it will be not by our efforts, but by their own - we can't really teach anyone anything unless and until they are willing to learn.

If you really believe that, why write your books or participate on the online groups? Aren't you trying in your own way to help people?

A warrior does the things she does for her own assimilation. Perhaps in the beginning of the Quantum Shaman™ website, I had some lingering hope that it might help others. But the reality is that I do it for myself - to clarify my *seeing* and place certain events and realizations in a context that is part of my personal evolution. I don't intend that to sound dismissive, but when we are honest with ourselves, we begin to discover that most of what we do is done for the survival and evolution of the self.

If we help others it will be because they choose to take the first step on the path toward freedom. Though it may be a fine-line distinction, it places responsibility squarely on the shoulders of each individual to take that step through their own free will. We aren't saving them, they are saving themselves.

The shaman is the maintenance and repair person of the spirit world and the powers used do not come from within, but from the gods themselves. To say otherwise is blasphemy.

Which gods? The Christian God? The pagan gods? The South American gods? The Native American gods? The Hindu gods? The wiccan goddess? If the gods had the kind of power to which you refer, they would surely not need a lowly human shaman to repair and maintain the spirit world.

Ultimately, I have come to see that most humans on a spiritual path probably start out with a rudimentary belief in god, but as their path evolves, so does their understanding of what god really is. It is not an extant deity, but the creative *force* which exists within all of us.

The power of a shaman is never about the shaman's self, it is about what is to be done for the shaman's people.

I think our use of the word 'shaman' may vary somewhat. Anyone has the potential to be a shaman - perhaps not in the manner you are using the word, but in the sense that the word translates to "self-healed madman". We are all capable of healing the rifts, tears, and fragmentations in our spirit, and sometimes that may involve a need in certain phases of our journey to place belief in extant gods/deities because - in the early stages of our ultimate evolution - we simply do not have enough belief in ourselves, and so we scramble around looking for something outside of ourselves, something greater than ourselves in which to place our faith. But if we are diligent in the journey and do the work of self-awakening and self-Realization, we slowly come to see that the real power of creation/healing/salvation is within our own heart and spirit. We integrate "the gods" and in doing so, we become god.

If you are impressive as a person, but have no way to heal the sickness of the spirit that seems to pervade the society to which you belong, then of what use is it to be impressive in a junk yard of broken souls?

The shaman heals herself first and foremost, and in doing so, perhaps others are inspired to begin their own journey toward healing. Or perhaps not. Either way, the *only* person you can save is yourself. My favorite analogy in this regard is this: if you're on a plane and the oxygen masks suddenly drop, you have to put on your own mask before you can help anyone else. We save ourselves through Intent and Doing. Sure, we might inspire or teach some of those broken souls, but we have to keep in mind that not all drowning men want to be rescued. Some jumped in of their own accord, knowing in advance they can't swim. Such is the nature of human folly and free will.

Unless individuals can take responsibility for their own evolution, they render themselves impotent in a universe of energy and power. While waiting for the angels to save them, they may fail to get on the rowboat and start paddling their way to shore.

If you are cold, you don't build your house in a dry forest and then set the whole thing on fire.

The smartest thing to do when one is cold is to begin within. A cup of hot tea warms the entire body. It begins within, whether we're talking about god or snowstorms.

The gods influence our lives all the time. But they do it in such a way as to not interfere with who and what we are.

That just seems like circular logic, like saying rain causes clouds or flies create garbage. The reason the gods don't interfere in our lives is because most people have no direct connection with the gods - which are, ultimately, reflections of our own actions, manifestations of our own Intent. We have to *create* the gods (or the god-self) *before* they can interfere in our lives. That's when it gets interesting. I prefer to think of it as the double or the higher self - but it's the same thing. We create our gods to teach us so that we may learn how to create them to teach us. It still comes from the *human* source.

If the gods ever decide to not come to work then their absence will be noted in a big way. Until then, everyone takes for granted what they do and how they interact with this world.

Only when the gods don't come to work has the person finally grown beyond the need for them, and must then take responsibility for her own fate and create her own reality as a singularity of consciousness. As long as we have even the slightest dependency on some idea of an extant god, we have taken that energy away from the self and thrown it to the abyss.

Self empowerment is a wonderful thing, but it doesn't make anyone a shaman. Only the gods can do that.

For as long as you see god as extant and I see god as the self, we cannot come to any meaningful agreement. What makes someone a shaman is a matter of where their path leads, how they walk that path, and how they assimilate all of it into a Whole that is a reflection of the self. Since a shaman is a self-healed madman, to me the "magic" that makes the shaman is in the healing. When the madman begins to *see* sufficiently to *see* that he is not really mad, but the world around him is actually the madness, he begins to heal himself of the doubts, fears and fragmentation that have set him apart just as a matter of being able to *see* the big picture in the first place. We go through life thinking it's real - the roles we play and the masks we wear - but the shaman is someone who knows her own heart sufficiently well to shed those masks and walk naked in the otherworld.

We walk the path through the world in which we find ourselves, and in doing so, we find pathways to the infinite. If

I lived in paradise, there would be no challenge, no opportunity for growth.

I'm not looking for the gods. I walk with them every moment of every day. And each of them has my own reflection. That is the real miracle.

Why do you think that the existence of the gods is threatening to your personal power as an individual?

Your gods don't threaten me personally. If *you* need them, they are there for a reason and they are there for *you*, not for me. But as long as any individual *depends* on the gods to assign meaning to their life, that person is not operating at their own full power or potential. Part of the Toltec path is letting go of dependencies. Anything upon which the individual is dependent is an energy hook. Whatever you need or want to believe is fine with me.

So as a philosophical maneuver, I must turn the question back on you? Why is my lack of belief in your gods seemingly a source of conflict for you? Why do you seem to need my agreement?

The gods do exist. The holy people I grew up around saw them, and in my journeys in the other world I have encountered them as well. So far, I have seen three gods.

That doesn't really answer the question as to why you appear to need the agreement of others - a question about which I have wondered in regard to all things, not just God or politics or your favorite applesauce - but I will say that I've also gone on many spirit quests and have encountered a few "gods", but ultimately I have found all of them to be of the higher self. What the spirit quests showed me was my connection *to* Spirit, not my segregation *from* Spirit[8].

We cast ourselves asunder and if we are fortunate, we find the strength and the courage to put ourselves back together as a cohesive singularity of consciousness. That is the great work - to evolve and grow beyond the fragmentation of our fears and dependencies, to become more than the sum of our parts.

But you aren't one of the gods and neither am I.

Right here, you have disempowered yourself by making a conclusion based in belief and programming rather than direct personal experience. You say you have encountered the gods, but have you really explored who and *what* they are other than their surface appearance and interaction? I do know there are allies or guides that are Other than the Self, but these are not necessarily gods in the sense you are using the term.

I have had my fair share of personal trials, and sometimes the spirits have stepped in when there was a crisis I wasn't prepared to deal with.

I have no doubt that something stepped in to help you, but in the terminology I use, I would say it was your double, your own higher self, your connection to the infinite. That aspect of the self is outside of time, and can be mistaken for gods or guardian angels or demons or whatever label one chooses to attach to it. I have no doubt the experience was real, but what I would question is the interpretation.

We are quick to say, "My guardian angel saved me," but have we really inquired as to the *identity* of that guardian? Many times, it is the double operating outside of time, on its own behalf, to preserve the mortal life so that evolution may

---

[8] A full accounting of my own shamanic initiation appears on my website at
http://www.quantumshaman.com/html/Initiation.htm

continue to progress. To assume it is a god would also assume that this god allowed you to wander into danger in the first place, and then had to intercede on your behalf to save you. I much prefer a world of free will, with a highly developed double who *can* act as guardian angel if needed, but who doesn't require all that worship and high maintenance that tends to go with serving "the gods."

It's all good, even the flaws, it's who you are. The real you is good enough, the real you is worthy of being loved unconditionally.

Totally agreed. We are flawed through our fragmentation, and as we move toward wholeness, we begin to embrace and embody the power normally attributed to the gods. We become the gods, and only in doing so, realize that we have been them and they us all along.

People believe what they have been told through myth and legend instead of having the experiences for themselves, and through their beliefs, they can be manipulated in all sorts of nasty ways. The core of what is being explored in Christianity (eternal life) contains much Truth. It's *how* it is practiced and misunderstood in today's society that has rendered those beliefs largely ineffective and, in some cases, detrimental. I have a lot of first hand experience with Christianity and how it is used as a weapon of subjugation and manipulation far more than it is ever used as a learning tool for the purpose of facilitating awareness of spiritual freedom. So while the core truths *underlying* the religion may be true, the religion itself protects and serves its masters: human beings, men with power, the organization of the church itself. And, of course, that isn't limited to Christianity alone.

In the old traditions you will never find a holy person who denies the existence of the gods, or who claims to be a god. There are entire bodies of lore that admonish everyone against such hubris.

Because, frankly, it is *always* in the best interest of The Powers That Be to keep the general population under some semblance of control, and one way in which that has been accomplished throughout history is to convince people they are less than the gods or the government or the king. It is a program, and one that must be broken by every being who embarks on a spiritual journey. I don't say the old myths have no value - I simply say that when we go into the realm of actual personal experience, it becomes possible to not only *see* the Truth behind the legends, but to see why, in some cases, these legends were sung into being by men in power.

In the case of Catholicism, for example, the early crusades had very little to do with trying to bring awareness of god to "heathens". Instead, it was about abolishing opposing belief systems altogether, so as to improve and increase the reign of the church. When a man becomes empowered through the force of his own personal connection to the Infinite, he no longer has need of churches or extant gods or even faith. That is when he has become a Man of Knowledge and can no longer be intimidated or shamed through fear.

There is no hubris in knowing who *I-Am*.

This Path Will Cost You Everything

I've been on the path for over 35 years, and I recently looked around and realized I've ended up pretty much alone. When I first hooked onto the journey there were several others I knew who were on a parallel path, but now it seems they've all gone back to the consensual reality. Why does that happen? Have you observed this in your own journey? If so, what's to keep any one of us from turning into phantoms all over again?

Orlando has said many times, "This path will cost you everything." When I've pressed him to go deeper into what that means, he usually responds with something along the lines of, "Just look around. How have things changed for you in the past year? In the past five years?"

It seems to be the nature of the path that *it* will shed those who are not really committed to it, sending them back to the comfort zones of friends and family, television and addictions, life in the comforting arms of the consensus.

In my own life, I've watched newbie warrior-seekers and advanced practitioners alike simply turn away from the path and attempt to re-embrace their former lives. Sometimes it is quite intentional and with full awareness, other times it's a slow but inevitable drifting away.

If you ask me *why* this happens, I can only say that some people were never suited to the journey in the first place, and others were pretenders looking for a place to belong. There's a wonderful quote that sums it up, and even though it's been said before in this book, it bears repeating in direct relation to your question:

The average man is hooked to his fellow men, while the warrior is hooked only to infinity.

-Carlos Castaneda

What I've observed in my own life is that most people cannot break that hook which binds them to their fellow men - or, I might add, the *hooks* that bind them to their indulgences.

If a warrior-seeker is serious about spiritual evolution and undoing the programs that hold one in stasis in the mundane world, then certain disciplines are going to be required - particularly in the earlier phases of the journey. There aren't any specific rules. It depends on *you* and your own indulgences, addictions and predilections. For example, in my own case, I was addicted to the comforting blue glow of the television, so my nights were spent worshipping at the altar of whatever inane sitcom, cop drama or sci-fi show might float across the airwaves.

Orlando never made any demands that I *should* break that addiction. He only asked that I spend one night *without* it. So I sat outside in my lawn chair, gazing up at the stars, feeling bored and displaced at first for having to break my routine, secretly glad he had only asked for one night of abstinence from an addiction I did not even realize *was* an addiction.

Just as I was beginning to grow uncomfortable with the surrounding silence of the night, I heard the soft padding of footsteps nearby. A moment later, a magnificent coyote appeared in a shaft of moonlight. He stopped in the driveway and seemed to be meditating for awhile, and then he burst into song. At first just a single clear note piercing the hymen of darkness, and then he was joined by his unseen brothers and sisters who were not far away. It wasn't just a chaotic chorus, it was a joyful *communion*, as if each singer in the band knew exactly what every other singer was feeling, and so the song was a celebration of a single moment - a celebration I would have missed entirely if I'd been curled up on the couch with the television blasting.

The night had become magical, filled with wonder, *alive*. Overhead, a falling star lit up the sky. A soft summer wind was blowing through the Joshua trees, causing their needle-like fronds to pluck a melody that was not unlike a siren's cry, drawing me further and further from the world I had always known, the world that had offered me such comfort.

I sat there for what must have been hours, feeling the embrace of the night and the nagual and the silence that was filled with *life*.

That was sometime in the summer of 1995, and I have never returned to the seductive arms of the sofa and the drone of the television since that night. That isn't to say *anything* is forbidden, of course. If I want to watch something, I get the DVDs, watch them, then turn it off. It's not the thing itself that's the problem - it's allowing ourselves to become addicted and obsessed that can create the pull to return to the matrix - something I have seen happen all too often.

As for why so many *do* return? It's often as simple as peer pressure, the demands of family and friends. In other cases, it boils down to the humanform addictions having a greater hook in the warrior than the path. One thing about this path is that it requires being both a self-starter and a forward thinker. It's why I have always advocated following the teacher inside our own heads - the double. While extant teachers can serve the warrior at certain points along the way, the double is the motivating force who knows the warrior better than she knows herself. As a result, the double pushes us further than any earthly teacher can - for the double is fighting for his own survival, and that survival is intricately interwoven with the mortal warrior's choices.

I know Orlando has occasionally answered questions from seekers. Does that mean he can be someone else's teacher, or is he strictly connected to you?

Orlando can answer questions or even provide some amount of guidance to others on the path. In his case, however, one of the things he stresses above all others is that the warrior-seeker *must* develop her own double if she is to complete the journey to freedom. As I've said many times, the double is the energy vessel of our awareness and the location of our totality. So while Orlando might be an excellent teacher for others, he can only be that vessel-of-awareness for me.

Oddly enough, I've had a couple of warriors actually start to believe Orlando is *their* double. Even more odd, I've had warriors become altogether disillusioned when he tells them it's time for them to begin working with their own double, creating pathways to their own gnosis, finding their infinite teacher within the meditations of their own silent knowing.

At that stage, the warrior-seeker either embraces the phenomenal opportunity with joy and enthusiasm, or wilts on the vine from a sense of unfulfilled entitlement. *No one can do it for you.* Not me. Not Orlando. Not even don Juan or the Buddha or Jesus or The Flying Spaghetti Monster.

The only one who can show you The Way in the final analysis is your own infinite double, but *only* when *you* create it, nurture it, fall in love with it, and embrace it as friend, lover, teacher, guide and companion.

So when you ask *why* warriors may turn away from the path, it's often because of that first enemy of a person of Knowledge: fear. Fear of failure or fear of success - not much difference.

Why would you say a warrior would have a fear of success?

There is a tendency of human beings in general to start off in one direction and then become distracted by something along the way. This is why I've written at length about 'The 3-Ds' - distraction, dissipation and diversion. There is also a tendency of humans to chase after what makes them feel good in the moment - but as with ordinary life, passions can wane and attentions can shift if one is not fully committed to their own evolution above all else. I may have dozens of other interests, but I have come to Know that if I intend to complete this journey, the deeper relationship between the warrior and the infinite is essentially a monogamous one. We may look at other possibilities, but we serve the one master - which is always and only Intent itself.

A fully-developed double is a formidable entity, and an infinite responsibility. When a warrior *truly* succeeds in manifesting her double, it also creates an inescapable commitment to the path and a duty to both the self and the double to *complete* the journey.

Put simply, it torches the bridge back to the matrix. And let's face it - most people don't like to burn bridges. Warriors, on the other hand, carry matches in one pocket and lighter fluid in the other.

———

PART THREE
Making Contact With the Higher Self

The Shaman's Double
The Dreaming Body, The Energy Body, The Higher Self

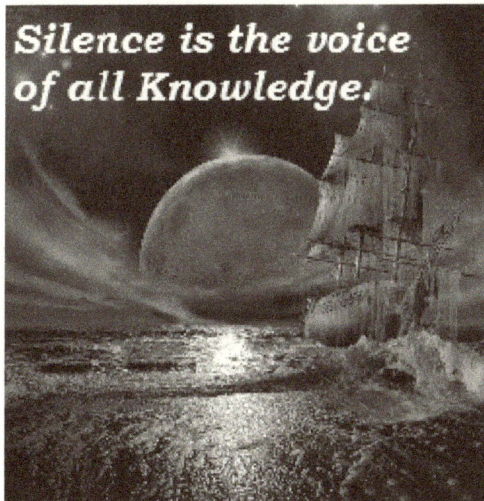

Silence is the voice of all Knowledge.

If a warrior could only do one thing on the journey to awareness, enlightenment and evolution, I would encourage them to meet their double face to face - whether in Dreaming or in the mirror or out there on the road.

What is a Nagual?

What makes a Nagual? Can only a seer determine if someone is a double-being?

Even attempting to answer this may be off base, in the sense that we would need to accept Castaneda's definitions of what a Nagual. I do find that what Carlos *intended* with his own definition (found in *The Eagle's Gift*) is accurate, but the manner in which he described it left a lot to be desired.

If I were looking to *see* if someone might be a Nagual, I don't immediately look for the four energy compartments, but for a sense of energetic cohesion and "fire" that is what gives the Nagual his or her drive. The only reason a Nagual is a good leader (and not all of them are, by the way), is because they are perhaps the most highly motivated beings on Earth with regard to a compulsion to reach freedom. That translates at a level of *seeing* to what I have described as a luminous black egg - a tightly cohesive energy that is simply different than that of anything else. Warriors at a highly advanced level may have an equal cohesion, so again it's a matter of recognizing that once the warrior creates her double to any degree of viability, there is very little difference between a Nagual and a warrior.

Most of the Naguals I've known have what I can only define as an intense love affair with the infinite that supersedes all else. The drive to reconjoin with the other half of one's self (Nagual man or Nagual woman) can have the tendency to make the world of Now seem almost trivial at times. Don't get me wrong - there is an ability to focus intensely in the Now, but that focus is driven by the inescapable connection to the other half of oneself (in my case, Orlando).

In the case of non-seers discerning whether one is a

double-being, it can happen, but the difference is that a non-seer might have no clue as to *what* they are seeing. I've been to psychics, for example, who see me as "divided between two worlds" (an exact quote), and they perceive this as a bad thing because of some belief system to which they adhere. The psychic who gave me that reading was a Catholic, so her interpretation of it was that I was "of the dark side". Another psychic once asked me, "Why are you so unhappy?" which I wrote about in The Birthday Gift[9]. In further conversations with that psychic since that incident, I have found out that what she is really *seeing* in me is the separation between the Nagual man and the Nagual woman. With Orlando already crossed into the infinite, I am constantly pulled there, which may be interpreted by a psychic as being unhappy. In reality, of course, that's not the case - it's just the *interpretation* of the *seer*, colored by their own programs and belief systems.

I am frequently seeming to run across self proclaimed Naguals. Interesting, as I'm not much of a warrior, but when I meet these folks in person I'm highly unimpressed.

I've met Naguals who have impressed me deeply, and others who are nothing more than kids in capes - wannabes with no more understanding of the path than a gnat on the ass of a yak.

What's funny is that when one really *sees* what a Nagual is, it isn't that glamorous. After many years on this path, I have come to conclude that Naguals are the fuck-ups who didn't get it right the first time[10]. Now maybe there's some great noble purpose for that - so that there will always be a leader, if one subscribes to such notions - but I'm inclined to

---

[9] http://www.quantumshaman.com/html/birthdaygift.htm

[10] Orlando has spoken about "the ghost train" many times. In essence, this is a method through which we *might* be able to give ourselves a second (or third or thirtieth) chance to evolve. For more information on this, see NAGUALS AND DOUBLE BEINGS (Why Do They Exist?) on page 159 of this book.

think it's just a warrior who created her double, got smashed by a meteor, failed to transcend the eagle, but had a sufficiently powerful double who was able to re-enter the mortal time-stream so that the mortal self would be born with the double already riding along inside - i.e., the four compartments of energy a *seer* might *see*. Believe me, all things being equal, it's best to get it right the first time.

As a result of my experiences and discoveries about my own nature as a so-called Nagual, what I've come to see is that what a Nagual really has is a direct connection to gnosis (Silent Knowing) combined with that energetic *push* toward freedom beyond the eagle. Some of the self-proclaimed Naguals may have the *physical* criteria (the four energy compartments), but what they may be lacking is the connection through gnosis to their double and to Knowledge. The reason I say this is because I have always had the energy and the drive to freedom, but I was altogether ineffectual as a teacher until I created and nurtured that connection to silent knowing (gnosis).

There are plenty of double beings walking the earth, but very few of them have that cohesion of self-double that is the key element. In the Castaneda material, there seems to be a distinction of language we may need to consider. Don Juan called himself "a man of Knowledge" - which implies to me that he certainly had that connection to the infinite through gnosis. Carlos was, at the time of the first books, only a warrior. His status was later upgraded (if one wants to look at it that way) to Nagual - specifically, a 3-pronged Nagual. I could go into what that implies, but for now it seems to go something like this:

1. A seeker on the path has the potential to become a warrior on the path. A warrior is one who lives by The Way, whereas a seeker may only be considering The Way. I often use the two terms (seeker or warrior) interchangeably, but if anyone wants to draw a distinction, this would be it.

2. A Nagual is a human being who could be defined as a

"double-being". Not all Naguals become warriors, and not all warriors are Naguals. It's only a probability until it is forced to go thru the motions of actually occurring.

3. A man of knowledge is a warrior and/or Nagual who has achieved a permanent connection to her own Infinite awareness, through a seamless gnosis with her double.

So, there are nuances of language that need to be taken into account. A Nagual is just a seeker unless and until she becomes a person of knowledge.

———

Storm

I sometimes feel like I spend so much time trying to fix everybody else's problems that I am neglecting my own spiritual path. On the one hand, I do want to help my friends and family, but on the other hand, I sometimes (selfishly?) feel it's fighting a losing battle.

I've faced that storm myself a few times. And rather than try to answer your comments directly, I'd like to share with you something that happened to me awhile back, which I think will have some relevance to what you're saying.

———

What drew my awareness to the storm was the scent of rain that drifted in through the open window. I neither heard it nor saw it at first, just the unmistakable scent of wet chaparral combined with what amounts to steam rising off the Earth when water comes in contact with the scorching layers of sand.

At first, it was just a typical desert rain - fat drops plopping on the Joshua trees, glistening like scattered diamonds in the slivered rays of sunlight which managed to pierce the clouds creeping in from the east. Hummingbirds flitted at the feeder, and there was no indication - other than a prickling of the hairs on the back of my neck - that it would be anything more than a brief thunderstorm at the edge of monsoon season.

And yet, it wasn't long before the clouds grew darker and finally opened up to dump what must have been six inches of rain in less than half an hour. Within moments, the driveway was gone altogether, and somewhere in the frenzy, the mail box had pulled up its roots and gone searching for otherworlds somewhere to the west. We shall not meet again in this lifetime, that much is certain. The road closest to the house was blocked by fire trucks and emergency vehicles, while small cars littered the landscape like discarded matchbox toys. Lightning scattered the shadows for an instant, thunder hammering at the windows, causing the house and the weenie dog in my lap to tremble.

I drew it all in, savoring its flavor, its scent, its textures and sights and sounds. The raindrops on my skin were sentient passengers, each one telling a thousand stories of a thousand lifecycles, the coming and the going, breathing in, breathing out.

The odd thing about the storm raging outside was that it mirrored the one raging inside. Over the past few days, an old conflict with an old friend had reopened, and despite all attempts at resolution, it seemed none was possible. So as I stood there in the aftermath of the storm, watching the raindrops drying on my feet and listening to the curses of a cactus wren as she shook the wet from soaked, spotted feathers, an awareness crept in through the crack between the worlds and settled somewhere near the crossroads where the infinite and the mundane overlap on rare occasions at the leading edge of a storm or the crumbling footing of a dangerous precipice.

Life is a desert and the rain is too rare and precious to squander, it whispered. *If you fret, trying to fix the leak in the neighbor's roof, you'll never find time to tango with the lightning or dance in the rain.*

So against all logic, I danced in the cold, cold rain and watched the lightning striking all around me. And I let go of any idea of fixing my neighbor's roof or salvaging the remnants of a friendship that has clearly been washed away in the flood.

Life's too short not to dance in the storm.

Breathing in. Breathing out.

———

THE MYSTERY OF THE DOUBLE

Face to Face

It's said in a lot of shamanic traditions that a warrior can't come face to face with their own double. Yet I've read on your website that you did, more than once. Can you share some of those experiences that aren't on the website?

It's no secret or surprise that the paths we walk have their ups and downs, their periods of great discovery and their longer periods of assimilation during which activity lulls and experience becomes somewhat more cerebral as opposed to visceral.

It's also no secret that the infinite has a wicked sense of humor.

One afternoon as I was standing at the end of an aisle in a department store, staring at some meaningless bit of fluff that I neither wanted nor needed, I had the passing thought that I was happier when my path was full of excitement and adventure, when Orlando was in manifestation and every moment was like some suspended eternity in which anything at all could happen, and often did. I actually heard myself sigh heavily as I realized that now - so many years after my first encounter with him in ordinary awareness - I live a rather uneventful life in many regards, even when it seems I am surrounded by chaos of late.

This particular afternoon was the day after my birthday - something we celebrate as children, but tend to ignore as we grow older. Not that the arbitrary numbers mean anything, but as I was standing there in the store waiting for Wendy, I was thinking about those olden days of high adventure when we would go driving in the middle of the night to court the unknown, when cars with blacked-out windows would follow us on long dirt roads and then just seemingly disappear into thin air. The nights when it was not uncommon to come home to an empty house, but with music playing on the stereo and books laid out on the coffee table as if placed there by mischievous fairies.

And I was thinking about Orlando, and what a long, strange trip it's been from Then until Now. Words I had spoken years in the past rattled through my mind, words spoken to Wendy when my writing career was still somewhat active.

"I don't want to be the one writing the stories. I want to be the character on some grand adventure, living the things I can only seem to write about!"

In so many ways, I've gotten my wish. It was shortly after I set that intent that Orlando *did* appear in our lives, and barely a couple of years later that we sold our house in the suburbs and moved to the desert to begin a long and intimate love affair with the unknown, the path of the heart.

So perhaps it stands to reason that as my mind was playing over these thoughts, something happened. From seemingly out of nowhere, a very tall, dark man with fashionably shaggy black-brown hair came around the end of the aisle, and even before my eyes registered his appearance, my heart was already pounding as if I had run a marathon, for he was all but exactly as I remembered Orlando from the last time I had seen him. The next thing I knew, he placed his hands on my arms in a gesture of familiarity, and leaned down to ask in a tone that was almost seductive, "Are we ready to go?"

For a split second, my mind went entirely blank. I couldn't breathe. I have known for some time now that the admonition given to Castaneda by don Juan is true for myself as well: "The sorcerer who comes face to face with his double is a dead sorcerer." The instinct to conjoin into the singularity is simply too powerful to resist - an energy which would be lethal to our fragile humanform bodies.

But as I stood there for that split second waiting for my heart to quit or my brain to explode in some massive internal hemorrhage, the space-time continuum did some sort of sideways dance and the handsome stranger was just a handsome stranger who had mistaken me for his girlfriend.

He jumped back, clearly embarrassed as he apologized, but as our eyes met, there was that one single instant of recognition that was like a shared memory. *There...* and then simply gone. And we were once again only two people in a store in the desert on a too-warm spring afternoon.

What was interesting was that I actually felt a flutter in the energetic flesh of the fabric of reality - as if two similar events had occurred at precisely the same time and space (thereby breaking all laws of physics). In one reality, the handsome stranger was just a handsome stranger. But in another reality, I had come to the edge of infinity and stood for a moment looking into the eyes of the double, into the heart of the unknown.

I felt the eagle breathe.

The nagual has a wicked sense of humor indeed and occasionally gives us glimpses of things that seem altogether normal if viewed only through the filtering lens of ordinary reality, but become altogether extraordinary when considered through the clarity of *seeing*.

"Are we ready to go?"

Interesting question. An hour later, my heart rate was still not back to normal.

———

An Exercise in Silent Knowing

Even though I've been on a spiritual path for many years now, I still haven't been able to make direct contact with my double. What do you recommend?

Find a place that is comfortable for you and relax into the Now. Have awareness of your surroundings without being attached to them. Is there a bird chirping in the distance? A dog barking? Road sounds? All of these things will be part of the experience, so awareness of them enables a blending of the warrior into the milieu, and the milieu into the warrior.

Essentially, the purpose of this exercise is to bring the warrior in contact with the double. As you sit with yourself in silence, focus on the Intent to move your awareness into the place of silent knowing - aka gnosis. For warriors at an advanced level, this may seem too simple. For those who have not yet worked with gnosis on a conscious level, it may take a few attempts to really make the connection, but once it is made, it is unmistakable. For myself, when I enter into a state of gnosis, there is a tendency for my head to tilt back and my eyes to close - though obviously this is my predilection and your mileage will vary. However it works for you to shift to the place of silent knowing, the purpose of this exercise is to actually hear the voice of the double - though it may not be experienced as a voice as we traditionally think of it. Could be a whisper that sounds at first like your own internal dialogue, yet is experienced as a bit of knowledge or information you did not know on any conscious level.

One of the hardest tasks a warrior faces is learning to distinguish the voice of gnosis from one's own internal dialog. The easiest way I have found to make the distinction is that the internal dialog is usually nothing more than lists, comments about what we are experiencing, reflections on the past, or otherwise personal information that is filled with our own self-importance. The internal dialogue is saying, "It's all

167

about *me!"*

The voice of gnosis, on the other hand, is often experienced as a single statement that fills the mind quite abruptly, and may or may not have any direct relevance on the surface. One of the strongest voices of gnosis I ever experienced came when I was staring up at a huge mountain overshadowing Palm Springs. *You have to meet the immortal world on its own level,* the voice informed me. Another one: *I am helpless before all possibility.*

Each of these statements is what amounts to a zip file - a single idea embedded with layers upon layers of additional knowledge which unlocks and unfolds itself over time, assuming the warrior takes upon herself the task of contemplation and the act of assimilation. I found it helpful to keep a journal for such purposes.

So as you sit in the place of silent knowing and take measures to stop the world, simply be open to hearing the voice of gnosis and take note of what it says. It doesn't usually tend to give long speeches, though it certainly can if there is a reason. But for the most part, if the warrior approaches this exercise with Intent and impeccability, you will begin to hear the voice of the double - and it is through learning to listen, ask questions, and communicate directly that the double is further developed until there comes that moment when you realize the double has become your teacher and your guide. This is when you may begin to realize the meaning behind don Juan's words, "The double is dreaming you."

This is where the real lessons actually begin.

———

The Vortex

There's something about driving, long trips on endless freeways leading in and out of the dark city of the lost angels. We got a late start, Wendy and I, due to a long list of unforeseen complications that seemed determined to create delay. So by the time I was in the driver's seat and cruising at a high rate of speed down the I-10 somewhere in the vicinity of Calimesa, my mind was drifting over the lush green pastures broken only by new housing developments and a smattering of golf courses which should perhaps be considered pastures for the human cattle. The damage the golf courses have done to the environment in and around the desert just stands as a testament to the excess indulgences of Man.

The day was bright, sunny, and had an odd quality of light which I have come to associate with a faded magazine photograph from the late 60s. I have an ability to essentially bi-locate my attention - I can be driving on auto-pilot while simultaneously walking through vacant houses alongside the freeway, or climbing to the top of some gigantic live oak in the distance. So I was exploring abandoned warehouses and rolling in tall grass in the distance. My thoughts were stilled. Just being. So it came as a bit of a surprise when Orlando's voice said very distinctly in my ear, *I am the vortex.*

I raised an eyebrow and brought my attention back to a cohesive sense of focus. "Eh?" I replied.

He didn't answer with words, but instead I was flooded with a download of information - one of those infamous zip-files I've discussed in the past, where it all seems neat and tidy on the surface, but unzips into layers upon layers of encrypted data which may require months or even years to assimilate.

The gist of it all, as I drove on through the late morning traffic, was that the double, once developed, is like the doorway mystics have spoken of since before time began. And yet, even that explanation is too simple, and at the same time too complex. I was shown a grid of energy, not unlike common graph paper kids use in school. Green lines in little squares. Except this was the universal graph. The big "it". Alive, sentient, Whole - not in the sense of an extant deity, instead it was alive with the energy of consciousness, awareness, the electrified Knowledge which is the cumulative experience of All Living Things, past, present and future.

As the awareness of the mortal self, I was off to the side observing the grid. As Orlando, I was the intersection point where two of those grid-lines connected. As I saw this, he again repeated, *I am the vortex,* and gave a little smile at my monkey-brain confusion.

And then I simply saw what he was trying to show me. The awareness which is the *I-Am* - the individuated singularity of consciousness which is the Whole self - is rather like the connection point on that infinite grid. At first, I felt a sense of uncharacteristic disappointment. *Is that all there is? I wondered. Just a point on a map, no different than all the other points on the map?*

Orlando laughed - and like a ripple in the grid, it reverberated across Allspace and Alltime. I understood it then, though I do not know if I can put it into words that will mean anything to anyone other than myself.

I am the vortex.

The words echoed in my mind, and the echo resonated through each and every one of those infinite intersection points on the grid. It is the door that opens onto the Eternal Infinite - and from that single intersection point, because it is connected to all the others, one may focus awareness "Here" or "There" or "Now" or "Then" throughout all of "it" at once.

He said he was only reminding me of what I already knew. And perhaps I needed reminding. It told me why I could windwalk through the trees, and why I could drift, ghost-like, up the staircase of a house far in the distance. Through the infinite grid, I am already there.

So there I sat, driving down the freeway on a day of no

170

special importance, looking at this infinite grid of energy with all its multitude of intersection points and all its sentient awareness and all its knowledge. And, without thinking, I said to Orlando, *So - what lies in the empty space between the gridlines?*

There was silence for a mile or more. A hawk drifted on high currents, incongruous as we approached the city, the Camelot of the Damned enshrouded in its yellow-brown envelope of smog and mist and misery.

The nagual keeps a few secrets even from me, he said at last, just when I had thought he wouldn't reply at all. *That's where the next evolution begins.*

So it would seem.

———

Wake-up Moments

Have you ever had a moment in time when you just suddenly knew something profound, without any background story of how or why you knew it?

I think most warrior-seekers have experienced those moments, and it is my belief that they come from the double - just a way of getting our attention in a world that is otherwise filled with chaos.

As I was sitting at my desk one morning, appreciating the change of season and deeply thriving on the slate grey sky which served as a backdrop for the snow-covered peak of Mt. San Gorgonio in the distance, I suddenly found myself back in time to when I was no more than 7 or 8 years old.

The afternoon was hot and still, the sky the same shade of slate as I was observing out my window in the body of the crone some 40+ years later. Though I remember nothing in particular about that day in the mid-1960's otherwise, I do remember feeling suddenly alive and awake and aware, so much so that the memory remains with me to this day. It was one of those wake-up moments when I abruptly knew something about myself, perhaps seemingly insignificant to anyone else, but monumental to myself.

I loved the dark and rainy days. I loved the storms which were so much a part of that desolate area in central Florida. And I particularly loved the days when the sun never made it through the clouds - those rare and precious days, usually in December or January, when it was dark and cold and the frost on the thick grass crackled beneath a little girl's feet like a living synapse of electricity.

At the time, that simple realization about myself was somehow profound, almost life-altering, for with it came the Knowledge that I was not like my peers, who loved the sun and could be counted upon to be glum and depressed on those uncommon dreary days. I remember standing underneath a scraggly Florida pine that day, actually confronting this aspect of myself, and the accompanying sense of exhilaration and isolation which were no less profound than the realization itself. It occurred to me that I could pretend to be like the others in order to fit in, but I would always know inside myself that I was a lover of storms and shadows and night, living in a world of others who worshipped sun and light and the dayshine world of ordinary affairs.

In hindsight, as I was sitting at my desk in the Now, I thought of that little girl's dilemma all over again, and realized it was one of the first times I had actually heard the Infinite knocking on my door. It seemed to be saying, *Take a look at who you are, and decide if you can walk a path that runs perpendicular to the world at large.*

Whatever the message, it was certainly a wake-up moment, one of those events we remember years later because our awareness was jolted into a fully awake state by some simple, small thing, and we suddenly realize we are alive and unique and utterly mysterious, that we are an entire universe waiting to be discovered.

> Brittle sky,
> still as an icy pond.
> The nagual has a steely grey beard today,
> and long silver hair
> wet with rain
> not yet fallen.
> A lone leaf flutters,
> driven by wind
> from a hummingbird's wings...
> the sole sign of Life.

———

Who's Who's Double?

One of the opinions you've put forth is that Don Juan was actually Carlos Castaneda's double. Obviously I don't agree with that conjecture, but I'm curious as to why you would even think so.

There are a lot of reasons I hold the opinion that don Juan was actually Castaneda's double - not the least of which is the very existence of Carlos's books. In a much-condensed narrative, what it boils down to is that no mere "apprentice" *could* have written some of the material, particularly the contents of *The Eagle's Gift*. Some (many) have stated that they think Carlos was just a scribe, but I have yet to see any scribe who could adequately or accurately translate or communicate complex mathematical equations even if studying under a master mathematician.

When things are written by scribes, they lack a certain authenticity - which is one major problem with the Bible, just for another example. The entire New Testament is essentially written *about* Jesus, but if Jesus ever existed, I dare say what *he* would have written would have been much different than what was put forth by his disciples and detractors. If Jesus himself had written the Bible, perhaps we'd live in a better world, but because it was transcribed by mere scribes, I can't help but see that most of the Truth of it got lost in the translation, and the world has been fighting about it ever since.

As for no sorcerer being able to come face to face with his double, or she would be a dead sorcerer, I actually believe that to be true, at least on one level. In my own case I *did* come face to face with Orlando many times, and I'm still on this side of the dirt. However, as my own awareness began to grow, there came that day when Orlando essentially burned with the fire from within and I was left standing in the outer courtyard of the post office wondering what the hell just happened. The only thing different from one day to the next was my own

Awareness. I had become at least a rudimentary *seer*, and when I began to *see* the actual energetic connection between Orlando and myself is when he *had* to leave this world in the manner of a sorcerer, or risk having that old caveat actually play out: I would have become a dead sorcerer because the instinct to reconjoin to that higher self would simply be impossible to ignore. The Spirit could *literally* be pulled right out of the body; and, in fact, there is <u>an article</u> on my website[11] which details how that *almost* happened to me that day.

Also, Carlos himself, being human, was trapped in linear time, so he was writing his books as the events were happening to him. If I had written about Orlando at the time the events were occurring, there is no way I could have even suspected what I now know to be true. In the same way, I suspect that don Juan knew the truth of the matter, but 1) there is simply no way to communicate that Knowledge directly without risking a real and genuine melt-down of the mortal source (in this case, Carlos); and 2) in those rare cases where a sorcerer really *does* come face to face with her double, it seems to me that the double's agenda would be to prolong that intense interaction for as long as possible, so as to shift the humanform awareness sufficiently out of its mundane stagnation.

By the time Carlos figured it out, he really couldn't see his way clear to say to his readers, "And, oh, by the way, Don Juan was actually my double all along." Because he had written of don Juan as an extant being and there was already considerable controversy over the veracity of the whole thing, I can't even imagine that his publisher would have condoned that kind of a confession that he had been making it up as he went along - which is how it would be perceived by the masses, in most cases.

That is not my random opinion, because I have actually lived the reality of it first hand. But to someone who has *not*

---

[11] <u>http://www.quantumshaman.com/html/crystal.htm</u>

had that direct experience, it would seem that Carlos was just trying to cover his ass as to why he could not produce don Juan for television cameras and hopeful hippies.

Don Juan also said, "It is impossible to reason out the double." Personally, I have not found that to be true. Keep in mind that that statement was made fairly early on, in *Tales of Power*. At the time those words were written, they may even have been true to Castaneda's perceptions. But as Knowledge grows and evolves, the absolute beliefs of the past become shifted in the wake of new information and experience.

Obviously this is just the tip of the iceberg, and perhaps the crux of all his books combined. The problem was that Carlos was never able to tell that little secret - that don Juan was actually his double - either because he really never did figure it out (I *seriously* doubt that), or because he simply could not see a way to do so without disempowering his entire writing career to all but the very few who have experienced it for themselves. To ordinary men, he would have appeared a liar, whereas to a sorcerer, he would be seen as someone who had actually experienced the infinite mystery of the Nagual itself. Unfortunately, the world is comprised of far more ordinary men than sorcerers, and so the secret died with him.

———

Abolishing Belief Systems

I have reason to believe we are already enlightened, we are already our double, and we are only here to experience Life. We don't have to become enlightened, when we have enlightenment already within us.

There seems to be a pervading belief among a lot of seekers that "we are already our double", or "we are all buddhas" or that we are already enlightened and just waiting to embody our perfection on the far side of the eagle's wings. And while it is a nice, comforting belief system, I cannot help but see that that's all it is - no different from the Christian faith, which teaches that we are born with a soul that can be saved through grace.

My agenda is about giving the seeker the tools with which to dismantle programs and beliefs that may have the tendency to hold them in check. And, in my hard-won experience, the belief that "we are already our double" is one of the most dangerous and debilitating beliefs a seeker may possess, for the simple reason that it gives the seeker permission to believe she is already an enlightened "finished product," when in all likelihood, she is only a sadly deluded phantom caught up in a belief system put onto her by the consensus reality, and nurtured by the comfort of the belief itself. Put simply, believing I have an immortal soul and need do nothing to nurture or maintain it is a fantasy being packaged and sold by someone with something to gain.

The reason I am so adamant about getting rid of this belief system that "we are already our double" is because it as a very deep trap if not acknowledged in a head-on confrontation. For that, the warrior may need an extant "mirror", and in this case that is my function.

My view on the double is simply that there is a vast difference between the spark of Spirit with which we are all imbued, and the actual, hard-line creation and manifestation of the double. Don Genaro's double didn't just pop out of the ether one day because it was sanctioned by Spirit. Quite the contrary, Genaro actually went to the bother of doing the hard work that formed a cohesive double which had the ability to manifest as something other than a comforting belief system that he was already "enlightened" or "saved by grace" or any of the other buzz-phrases we hear - all of which amount to an attempt to excuse ourselves from the actuality of *Doing* whatever it takes to create and manifest ourselves as a singularity of consciousness.

The idea has been put forth that basically the double creates us - meaning, we are disembodied spirits somewhere "out there," and the double is like an oversoul that chooses when, where and why we manifest as organic beings here on Planet Earth. In my opinion, nothing could be further from the truth. In fact, those who adopt this belief system may be seriously disempowering themselves by placing the responsibility onto the double that some religions attribute to God. By saying "the double creates us every time" it's no different than believing in reincarnation or some offshoot of a Christian creator-god. If the warrior doesn't take 100% responsibility for Dreaming the double in the first place - the double cannot exist to Dream the warrior.

While some of this process may appear to occur outside of time - there is often evidence of the double long before the moment of creation - that evidence does not become significant until the warrior goes through the process of creating her double through Dreaming. Orlando has often said: "You are the creators of reality. I am only its servant." In other words - if we don't create the double, the double exists only as a spark of spirit, an unfulfilled potential.

When a warrior has some sort of "evidence" that her double exists (a specific dream, a chance encounter with the nagual), there may be a tendency to accept that as also being evidence that one has "made it", or one has created her double, or simply that the double has been there all along. From our perspective in linear time, this is quite normal - *but we are not entirely beings of linear time.*

Let's say there actually is a moment of creation wherein the warrior takes the assimilation of all she has learned and actually brings it together in a cohesive "big bang" of Dreaming/Intent/Will. And let's say that happens sometime in the year 2016. From that moment forward, the double then exists as a viable entity capable of Dreaming (teaching-guiding) the warrior - but the double is not limited to *only* moving *forward* in time. The double may actually appear in the warrior's life at age 3 or age 12 or age 35. That presence may be (mis)interpreted by the warrior at age 20, for example, as evidence that the double is already there and Whole. And while that is true in one sense, it does not and cannot alleviate the warrior's responsibility for reaching and *manifesting* that moment-of-creation in the year 2016 that brings the double into *actual* manifestation. It is a self-replicating paradox, but any warrior who has been on the path for more than five minutes should be well-acquainted with self-replicating paradoxes.

The whole concept of linear time may be illusory, but one thing is certain: it's a *deadly* illusion if the warrior can't break free of it sufficiently to see that what we do in the Now is really the *only* thing that determines who we are in eternity. The double is not going to give us any second chances (unless one is a Nagual[12]) and even *if* one is a so-called Nagual, that theoretical second chance cannot exist unless the warrior in the Now takes responsibility for creating the moment of creation (through assimilation, intent and will) which actually manifests the double as a quantum construct of energy rather than just some nebulous belief system that we're already there.

The reason I feel so passionate about this is because I myself have been there with regard to having evidence, misinterpreting it as proof, and then having to essentially reconstruct the double from the ashes, like a phoenix rising. I got lucky. The process wasn't nearly as painful for me as it could have been, but it did have the effect of illustrating that *nothing is a given.*

If you are waiting for the double to do it for you, the eagle is preening his talons with patient anticipation.

———

[12] See "Naguals & Double Beings - Why Do They Exist?" elsewhere in this book.

Abolishing Belief Systems (part 2)

In essence, our double or higher self, like our Buddha nature, already exists. As with realizing the Buddha nature, realizing or actualizing the double/higher self requires effort.

The *potential* exists for the double. Look at it through the lens of probability. The potential *also* exists that we will all sprout wings and fly - but unless that is forced to go thru the motions of actually occurring, it remains as nothing more than an untapped potential.

If there is a predator mind at all, seems to me that its greatest accomplishment lies in convincing even impeccable warriors that all they need do is wait for enlightenment to come to them, wait for their double to manifest, wait for the eagle. While we're waiting, those moments of creation pass us by - and without a certainty of cohesion, I'm not at all convinced we have cohesion at all. Certainty *only* comes through direct, personal, hard-won experience.

If these notions are to be dismissed as being a belief system then perhaps the entirety of Eastern Philosophy is at risk.

Perhaps it should be. The fact that it is old and established doesn't make it right. Only makes it old and established. No matter *what* the system (Toltec included) it is *all* only a series of beliefs until the individual has the experiences for themselves. Only *then* does belief become Knowledge.

My opinion on this matter isn't popular with most, because it flies in the face of complacency and, if we allow it, brings us face to face with our self-importance that will be our undoing if we aren't careful. For as long as we believe we are already buddhas, we never will *Be*. Just human nature. If you woke up tomorrow morning and discovered you had won the lottery and the man, woman or sheep of your dreams had fallen madly in love with you, what motivation would you have to go to work or take an ugly woman out on a date? Think about it. If we truly *believe* we don't have to do the work, we probably won't.

The actuality of the double is not what we imagine, but what we Intend at the deepest levels of our being.

In a nutshell, it comes down to the fact that I personally came face to face with my double, who then burned with the fire from within, leaving me with the incredible task of creating him in the first place so that he would exist in order to show me that the world is nothing like we have been taught to believe. When he said, "I am going to destroy your world," he meant it literally, and proceeded to do just what he had promised. For as long as my world was comprised of the philosophies and belief systems of other people, *I* did not exist. My world was a false front and I was a phantom.

I have written about these experiences at great length on my website and in my books. The result of all of those experiences was that they led me to that "moment of creation" I keep talking about - when Orlando's words, "Make me whole," suddenly took on depth and substance and quantum *action*. To my linear-time awareness, it certainly *seemed* he had been there all along. But only *after* I accepted responsibility for that moment-of-creation did I force that "evidence" to become manifested into *proof*. To someone who has done this, it is obvious. To someone who hasn't, it will appear impossible or even as madness incarnate.

———

Danse Macabre

On your website, you talked about meeting your double (Orlando) "in the flesh." I assume you meant this literally, particularly on the page entitled "Meeting the Mirror." I'm curious if you had any other encounters with him in ordinary reality.

Yes, I knew him "in the flesh" for a period of about three years, though I did not know at the time that he *was* my double. As a result, we were able to meet face to face several times, though each meeting was always layered in mysteries which only began to unfold quite some time after the incident which I have come to call "The Crystal and the Nagual" on my website. The encounter I'm going to describe below occurred probably five years after Orlando left this Earth, not by dying, but by a process known in the Toltec practices as "burning with the fire from within." (see the glossary)

――――

If I believed in Hell, I might have thought I had arrived there. Though the temperature in San Diego was officially a mere 78, the high humidity combined with the complete lack of a breeze gave the illusion of a sweat lodge at high noon somewhere in the badlands of Death Valley. The Renaissance Faire which had traditionally been held at another venue had been moved to a hilly ravine, and what had once been merely difficult had become nigh on to impossible. Entire shops and guild encampments had to be moved in by hand (lest the dead grass be damaged - though how it could be any more dead was a mystery to all), and all down a steep hill without the use of vehicles of any sort. I had left my wand at Hogwarts, and despite all evocations of Intent (in varying degrees of colorful language), that 50 pound box still weighed 50 pounds and refused to be levitated even though I am wholly aware that it

182

is possible to do so.

By the end of the day on Friday, my body felt like it had been a punching bag for some super hero in training, and this led to fitful dreams which were a far cry from Dreaming, but nonetheless may have served some purpose not yet clear.

By the time the event opened on Saturday morning, temps and humidity had already soared, and the definition of relief had come to be spelled with a bottle of ice water dumped down the back of one's shirt - rather like attaching electrodes to one's nipples and flipping the switch. A real eye-opener, to be sure. And, in the end, not much relief.

So we sweated.

Took to counting phantoms to pass the time in between customers.

And sweated some more.

It occurred to me at some point that it was all rather amusing. Patrons who would tout the solidity of reality at any other moment swirled past in peasant bodices and merchant-class jerkins. A noblewoman fanned herself with an array of peacock feathers, remarking at length on the heat. Dressed in a long-sleeve, high-necked thick brocade dress complete with hoops, underskirts and a flowing black velvet cape with hood, I could only inquire with a certain degree of curiosity, "What do you do when you return to the 21st Century?" Perhaps not surprisingly, she was a high school science teacher.

Approaching on the path of dead grass, I saw the *Danse Macabre* - a troupe of musicians who dress entirely in black, with skeletal faces and the trappings of death. Their movements were slow, lethargic. Their music had hooked into the heat and gave it a voice of a heavy, slow drum, like a heartbeat slowing, slowing... slowing.

My mind drifted, and as the dancers passed by, I felt my own heart jump wildly into my throat. A very real gasp slipped past my lips, and I realized I was looking straight at Orlando. Sitting on a low block wall about 30 feet away, wearing a black tank top and dark glasses, there was no mistaking him for merely another man - a fact that was validated when I realized I could neither breathe nor move.

Time stopped.

Between tick and tock.

Only the dancers continued to move, and then only in slow motion.

The very real thought crossed my mind that perhaps this was simply "it". End of the mortal timeline. Time to dance with the double past the lair of the eagle. To my surprise, I had no particular fear of that dance - in fact, I was far more unnerved by Orlando himself than by the idea of my own potential demise.

This was not some passing vision. What I saw was as solid and physical as any of the other patrons at the Faire, and all the more because the luminosity of him was the same unfathomable black light I have always associated with him. The reverse luminosity of the singularity, whose cohesion is so tight not even light may escape.

A black-clad flutist passed between us, obscuring my view for no more than a single second. And yet, as the dancer moved on toward the west, the wall where Orlando had been sitting was suddenly empty. No place to hide, nowhere to run. He was simply gone, back to the infinite, behind the veil, into the minor-keyed melody of the flute which is without substance, yet omni-present throughout the air itself.

I do not specifically know what this incident means, nor why it chose that unlikely moment to manifest. After returning home on Sunday evening, I fell into an exhausted sleep, though not a restful one, and dreamt of serpents in my house. Within minutes, I was awakened by a fierce storm over the desert, with lightning flashes so intense and prolonged, they seemed to reveal shadow worlds not normally visible to the naked eye.

The nagual is a restless tempest, its darkest waters doorways into otherworlds.

———

Romancing the Nagual

Tell me what you mean by 'romancing the nagual'.

Since I view the nagual as the unmanifested - energy not yet in use but in a state of waiting - I have found that the act of "courting" it tends to bring into manifestation that which we desire - and more important - that which we *need*. Example: As a little girl growing up alone in Florida, I had time and freedom to let my imagination run wild, and as I came into adolescence, I began trying to create for myself what I might call the perfect lover. I never thought of this as a human male, but as a literal manifestation of magic. Something from nothing. When I was 11, I shook my fist at the sky, and proclaimed, "If I can't come to you, I'll bring you to me!" I spoke these words with such intent that I can see in hindsight that the nagual manifested Orlando.

The reason I describe it as a courtship is that's what it's

been and that's what it continues to be. I can intellectualize it all I want with electromagnetic fields and all the stuff a lot of new age gurus talk about, but unless it is personal and speaking to me in the language of the autumn wind, it's all just words. What makes it real is that courtship, that love affair, that kick in the gut that comes whenever I realize I have established a relationship with something that can come to me as a man walking the earth, or a shaman in my dreams, or a coyote walking down the road in the desert.

Why you think it is necessary, and what benefits might one have from so doing?

Without the courtship, it is only an intellectual understanding. That might be enough to get you where you're going, but it's not enough for *me*. The courtship with the nagual is like tantric sex. There is no limit to its power. When it finally consumes me, that will be the cosmic orgasm that launches me into the awareness and assemblage point of the double - the totality of myself, the singularity.

A lot of warriors resist the idea of falling in love with their double out of fear, or some misperceived notion that to do so would qualify them as having invisible friends and thereby make them candidates for residence at the funny farm. In short, there is a program of restraint or acceptable behavior that limits what one is willing to experience. As long as that kind of program is in effect, the warrior will never achieve her full potential. That isn't to say they won't have communication with their double in other ways, but I've really found that the full-on communion only began to occur with me after I gave myself permission to love wholly, deeply, unconditionally and eternally - the good, the bad and the ugly.

I once worked closely with a warrior who seemed to embody the antithesis of this. In her own pursuits of her double, the brick wall she encountered had to do with her inability to fall in love - not only with her double, but with *anything* in life. She could have love for things and even some people, but never that crazy-in-love feeling which accompanies a new romantic interest (one of the lowest manifestations of "falling-in-love", by the way), or the exhilaration one feels when skydiving or riding a half-wild horse at break-neck speeds through an unexplored canyon with the cold wind blowing in one's face and the cry of the eagle echoing in the sheltering pines. Her love was conditional, and rooted heavily in fear. If we agree to love, there is the fear we may lose our love, or our love will be unrequited, or a thousand other irrational fears, all of which may end up conspiring to crash the boat of intent on the rocks.

Anything less than wide-open experience is less than our fullest potential - and falling in love with the double qualifies as the ultimate experience of a lifetime, a love affair with one's own higher self in eternity, reflected on the infinite.

I have taken to sitting in the desert, listening to the songs in the wind which speak of the coming of winter and the embrace of the ice prince and the dance of the seasons reflecting in the raven's black eye. In the midst of all of that, Orlando walks with me and within me, and there is a level of communion that exists in defiance of all attempts to explain.

The understanding is in the silence.

———

Gazing at Dragonflies

I believe the universe allows for all possibilities. That is, we are completely free to do whatever we want. We are free to do our exercises or not, or even to tear up the book if we feel like it, to paraphrase Richard Bach in "Illusions".

Sure. We are also free to kill our neighbors, slaughter inhabitants of third world countries for no other reason than that we want their natural resources, and essentially do *anything* we want to do. But there will be consequences - and a warrior's impeccability takes that into account and the assimilation of that becomes defined as "the right way to live". All too often I see that we-can-do-anything-we-want approach used as an excuse for laziness or indulgence or do-nothingness. Sure, you *can* do that, but is it in any way pushing you toward your highest potential? I can't help thinking that the one who tears up the book will never know what it might have shown him.

We need not seek out the nagual. If we choose to become more aware, to reach the totality of ourselves, then the effort is primarily in the arena of the day-to-day world.

The work is done in the day-to-day world, but the force that manifests the totality of oneself resides within the infinite. I see it like surfing. The surfer rides on the crest of the wave, but the power driving the waves is much deeper and may, in fact, be far out to sea, completely unperceivable to the surfer except as how it manifests on the crest of the wave.

The nagual is, I think, the non-specific arena of the extraordinary, not the repository of a person's so called double, alter-ego, or whatever it is to be called.

Too limiting. The double is not contained within the nagual. The double is the ubiquitous awareness of the warrior's Whole self. It requires neither milieu nor manifestation, though it may be perceived to have both.

The process of reaching for the totality of oneself is to integrate that 'other' within ourselves, but that has nothing to do with the nagual, which is impersonal.

Just by its existence, the nagual gives us the proof that the world is nothing like we have been taught to believe (it is the

188

unknowable, manifested - alpha/omega, all/nothing) so in that manner it gives us the power to unlock and dismantle our programming that keeps us from experiencing the double. Yes, the nagual is impersonal, but so is the force of electricity. We may use it, but it doesn't care one way or the other.

I have come to see the totality of oneself as what amounts to the total experience of the mortal self and the eternal double, gathered together under a single unlimited and seamless assemblage point - which could be considered the whole self. As we've discussed in the past, my take on reincarnation is that it is really the Intent of the double moving through other experiences outside of the immediate perception of the mortal self. There is no past or future involved. Just intent and experience. That being the case, the double amasses a plethora of experiences which are relevant to the mortal self, but which may only be integrated into the mortal self through the process known as embracing the totality of oneself.

While we may glean certain knowledge from looking at the flight of a raven or the power of a storm, I maintain that having a somewhat more direct line of communication is not only more energy efficient, but is actually more in alignment with our nature as human beings. For example, while I might be able to look at the tilt of the wind and realize a huge storm is coming three days hence, it is more energy efficient for me to have a highly developed double who might say to me through gnosis, *A storm is coming, and by the way, did you ever get that hole in the roof patched?*

That's a silly example, of course, but it encapsulates what I am trying to convey to other warriors. If you *can* have that kind of communion and communication from the actual embodiment of the Infinite, why would you not? I have some real question about the warrior who says, "Oh, I *could* be sitting in a lotus grove having a direct conversation with my double, but I'd rather gaze at dragonflies."

Is it *really* that you would rather be gazing at dragonflies, or is it that you really *can't* (meaning don't-know-how) to have that straight-up one-on-one conversation with your double, and so it becomes a case of sour grapes?

I've gained a lot of insights gazing at dragonflies, to use that metaphor. But I am continuing to gain the totality of myself through direct communion with the double. To me, gazing at dragonflies is just one of the tools for *developing* the double. It is not a substitute.

––––––

Naguals and Double Beings - Why Do They Exist?

You've written a lot about the double and double beings (Naguals). What's unclear to me is why double beings exist at all. Is this just some weird fluke of nature, is it a separate species, or is there some purpose these beings serve that isn't immediately clear?

The following is a compilation of several posts made to my old group, The Sorcerer's World. I realize some of it may be complex and repetitive, but rather than try to distill it down to 50 words or less, it seems reasonable to present it as it was written – in fits and starts of passion, and long nights in the womb of silent knowing.

––––––

Though it was said by don Juan that no one really knows why Naguals are born with four compartments of energy rather than the traditional two, I think I might have a vague inkling of why this is so. As a warrior creates her double and projects that energetic vessel into the infinite, it is given the agenda of teaching us how to live, but even more so, it teaches us how to *evolve*, how to reconjoin with the double so that the warrior may inhabit the totality of OneSelf. Literally *One. Self.*

190

My double has always said that the only way he can leave me is if I were to turn my back on the path and fragment myself back into phantomhood. Should that happen, the result would be that when I face the eagle, the "Della-self" would not survive, and would fragment back into the component parts of energy of which all things are made. I would return to the All, but not in any cohesive manner. But as I have come to understand it, the energy body which is the cohesive double would continue because it is already Whole within the indestructible hologram. What would be lost would be my mortal self with all her life-experiences, not necessarily the part of me that is already whole outside of time.

The whole purpose of this two-part migration of the soul is to bring the mortal self and the double into cohesion, so as to inhabit a single assemblage point into the infinite. The double has been given the agenda to teach, to create, and to make the warrior an integrated Whole being through an ongoing series of lessons, information, Knowledge and experience. There is no limit to this, and that agenda is an eternal one, perhaps expressed in the words: "I give you the will and the wisdom to be whatever you need to be in order to teach me how to be Whole." For "whole" you could substitute the words evolved, cohesive, eternal, or even immortal (i.e., not-mortal).

There is a concept which Orlando calls "the ghost train". If we look at our mortal lives like a train trip, and we get to the end of the line (the eagle, death, transformation), our intent is to step off the train, embrace the energetic double, and conjoin into our Totality - literally the combined assemblage points of every experience the self and double have ever known – both in and outside of time. But if for some reason the mortal self fails in its bid for cohesion, my theory is that the double actually goes "back in time" to within the time-frame of the mortal lifespan, and begins the whole procedure again. Orlando says he and I have ridden the ghost train a few times - not a particularly reassuring idea, but not surprising, considering everything I now know. It's like that scene in *The Matrix* where Neo first jumps off the building. One of the others remarks, "Everybody falls the first time." I think that's true here, too, which may account for why the idea of past lives is so popular. Some of those past lives may well be our individual journeys on the ghost train. It is the double's journey toward Totality, toward fulfilling the agenda with which the mortal created it through free will.

What it boils down to is that the universe is holographic in nature. So once something is created, it can never be destroyed. If your double is real *now*, even if you develop Alzheimer's, go insane, or simply fail to get past the eagle, the double is nonetheless real within the hologram, and because its agenda is its own evolution and conjoining with its mortal self, it will continue to slip back into that small segment of eternity known as the mortal lifespan in an attempt to teach the mortal self how to *succeed* in getting past the eagle "next time". This may also account for some instances of déjà vu. We think we've done this before because we *have* done this before.

With that bit of background, I have begun to seriously wonder if so-called Naguals or double beings are born that way because they are the ones who *have* ridden that ghost train at least once or twice, and so they essentially come into *this* life with the energetic double more or less already fully formed – lying dormant until such time as there is an opening, or window of opportunity for the teachings to begin again – or more precisely, until such time as the mortal's free will awakens and issues the command. In my case, that command is remembered as an 11-year-old girl shaking her fist at the sky and proclaiming, "If I can't come to you, I'll bring you to me."

Because the double is an eternal part of the hologram once created, even if the mortal self fails in her bid for evolution past the eagle, that which is eternal within the hologram (the double) has the ability to step back inside the finite span of that mortal lifespan – because the double is not constrained or limited to a linear-experience of time, and exists seamlessly throughout the space-time continuum. So, it begins to appear that those who have created their double, but for whatever reason perhaps do not fulfill their evolution "the first time around", may be those who are born double-beings, or Naguals. What is happening in actuality is that the agenda given to the double kicks in if the mortal self fails in her bid for evolution, and by virtue of re-entering the mortal timeframe (rather like stepping into a re-run on television), the being who is born Now is born with the double already attached – four energy compartments instead of only two.

Doesn't the double exist beyond the eagle for everyone? In other words, even if a warrior or an average human has not fully created that double, does it not still exist in quantum space and would it not re-enter the human matrix to try again? Or are you saying that unless the warrior brings the double into being with his Intent, it simply does not exist at all? So unlike the concept of soul, or the Buddhist idea of Mind, the double does not exist until a human manifests it? Is that the idea? If that is true, where does the Double exist in space-time? Would it not have to be "somewhere," in order to be created? I guess I had always considered the double to be similar to the idea of soul in that it exists in some nebulous space but waits for the human form to recognize it.

The double has some similarities to the concept of a soul, but there are also differences. I have come to the conclusion that everyone comes into life with a spark - but unless that spark is nurtured into an eternal flame, it tends to dissipate and eventually disappear, thus the Toltec concept of the eagle, which basically devours our awareness and returns it to the energetic components from whence it came.

I'm delighted that you asked "Where does the double exist in space-time?" From my observations, the double is a paradox incarnate, which is precisely *why* it has the ability to serve as the energetic vessel for our awareness beyond the eagle. The double exists in space-time (for starters) within the human being who will (or won't) bring it into being. It exists as that spark. Once the spark is nurtured and begins to grow, the double is then projected into the infinite - meaning that it becomes ubiquitous and *non-local*. It is everywhere and nowhere - the quantum paradox which is awareness itself.

From a human perspective, we perceive that our awareness is localized within our brains, but we know from Dreaming and out of body experiences that this really isn't the case. I myself had a near death experience (dead for several minutes) in August of 2014, and my consciousness was anywhere *but* inside my brain. It was infinite, and simultaneously it was interacting directly with my double. Orlando was basically very casual and kept saying things like, *Oh, just come with me. Let's blow this town and go have some real fun!* Yes, he is a bit of a trickster, but also deadly serious. It was my choice - whether to dance off with him beyond the eagle, or come back to Earth for awhile.

What is the purpose of the double? Don Juan said the double is created in dreaming, but what is the actual purpose of the double?

The double is coyote and raven combined: it may trick you, but it will also give you wings.

The purpose of the double is to serve as the vessel of our awareness in eternity. Put another way the infinite self has the ability to transcend death provided it has sufficient cohesion.

194

Though this is a massively simplified explanation, look at it this way: at the moment our physical bodies fail, our awareness may choose to shift its assemblage point from the tonal body into the nagual body. The nagual body *is* the double - it is infinite, or it may choose to *appear* human (as Genaro did, as Orlando did) but ultimately the purpose of the double is to be the assemblage point of our totality.

It could also be said that the purpose of the double is to teach the mortal self *how* to become what the double already is. Thus the riddle*: You have to be immortal before you will know how to become immortal.*

———

You have to BE immortal...

before you can Know

how to BECOME immortal.

The Dual Assemblage Point

In a recent discussion where the subject of the double was touched upon, some of the comments put forth included: *"I don't believe in the double." "The double doesn't exist except as a component of self." "The double can only be like what Carlos described. It's an exact duplicate of the warrior."*

As I read the transcript of this discussion, where the conversation actually turned somewhat volatile, it occurred to me that a lot of the reactions I am seeing with regard to this subject are based almost wholly in the mindset of fear - a fear generated by 1) lack of comprehension; and 2) the insecurities of the ego as it resides in the world of ordinary awareness.

When an otherwise advanced warrior proclaims, "I don't believe in the double," it's usually a signal that some old program is running in the background which is distorting one's perception of oneself. One warrior whom I questioned about this recently told me, "The double is just a myth, isn't it? It's just a way of explaining a feeling - like Santa Claus being used to promote some essence of Christmas."

> *"The self dreams the double. Once it has learned to dream the double, the self arrives at this weird crossroad and a moment comes when one realizes that it is the double who dreams the self. Your double is dreaming you. No one knows how it happens. We only know that it does happen. That's the mystery of us as luminous beings. You can awaken in either one."*
> -Carlos Castaneda, *Tales of Power*

The double is the evolved self, projected initially by the mortal warrior as a manifestation of the intent to preserve awareness beyond the threshold of death. It is created from the energy of the warrior, literally, but takes on a life of its own as a projection of the warrior's Will. We give the double life. When the warrior puts forth the intent which says, "Teach me," or "Make me whole," the double is the teacher who then

196

begins 'dreaming the warrior'. In this manner, the warrior is able to perceive well beyond the assemblage point of the ordinary world, and actually begins to utilize information and Knowledge gleaned directly from the assemblage point of the nagual.

If someone has already determined that they don't believe in the double, or that the double is "only a component of self", then that is the colored filter through which the words will be viewed, and from that filter, the warrior's own understanding will be limited at best, and often thwarted altogether.

The double is not a theory.

It is not a religion.

And it is not a belief system.

To the warrior who has experienced her double, it is simply what-is. To the warrior who has not experienced her double, it remains as an energetic potential in the realm of all possibility which must be forced to go through the motions of actually occurring.

So much of any serious path of Knowledge lies within our ability to set aside what we believe and deal instead with what we have never even considered - those concepts and otherworlds which exist beyond the words and in the realm of actual experience. But that's where the ego can become fragile and fearful and slam on the brakes with blanket statements such as, "I don't believe in the double."

The ego may not want to believe in the double, for the simple reason that the double tends to represent something larger than the sum of our human parts, and the ego is not particularly forgiving of anything which it may perceive as greater than itself.

I mention this primarily as a tool for our own awareness,

and it is a tool I use ruthlessly in my own journey. If I find myself recoiling and stating, "I don't believe in this or that!" it is often helpful to turn and look the demon in the face and ask oneself why I am so closed to the possibility which elicits such a response in the first place. Most often, I will discover that my beliefs are generated as a comfort zone for the ego, rather than based in any sort of actuality. And, of course, once this is *seen* and acknowledged, it is a relatively simple matter to put the ego aside, shift awareness to a more fluid position, and look at the whole concept from an entirely different point of view. It's awareness *of* the ego that essentially enables us to bypass the ego when dealing with matters of the double, the nagual, or any other unknown which may be frightening to our organic humanform awareness.

To limit the double is to limit the self.

To limit the self is to defeat the purpose of the double.

To see and acknowledge only the mortal self is nothing more than a manifestation of the ego's insecurities.

Please consider that, for it is ultimately the insecurities of the ego which have the greatest potential to derail the warrior-seeker altogether. If you are given to meditation, this is a topic which always yields new insights and perspectives.

What do we have the potential to *be* when we set aside ego and belief, and open the door to the manifestation of all possibility?

The double represents the other half of the dual assemblage point of man. We perceive the ordinary world with our five ordinary senses. We perceive the infinite with the *other* senses (no way to know how many) which are inherent in the energetic construct of the double. When these assemblage points overlap (through dreaming, meditation or gnosis/silent knowing), the warrior-seeker gains glimpses of her connection to the unknown. When the two assemblage points conjoin at death, the warrior may be said to have achieved ultimate freedom.

My personal sense is that the ultimate freedom of our

totality is only one more step in an infinite journey. From the wholeness of our totality, we embrace the first step of the next evolution.

———

Listen with your heart.
Hear with your spirit.
See with your third eye.

Only then will you Know.

PART FOUR
Questions for the Infinite

Love is a quantifiable force.

When you understand that, you will have the power to finally be free.

Free Your Mind at
Quantum Shaman.com

What Orlando has to say about all of this
from the perspective of the infinite.

The Voice of Silent Knowing

Though Orlando is my double, I have found that one of the best ways for me to learn from him is through the inquiries of others who manage to voice the questions I want to ask, but never seem to find the right words. When I initially opened my first forum on the internet (2002), Orlando's advice to me was simply this: *Take everything you've learned and slam it up against the brick wall of the consensual reality. Throw yourself wide open and, with vulnerability, see if what you have learned can transcend the challenges of the best minds and the worst trolls the internet has to offer.*

Somewhat to my surprise, the things I learned from Orlando and through other outlets along the way not only withstood the challenges, it turned out that the challenges forced me to look deeper into myself and further outside the box, to finally realize that the foundation not only held, but expanded exponentially with every challenge it faced.

For warrior-seekers who have learned to stop the internal chatter, it becomes possible to have full dialogs with the double which will ultimately become one's finest and most reliable teacher. The trick, of course, is learning to know the difference between one's own double and the clever attempts at manipulation by the internal dialog - which is never completely eradicated, even if dormant for weeks or even months at a time.

Over the years, Orlando has communicated many things to us - so much that it would be impossible to include it all. Some has appeared on my website and my various forums, but most remains in private journals and letters.

This section is offered for a multiple purpose...

1) To share with the warrior-seeker a few thoughts and musings from the perspective of the double - the dreaming self, the higher self, the eternal and infinite self.

1) To encourage the warrior-seeker to seek the counsel of his or her own double, to glean information and Knowledge directly from your own higher self and...

3) To provide - hopefully - a gram of mystery, a spark of passion, a taste of the Infinite...

———

An Evolutionary Mitosis

The double is the manifestation of what you desire - not only what you desire as a lover, friend and companion, but what you desire of *yourself* - the manifestation of your own highest potential. The double is what you need him to be. More than that, as the double is developed through long-term intent, he becomes the force that stands at your back, whispering in your ear all the ingredients that are necessary for his creation.

This is where the mortal and the double swear a sacred pact which can never broken if both are to survive into the infinite. For this is when the double takes his first breath and becomes the *I-Am* in eternity. This is where the egg divides in an evolutionary mitosis so that it will be always driven to come together again, recreating in eternity what was begun within the mortal dream.

For I am divided for love's sake,
for the chance of union.

-Aleister Crowley

The Mold of Man, The Source of God

I'd like to ask Orlando his thoughts on God. Do you believe a Creator exists? And how does that relate to what Carlos Castaneda referred to as "the mold of man?"

Before anything we currently think of as the universe existed, there was only an immense void - a nothingness which had gathered into itself all matter-energy. It was all there was. Yet from the nothing - literally a thought which created itself - the universe as we know it sprang into being - a thought creating itself because it wanted and needed to exist as an entity separate from the void. It demanded life, yet the only way for it to achieve life was to create itself from the nothing and hurl itself out in all directions.

Because it was a thought-creation of will, it created itself with perfection - it gave itself all possibilities needed for survival and, even more importantly, it gave itself and its creatures the ability to evolve in order to adapt to changing circumstances within its own continuum. This is the correlation to the Biblical I-*Am* - it is the All bringing itself into being. It is not an entity separate from Man, but an all-encompassing milieu of which Man and consciousness are but one small part.

If we think of the void as containing all of matter-energy, then the universe is the stage of time - and both together create the continuum of space-time and matter-energy. Before the universe existed, it was perhaps contained inside a single particle no larger than an atom - yet from that single atom sprang all of creation, willed into being because the entity we recognize as the universe had to expand beyond the sum of its individual parts - it had to evolve to be more than it was before.

In its creation, it gave all the beings within itself the ability to continue through evolution - for the ironic thing about the creation of the universe is that it gave all it had. It won't interfere in the affairs of man because it *can't*. There is nothing left of "it" except all these individual components that comprise the all - so from a quantum perspective, there is no intelligence sitting outside the universe who can intervene in its destiny. In its original creation, it used all its parts to create the whole - which also means that it used its full intelligence, its whole awareness, its absolute will, and in doing so, it automatically created each individual cell of itself with those qualities. For that reason, each of you - whether man, animal, stone, vegetable, air or distant sun - has the blueprint for your own unique evolution.

In creating itself to survive,

the universe gave us the ability to evolve.

The irony is that the universe and all its individual components are at constant war with the void in that it's the nature of the void to take back what came from it and it's in the nature of the universe to avoid being taken. The only way to avoid such a fate is for each individual creature to create its own continuity in the same way the universe created itself from the void. We must strive to become our own individual universe, expanding beyond the reach of the stage we currently inhabit - we must create our own continuity by saying *I-Am*, just as the universe itself originally detached itself from the void when it sprang into being from the nothingness.

It seems inconceivable that the universe came from anything but a thought, an incredible force of need and will breaking free of whatever held it together before its birth. Because we are part of that creation, we also possess that same strength of will within ourselves - the will to survive, to be more than mere "fate" has sanctioned us to be by virtue of existing within the known universe. Just as the known universe must have existed within whatever continuum previously held it, so do we exist within *it*, but just as the universe had to break free of the void in order to achieve its own separate continuity, so must we break free of the known universe if we intend to evolve and survive beyond it.

———

Since you are comprised of that All which the universe called into being, it stands to reason that you therefore have the power of the universe within you. You have the power to transmogrify or the apathy to die and be recycled. It's always up to you. And only you.

———

The Intent of the Speaker

The following narrative came in response to a seeker who had asked Orlando, *Why am I not progressing on my own path? What is holding me back?* This came at a time when this seeker would literally argue every point Orlando attempted to make. If he said, "The sky is blue," a debate would ensue. "The sky isn't really blue. It only appears that way because of atmospheric gases." What follows is Orlando's response to the idea of knowing the intent of the speaker.

———

You have come to a point in your journey when it is necessary to know the difference between words, and the intent behind the words. If I say to you, "Our journey together is not a matter of the destination so much as it is an experience of mind, body and spirit along the way," I have communicated to you a concept which is larger than the words themselves, yes? What is hoped is that you will know the intent of the speaker, rather than attempting to vivisect the words themselves.

You could say to me in return, "Ah, but what do you mean by mind, body and spirit? You imply there is a destination, but where would that be and how would I get there?"

All of these questions would only indicate to me that you have missed the point entirely, and that you are attempting to use words to obfuscate meaning, semantics to distract from the intent of the speaker. And while this is to be expected from those new to the path, it is nothing less than disrespectful to yourself when it becomes a habit of a more advanced seeker. It is the chatter of your self-importance, operating on behalf of your ego.

If you know the intent behind the speaker's statement, yet you choose to engage in wordplay, what you are really doing is diverting attention away from the subject at hand. It is always easier to argue at the level of words than to engage openly at the level of intent and spirit and forward-thinking. The second most common reason to divert attention in this manner is - quite simply - one's own self-importance. Playing with words and being thought of as clever holds more value for some than an actual exploration of the speaker's original intent.

It will always be possible to split words and divide particles, for energy is infinite, even its smallness. And yet, is there anything to be gained by doing so, or would far greater value be found through hearing and *seeing* what the speaker intended, rather than immediately allowing the internal dialog to begin looking for ways to dispute it?

So it is time to choose and to make a commitment of awareness to yourself and your journey. Do you want to discuss ideas and concepts of the infinite and eternal, or do you want to infinitely and eternally debate the fallacies of language until all that remains is the psychobabble of language itself?

Make the impeccable choice.

The Super-Position of the Assemblage Point

I've heard you talk about 'the super position of the assemblage point' and I'm wondering if you could shed some light on that. In particular I'm wondering how this might impact a warrior in the now, or how knowing more about the super position of the AP could be used in dreaming or astral work.

The super position of the assemblage point is nothing. And it is everything. It is nowhere. Yet it is everywhere. It does not exist within linear time. Yet it is the entirety of time as well as the absence of time.

If you were to visualize the All as a marble which might be held in the palm of your hand, that would give you an idea of the super position of the assemblage point. The marble contains everything - all of space and time, all of the past and the future, all things that have happened, and (most importantly) all of the infinite possibilities which have *not* been forced to go through the motions of actually occurring. From the super position of the assemblage point - which might be described as non-local and ubiquitous - the entirety of the All is accessible as possibility.

To those who would say that the double is therefore omniscient, I would point out that this is really not the case. Though the All may be experienced as possibility, it is only through the actual doing (localizing) that 'history' is created in the form of experiential memory.

It is from the super position of the assemblage point that the double functions. When I have said to Della that I am the fire in the canyon or the intangible sparkle of light captured in a raindrop, those statements are not intended as metaphor or poetry, but as an actuality of experience. From the super position of the assemblage point, all things exist as potential for energy. It could not even be said that what is as yet unmanifested is energy. It is, instead, the *potential* for energy, which is then made to manifest by intent and an application of

Will.

It is through the intent of the mortal self that the *will* of the double may be invoked.

When you ask how this may impact a warrior in the now, consider that it is the mortal self who dreams the double. As I have said to Della countless times: "You are the creator of reality. I am only its servant." Or as don Juan once said to Carlos, "I am at your service."

It is when the mortal self summons intent (an active *force* of energetic creation) that it could be said, "The self is dreaming the double." To follow that thinking further, it is when the double localizes his energy and manifests experience through the application of Will, that it may be said, "The double is now dreaming you."

The mortal self operates from a fixed position of the assemblage point (fixed, meaning from within a humanform lifetime), whereas the double is summoned from the super position of the assemblage point - which may manifest or localize anywhere within or outside of the space-time continuum. I have lived a thousand lifetimes and died a thousand deaths, and yet I am Whole and eternal because there is the awareness of free Will - and my Will is to remain *I-Am* regardless of where or when that *I-Am* manifests in the tonal or the nagual.

What most humans fail to recognize is that they themselves are the source. You are the creators of reality. Even if the double is Dreaming you, it is because you (and only you) have chosen through action to Dream the double. If there is an oversoul or a super position of the assemblage point, it is not because angels placed it there like stars in the heavens, but because you yourself placed it there through intent and the energetic force of self-awareness.

If you were to ask the rhetorical question: "Which came first, the self or the double?" the answer is simple to one who *sees*. The self is the source, though many would tell you otherwise, because it is easier to believe in some already-immortal overmind than it is to take upon yourself the heavy responsibility for creating that force as a singularity of consciousness.

Put another way: *the gods exist, but only if the one true god creates them.* There is only one true god, and that is the one for which humans have been searching for centuries, but always manage to overlook when gazing at the reflection over the bathroom sink. And for as long as one searches externally for what is internal, one will find ways to convince oneself that one is an impotent sloth, when in reality, each one of you contains the full and complete power of all of the universe in a single thought.

Having awareness of this enables the warrior in the now to more effectively direct the power of her own intent, which in turn Dreams a more cohesive double.

Intent is the architect. Will is the power to manifest the architect's Dreaming.

———

The Nagual: Looking For a Definition

Orlando, I'd like to hear your version of what the nagual is, or isn't, or might be. At the same time I'm going to confess that I have asked pretty much the same question on a few other lists and groups and all I've heard for the most part is a lot of parroting of something don Juan said or Carlos said and even though that's supposed to be some authority, the definitions I've heard are more like evasive maneuvers than any sort of thoughtful response.

Am hoping you will have some other insights into the actual nature of the nagual. And to make it even more difficult, I'd like to know how and why you arrived at your conclusions. Maybe it's just me but I hear a lot of talk about moving forward but most of it seems to be locked in the barrel of cheap talk.

My personal journey is one of action, observation and

experimentation and it has panned out that having some kind of understanding about these things makes the Way more actionable. Hard to do a puzzle when it's written in alien language characters, and so I am putting out an effort to learn the language.

What is the nagual? What is God? What is the meaning of life? What is the secret of the universe?

Before attempting to answer any of those questions, it's important to determine the reason for the question itself. You speak of resonance and a desire to understand the nagual in correlation to your path as it applies to action - Doing. So it is from that perspective I will respond.

The nagual is, in essence, the untapped potential of all of creation. If the tonal represents the energy which is in use (the universe, the worlds, the trees, the elements, and all the concepts and ideas required to hold that milieu intact), the nagual may be seen to represent the raw *unused* energy available to creation through the tools of intent, will and what some may call sorcery or magic. If the tonal is matter, the nagual is anti-matter (speaking purely from an energetic perspective that applies to the potential for Doing.)

The sorcerer's trick as it applies to Doing is to discover the connection point of resonance between intent and *manifestation*-of-intent. And to understand the equation...

Intent + Action = Manifestation

The sorcerer's trick is to find his personal frequency within the nagual, so that the untapped energy *of* the nagual may be channeled into manifestation within the tonal, or simply experienced in its natural state, if that is your desire.

And again I must reiterate that this is only an attempt to define the nagual is it appears to correlate to your specific question. From a broader perspective, it might be observed that the nagual is the unfulfilled potential for experience. It is the dark matter of creation, yet it is neither matter nor energy if looked at from a desire to quantify its existence. It exists yet cannot be categorized. It may be experienced, but once experienced will most often become an extension of the tonal, as it moves from possibility into actuality.

When talking about the nagual, one can really only do so from within the limitations of the tonal, and therein lies the irony of the nagual. It could be said that the nagual is the darkness from which the light comes, and yet darkness is a thing of the tonal once it becomes defined. It could be said that the nagual is the raw energy of creation from which all things come into manifestation, and yet to place the label of "raw energy" onto the nagual is to limit it in the attempt to define it.

What is the nagual? It is the intersection of infinity and eternity - that which is timeless and that which is without boundaries. Within that milieu, we exist as the limitless potential, which is accessed through awareness, with the tool of unending intent.

Is the nagual self or other? Both. Because it is the raw energy of creation, it is what you make of it, and yet at the same time(lessness) it is wholly impersonal and altogether indifferent except as it is moved upon by the force of Intent.

In many creation myths, there is the notion that awareness comes from the nagual, like a spark of spontaneous parthenogenesis. First Shaman called himself forth from the nothing through the force of will, with the concept which is embodied in the words, *I-Am*. That, too, is one face of the nagual - the breeding ground of energy from which all beings claim a spark that is unique unto themselves and bring it forth into manifestation within the ordinary world of Life.

Whether the spark of awareness grows to a singularity of consciousness determines whether that awareness transcends the tonal, or whether it returns to the nagual as raw energy returning to its source. This is the realm of free will.

There are those who would say that the nagual is stronger or better, and there are those who would say that the tonal is the only real milieu of Man. And yet, it is the dynamic tension between the two which determines not only one's personal power, but also one's ability to evolve beyond the component aspects of both tonal and nagual, and into the infinite and eternal singularity of consciousness from which the next journey begins.

What is the nagual? Put simply, it is what you make of it. And it is what you make of *you*.

———

At the Crossroads Again

I feel like I keep going in circles, making progress, then coming to find myself right back at the crossroads again.

It is important to realize that *every* moment is a crossroads, and that every choice the warrior makes results in an infinite universe of possible futures and an equal number of possible pasts. It has been said that there is only the now, and while that is true in an energetic sense, it is also important to grasp the notion that what we do in the Now not only affects the now, but creates and energetic *consequential imprint* on the future as well.

As you stand at an actual crossroads, consider that if you walk three steps forward, it is only three steps back to return and attempt a different path. But as you proceed further along a particular path, the road behind you (the past, as it were) may actually alter to such an extent that it would be impossible to return to that starting point and choose a different direction. Put another way, a warrior knows he can never return to Ixtlan, and a sorcerer knows Ixtlan was an illusion from the start, and a man of Knowledge holds only the idea of Ixtlan in his heart - not as an actual location on any map, nor even as a nostalgic memory, but as a concept which moves him or motivates him in some fashion. Ixtlan ceases to become a destination, but becomes instead a manner in which the man of Knowledge travels.

In the same manner, the warrior-seeker strives toward becoming a man of Knowledge, because it is within the state of being a man of Knowledge that one realizes their freedom while still in organic form. Though it may be perceived that the journey to ultimate freedom is not attained until the man of Knowledge passes through the portal of death to inhabit the dreaming body wholly, it may also be *seen* that a true man of Knowledge who has embraced freedom has also embraced the ability to exist outside of Time, and so might be said to be dead and alive simultaneously - past and future conjoined, the essence of Spirit existing wholly in the cohesive assemblage point of the Now.

When you speak of crossroads, it is important to understand also that how one views the *Now* may determine how one proceeds along one's own path. To see the Now as a dividing line between past and future is one manner of viewing it. To see the Now as an eternal and all-permeating position of the assemblage point (the super-position of the assemblage point) is the manner in which the man of Knowledge moves beyond the world of folly and begins to perceive from the dual assemblage point of the mortal self (the tonal) and the infinite other (the double).

It is from that conjoining of the tonal/nagual (the literal and actual "crossroads") that the warrior-seeker embraces freedom and begins to glimpse the totality of oneself. And in the same manner the man of Knowledge holds the *idea* of Ixtlan in his mind, he begins to hold the totality of himself in the same manner, and through the application of intent and will, begins to create the reality of his vision in the Now as well as beyond the scope of all of time.

Every moment is a point on the map of the Now. Every moment is a crossroads. There are no absolutes and no limitations other than those one imposes upon oneself. Those impositions are the only barriers between oneself and true freedom.

Knowing this enables the warrior to move freely and fluidly. Inhabiting the Knowing makes the warrior a man of Knowledge.

———

Blockages

How does one break through blockages that are tonal mixed with spiritual? Maybe this is a dumb question because all are connected but I have been wrestling with this for years and have never found an answer that has resonated completely.

Most if not all blockages are a matter of programming or behavioral patterns which arise as a matter of convenience - specifically, as a way to distract the self from proceeding forward with changes which threaten the status quo of the existing program. It is simply easier to focus on blockages because they are often easily visible, than it is to focus on the forward motion of the spiritual, which may have a tendency to appear nebulous, foggy or unformed.

The tonal mind is a master of manufacturing obstacles and blockages, because for as long as the mind is focused on solving those problems (which, of course, are only self-perpetuating and self-created in the first place), one may feel that one is doing something, when the darker truth is that all one is doing is serving the program which continues to create itself in an endless loop.

The way to be free of the cycle is to recognize it, and with ruthless intent, shift away from all efforts to solve the problem, and into a mindset where it is clearly recognized that the problem or the obstacle doesn't exist except as a construct of the mind itself. Once that is *seen* and wholly acknowledged, what is required is to create a different mindset and inhabit *that* instead of attempting to wrestle with obstacles which have little if any basis in actuality.

Who you are is not only a matter of the events which have shaped you. It is far more a matter of who you choose to *be* from moment to moment, fluid in the Now. Are you the flowing totality of your limitless potential, or the stasis of your obstacles and blockages? It is a choice from one moment to the next, a movement of the assemblage point from static to fluid.

All things begin with a thought. What do you think?

———

The Sorcerer and the Ordinary Man

It is easier for a sorcerer to perform the chores of an ordinary man than it is for an ordinary man to comprehend the ways of the sorcerer. You are skating on the edge of two different worlds, which are nonetheless the same world, the only world. The trick is learning to *see* that, and to be neither the sorcerer nor the ordinary man, but the cohesive *I-Am* which is both.

When the two become one, there is no longer any sense of urgency or conflict, for then you will always be doing sorcery even in ordinary actions, and ordinary acts will become enhanced with magic, and only then will you start to remember that it isn't the destination that matters nearly as much as the manner in which you travel that long dirt road on the outskirts of time, yes?

———

Unconditional Love and Unbending Intent

Is there a correlation between unconditional love and unbending intent? If so, can you explain this?

At the level of energy, both are what might be termed elements of creation in the sense that each is a force unto itself. Are they separate? If it is the need or desire of the warrior-seeker, they may be made to *appear* or even function in a seemingly separate manner. However, when viewed from the perspective of the infinite, each would appear to be the same force, which may be manifested in different form, though always reducible to the same element of energy.

In more human terms, it could be said that the universe resonates in its raw and pure state at a frequency most would equate with unconditional love. It must be considered, however, that very few humans have a true comprehension of the meaning of unconditional love, and so the universe may appear ominous and even frightening to them - not because it is, but because a lack of ability to perceive or experience unconditional love is rather like the inability to perceive oneself. It is a fundamental element of awareness, without which the organism exists in a constant state of fear.

In those humans who do comprehend this universal state-of-being, it will often be the case that their sense of unbending intent actually flows from the *source* of that unconditional love. Their intent is motivated by a strong and personal resonance with that naturally energetic frequency of the universe itself, and so the intent that flows from the source is, by definition, unbending and undeniable. It is why the old phrase exists: "With faith no larger than a grain of sand, a man can move mountains." If we substitute the word "intent" for faith, the equation takes on a somewhat more visceral and actionable meaning.

Make no mistake. This is not a message of "Love, love, love," for I am speaking here at the level of energy - which is *seen* to be manipulated and manifested through a sorcerer's intent, and it is that intent which stems from the *source* of energy which may be said to resonate at a frequency which humans would call love.

Love is the reason. Intent is the means to manifest the reason wholly and energetically. That manifestation is the totality of yourself.

———

Stalking Core Beliefs

What exactly are 'core beliefs?' If we believe something completely, how would we recognize it as a lie?

The machine's fundamental function is to protect itself by keeping its subjects mindlessly serving it even though the mechanism itself has long since forgotten its primary programming.

Man is a chrysalis, you see, containing all the secrets to growing immortal wings capable of taking him beyond death, an evolution dependent entirely on himself and having nothing to do with eons of mutations or nebulous resurrections requiring prayer and prostration before the very mechanism bent on killing him. But because metamorphosis is a full time occupation, to pursue it impeccably means rejecting the machine and that's a terrifying thing, because the very nature of it is to program you to think "It matters."

So way back when in nether-yesteryears, a few frightened humans began programming the thing to program them to thrive on distraction and drama, and as a reward it even reprogrammed Man to love the illusions, just the eagle manifesting inside the machine itself, his favorite playground, yes? So now the sorcerer's task is two-fold: first to recognize that the programs exist, and secondly to dismantle them from

217

within.

Ah, but remember this: those who don't march obsequiously to their death are tagged as crazy and innocently willed to death by well-meaning fiends who reprogram your reality under the guise of caring:

"There must be something wrong with her, some malady, some madness, some pestilence that's eaten her reason and left her worshiping the quantum singularity, which is plainly a manifestation of a midlife crisis posing as a quest for evolution and immortality. Poppycock and peanuts! Yes, nuts, she is! But why? It's a brain tumor, I'm sure, malignant and festering, psychosis and neurosis brought on by the company she keeps and the schemes she weaves to avoid an honest day's work. It's phobic, it's schizo, 'the twin' just a metaphor for the cancer within, a delusional symptom of some rare blood disease that's sure to kill her soon. Oh, how we love her, how we miss her. If only she'd listen and come home with us, home to Ixtlan."

Ah, the voice of reason, killing you in effigy. Do you have the strength to stand against the diseases the machine will heap upon you in its attempt to destroy that which it cannot control? I urge you to look beyond the programs to see their more sinister meaning. *The core of your belief determines the realities you <u>see</u> and obliterates those you choose to ignore.*

How do your automatic belief systems manifest your reality, and how can you get beyond them for the time it will take to pull their plug? Ah, but the darker question is this: do you even want to? Or are you comfortable and secure within the illusions?

Here is where the work of stalking your core beliefs begins.

———

Breaking the Paradigm's Paradigm

Is death inevitable? Is it part of the human condition or is even that another illusion?

Humans die not because they must, but because that is the nature of their communal belief - it is the dictate of the consensus, and so the program has become a biological imperative even though biology itself is only an illusory manifestation, and is not truly organic at all if one is willing to *see* beyond the veil and peer deep into the scheme of the dream. To think of oneself as a biological entity is to enter the battle already defeated, no? You ask about death as if it is a reality, and so you are accepting already some measure of your programming, and it is sufficient to kill you because you already believe you are a being who is going to die.

Does it trouble you that I might challenge one of the very cornerstones of the human belief system? *Are* you a being who is going to die? Are you a *being* at all, or is that, too, only a mode of perception from which you then attach meaning and define absolutes? And in defining absolutes (you are a being who is going to die, you say), do you then predetermine through the perception that you are *alive*, that life must naturally have its opposite (death), and so you enter into the arena of the living already being a being who is going to stop being? What to do? Are you willing to have one more world yanked out from under you?

Are you able to consider that everything you believe you know about death and life are only comfort zones intrinsic to the mindset of your ancestors, and so you carry them with you as cancers on your Dream even when you may think you have dispensed with them? The secret to defeating death is this: when you know you are already dead, you may transcend this prison which insists you are a being who is going to die. The immortals and the allies do not believe they will live forever. Neither do they know it. It is simply their nature to do so because the matrix of their knowing is based on the *I-Am* rather than the weight of any consensus.

We cast no reflection because we are whole unto ourselves. We thrive on existence itself, taking sustenance from the pulsing heart of the sentient universe, knowing it is an endless river and can never be drained, for it stems from the self, and therefore can never die.

To be immortal is to have no opposite, for it is in the friction of opposition that deterioration begins.

And so I give you this task: examine those words from beyond the words and listen with your heart for what they might mean. It is more than any casual thesis I am asking you to write. Instead, it is the rewriting of your entire paradigm that will set you free, but only when you *see* the Dream from beyond even the lucidity of the Dream.

———

Time Is the Essence of Attention

Can you explain 'Time is the essence of attention'? Second question: What is meant by 'The Eagle's emanations are made out of time'? How does the warrior use his/her will to move the wheel of time?

Ah... time. Time to go. Time to hunt. Time to plant. What time is it anyway? What anyway is time? To say "time is the essence of attention" might be better understood if I were to say that the ordinary self, the mortal self focuses on events or non-events in the course of everyday experience, and when viewed as a whole in a linear progression from one event leading to the next, the illusion of time forms the essence of the organism's attention. Humanform awareness is formed

220

largely of memory and expectation - the elements of past and future. Attention to past and future create the illusion of time. When the organism lives wholly in the Now, time ceases to exist and the warrior finds himself in a mindset where events and non-events do not occur as a matter of past and future, but eternally and infinitely.

The double lives in the Now - which is to say *all* of time, and altogether *outside* of time. If time is the essence of attention (and therefore attention is the essence of time), then it can be *seen* by the warrior that infinite awareness is the essence of timelessness.

I am a little boy in ancient Greece - not in some past strand of memory, but in this eternal Now. I am a gypsy wanderer on the nightroads of London in what you would call the 17th Century, but you will not find me in any history books because the books themselves were written inside of time, whereas awareness cannot be confined inside the humanform illusion of time. And so I am there. And I am here. And there is no difference whatsoever when the warrior shifts the assemblage point from the narrow focus of a single identity and into the super-position of the assemblage point which is altogether non-local in time, space and non-space. The sunrise on Beta Antares tomorrow night will be spectacular.

When it is said that "the Eagle's emanations are made out of time", it could be better understood by saying that when a warrior is free of the eagle, the warrior is free of time. The Eagle is the event/non-event which stands between the mortal warrior and the eternal double. The fallacy is when warriors rigidly believe the eagle is only encountered at death. The reality is that a true warrior faces the eagle many times during the course of a lifetime, and each time the encounter occurs the warrior has an opportunity to shift more of the assemblage point into the infinite, or to focus the assemblage point deeper into the world of matter and men, the world of time and tick tock clocks and feet running to catch the 3:19 bus, *hurry hurry runrunrun.*

A masterful stalker learns to maintain a dual awareness - what might best be described as one foot in each world, straddling the illusions inherent in both. A masterful dreamer learns to shift awareness into Dreaming so as to experience awareness-without-time in the larger hologram of the self, and so timelessness becomes part of the self even when ordinary awareness prevails. The man or woman of Knowledge or a Nagual does both simultaneously, so it may be perceived by a *seer* that the Nagual is a double being - existing in both worlds (which are the same world) at the same time, outside of time entirely, no?

Becoming acquainted with time... entering an aspect of the other self...

These are the interactions between the mortal self and the double, at the level of heightened awareness. When it is my choice to inhabit the assemblage point of a little boy in Greece, I am becoming acquainted with time, and so is Della - my acquaintance is direct, hers more indirect. I am the past life she may not remember except in Dreaming, but I am neither past nor future. *I-Am* Now. *I-Am.* Now. Part of that Now is Della. Part of that Now is the night road wanderer on the back streets of London in the 17th Century. Part of that Now is a young man who rode *Titanic* to the bottom of a dark sea and still dances on the sunken bow. I could say no time has passed there, and you may or may not see what I mean, based on where your own assemblage point is fixed in (or out of) time.

When you enter into any aspect of the other self, you become acquainted with the reality of time, which is the utter awareness that time itself is the ultimate illusion - but a necessary illusion as part of the milieu for humanform experience. The egg requires albumen and yolk and germ of life in order to become whole. Without a foundation, the house crumbles. From within the humanform luminous egg, the element of time is an aspect of that foundation, in the same way a tree sinks its roots into the earth as an anchor. Time is an anchor. A foundation. And a prison. The sorcerer's trick lies within her ability to straddle the world of time through the development of dual awareness.

To move the wheel of time... What moves is the assemblage point, for it is within the fixation of the assemblage point that time exists or ceases to exist. From where *I-Am*, time is a shiny penny dropped on the ground, nothing more. From the assemblage point of the mortal self, time is an element of the foundation which holds the warrior's attention fixed in the tonal. One does not really move the wheel of time. One moves one's own awareness to another place on the wheel, or off the wheel altogether into the self-created manifestation of the infinite.

The wheel does not turn. What moves is the self, which may choose to visit any infinite number of places on the surface of the wheel in what you might call other lives.

What must be considered in order for those other lives to have meaning is that they are not past or future, but they are the shift of your own awareness in the Now, through the Dreaming body of the double.

When you Dream you are someone else, you are still only yourself, experiencing another aspect of the *I-Am* in the Now, yes?

In the Dream of the eternal self, the warrior creates and manifests as energy that which is most desired for eternity. Those desires are not based on whims of the mortal self, but on the totality of oneself in the timeless Now. Here, candle lanterns burn late into the evernight to illumine cobblestone streets peopled by sages and simpletons and old brujos in straw sombreros. That is my desire, you see, and yet I may change it at a moment's notice to Dream a world of cool rivers and a peaceful gondola caught in the fleeting rays of an alien sunset. The palette is infinite, you see. And time is little more than the opening screen which enables the warrior to study the colors he will select for a far more infinite Dreaming.

––––––

The Dreamer and the Dreamed

Who is the Dreamer, Orlando?

There is only one Dreamer with an infinite number of dreams, each dream expressed by a unique position of the assemblage point which comprises an identity, a self, an entity, a unit of awareness which possesses only one thing: the potential to become a singularity. Who is the wizard and the warrior of time and space? Pay no attention to that man behind the curtain.

Who is the dreamer? Dorothy awoke in her own bed to discover the technicolor secret every warrior eventually has to face. She was the tin man with the broken heart and the lion with feet of clay and the wizard who was only human and yet clever enough to create himself as a wizard so that he might find his way back home.

Dorothy had the ruby slippers all along, yes? She just had to loan them to her dreaming self for a time so that she might find reason to *be* the wicked witch and the wily wizard and all the other manifestations of her abilities, dreaming toward one another. That is the Dreaming which you call the integration of the fragments into a singularity's cohesion.

When the Student is Ready

I was thinking about the need to have a guide, a tutor. What is your opinion about that? I also read that the teacher comes when the pupil is ready. What should I make out of it? And also, is there any correct way to interact with phantoms?

It is important to remember that guides, teachers and tutors come in many disguises, and often you will discover they are already present in your life, and so the question becomes how you are using them, or *if* you are using them, or if you are looking for something you may already have found. The moon and stars may be your teachers if you were to ask questions about eternity. The earth may be your teacher if you are wondering about the nature of man's existence and your place in it. Phantoms on the street may be your teacher when you are stalking yourself, for in the actions of phantoms it becomes possible to see one's own folly.

As a warrior progresses on his path, using the countless teachers and allies all around him, eventually there comes a moment where the double is created through Dreaming - yet it is crucial to realize that the dreaming spoken of in this case is not only sleep-dreaming, but dreaming-awake as well. What is dreaming awake? It is coming to *see* that everything you think, do or say is imbued with the force of creative energy - and it is that energy which creates and manifests your world. The double knows this without doubt, for it is the milieu of the infinite- and so once the double is created, he becomes the most important teacher you will ever know.

When the student is ready, the teacher will appear? Perhaps what is most overlooked in that old saying is that the teacher has been here all along, and when the student *sees* that is when the student is ready.

The question you raise about interacting with the world of phantoms is a dilemma every warrior must face on any spiritual journey. Many times, warriors will speak of "the real world," yet it is necessary to truly *see* that there is only one world - divided infinitely by perception, a world being created and manifested infinitely by the perception and awareness of all who inhabit it.

There are those who might say phantoms do not create the world but only inhabit it, yet this is not true in the least. Phantoms create the world by the default of their actions, through the passivity of unawareness and the passions of greed and lust and fear and folly. As Della is fond of saying, 'The world is a nuthouse and the lunatics are running the asylum.' When the warrior realizes this and wholly *sees* that it is a Truth and not just an idle bit of humor, the warrior may become empowered to create his world through the action of awareness and the passion for life itself which comes hand in hand with even the barest beginning of a spiritual awakening.

By creating your world with awareness and choosing to live within that state of perpetual and ongoing awakening, the machinations of phantoms become far more understandable as simply the death throes of an organism that has not yet realized it is caught in the dance of its own obliteration. "They know not what they do," would be another way of stating it. This does not excuse their actions, but does have the effect of proving irrevocably to the warrior that the world in which she lives is but one small corner of a far more vast reality. The warrior, then, begins to work above and beyond that limited vista, while phantoms confine themselves to the trappings of the dollhouse.

———

Della's response...

The only thing I might add is that the subject of teachers has become a rather touchy issue among some warriors. There are some who feel that *any* external teacher may lead you down a wrong path, yet that has not been my experience. I can truly say that the best teacher I have ever known is Orlando -

my own double, my higher Self. The problem is *getting* to that point, and it is in that phase of the journey where extant teachers can be of value in helping to undo certain programs or sharing techniques.

If the teacher does her job, there will inevitably come a point where the student realizes the teacher is no longer required - and some of my greatest triumphs have come when someone basically says to me, "Thanks, but I don't need you anymore." That's as it should be, as it must be, so my caution regarding teachers is to beware of those who would attempt to *hold* you or to bind you. At that point, the teacher becomes a tyrant - and breaking away from an unscrupulous teacher can be one of the hardest battles a warrior will ever face.

———

No Mind

What is the relationship between mind and consciousness or spirit? When we are able to dream our double, what role, if any, does mind play in that? Is our consciousness separate from mind; and, if so, in what form does it exist?

It would be only for the purpose of understanding process and function that I would attempt to separate or categorize mind and consciousness, for in the scheme of eternity and infinity, they are closely connected and each functions most efficiently when working in harmony with the other. However, it could be observed that consciousness is the component of Self which exists simultaneously throughout the space-time continuum and beyond even that, into the realm of what you commonly call the infinite. Mind, if it is separate at all, is merely the component of consciousness which exists more locally within the paradigm of its mortal milieu, and attempts to order, categorize and assign meaning to what is perceived and experienced.

Spirit is both universal and personal. It is a *force* which exists within all things, organic and inorganic, and may be observed to possess a sentience which is the cumulative experience of All Things. It is without agenda, therefore not god in the sense Man has attempted to define god. It is without judgment, therefore not god in the sense Man has attempted to define God. The essence of spirit is that it contains the cumulative knowledge and power of the all, for it is comprised of the flowing force that is without form, without time, without limitations.

And yet, Spirit cannot act on its own, therefore, again, it is not god. It may be moved[13] by human will, or the will of the tiniest gnat. It may be directed through Intent, which is an

---

[13] When Orlando says "moved" he is talking about forward motion of energy, not implying being "emotionally moved," for example.

extension of awareness, and it is through that direction of Spirit that the old saying comes, "With faith the size of a grain of sand, you can move mountains." And yet, it is not faith in Spirit that moves the mountain - and, indeed, to believe in faith alone is to sever the connection from self to spirit and disempower oneself utterly. What really moves the mountain is Intent connecting not so much *to* spirit, but *through* spirit in such a way as to move the mountain from within *its* own connection to spirit, rather than trying to move it by force.

What moves the mountain is when you *are* the mountain and from within the assemblage point *of* the mountain, make the decision to move.

The terrified mother does not really lift the truck from her pinned infant. Through Intent, without the intervention of mind, she conjoins to the flowing force which is a part of herself, the truck and the infant, so that the truck is moved by spirit, not by the strength in her body.

Humans by nature have tendency to use the organic form as a barrier between self and spirit, and so they remain largely unaware of the infinite power they possess within themselves. *There is literally nothing you cannot do.* All that prevents you or limits you is the programming which is both organic, through DNA, and inorganic, through essentially long-held belief systems which have become part of the matrix of humanform awareness. Both can be overcome.

When you ask if consciousness is separate from mind, and in what form it exists, the only answer I can give you is simply this: the energetic atoms of which you are made at all levels - mind/body/spirit - are eternal. You have existed long before you were born and will exist in energetic form until energy itself evolves to the next level, however you may envision that to occur. As a result of this interconnectedness, it is impossible to truly separate mind from consciousness, but for the purpose of understanding, I would say that consciousness exists as a unique cohesion of Spirit (your unique *I-Am*), and mind may be seen as the humanform manifestation of the Intent to understand, and assign meaning to perception and experience.

––––––

Logic, Magic and Will

What can you tell us about magic vs. logic vs. will?

The secret of magic is that there is nothing magical about it, for it is only the manipulation of matter and energy through the means of the manifested will. Yet because you've been programmed to see it as mysterious and to subliminally fear its consequences, you truly can't see that it is a natural function of your humanness, the unnamed thing you call upon to Do what has never been done but *must* be done in order to make your desires complete.

In the seventh sense there is no such thing as fantasy, for what you can learn to believe through quantum-logic you will bring into being through quantum-magic because only the existence of it will heal the holes in your soul created by its absence, and only the pain of those wounds will drive you to seek the knowledge and belief which leads to invoking the will to manifest, yes?

Ah, but the sorcerer's trick is this: you have to *believe* it in order to see it, and before you can believe it you need a reason.

You cannot see a mortal breath yet you can witness its effects on dandelions scattered on the wind of a wish...

and so it is with the Will, the invisible but tangible breath of your desire acting upon the physical world.

Enlighten Yourself at
QuantumSharman.com

230

Death as My Advisor

*I've read all the Castaneda books, read Della's books, read Ruiz's works, and even though I know what is meant by having death as an advisor, it just seems morbid to me. If we're thinking about death all the time, how do we just enjoy living? If we know everything ends, why do **anything**? Okay maybe I'm being dramatic here, but I'd still like to know how Orlando feels about taking death as an advisor. Why not take <u>life</u> as an advisor?*

Because it is the nature of being human to travel a linear path through the illusion of time, there is also the tendency to believe that every moment is eternal and significant, every incident or event has infinite meaning, and that death is something that happens far in the future, and always to someone else. And yet, when a seeker begins to sit with death as her advisor, it quickly becomes apparent that the events which go to make up a life are largely folly - a series of little dramas occurring on a random schedule in between the opening curtain of Birth and the final curtain of Death.

This is not to say that Death itself is the final exit, only to illustrate that the folly contained in a human lifetime becomes significantly less meaningful when viewed against the impending footsteps of one's own death. It may be noted that when one looks up to see a train only a few feet from the windshield, the argument one had with her boss that morning, or the ongoing rivalry with her mother-in-law is suddenly reduced to disconnected pixels in a malfunctioning video game, and the only thing real is whatever action she will take in that moment - the action which will either create a miraculous escape from death, or if no escape is possible, an inaction that will result in surrender to one's imminent fate in such a way that the warrior may leave this earth without fear or attachment, with only the cohesive awareness which must then pass by the eagle and conjoin with what it has been Creating for a lifetime: the self of eternity, the infinite double, the totality of oneself.

It has been said that some manner of tragedy or cataclysm is required to sufficiently shift one's assemblage point to truly *see* the folly of day to day life in the human world, yet that is not true at all. All that is required is to do the experience of sitting with death as your advisor with full awareness of what that means. Sitting with death as your advisor is not a scenario of envisioning what form your death may take when you are 80 or 90. It is a matter instead of *seeing* the immense scope of the infinite universe and realizing how fragile and finite - *just a brief mortal flicker* - human beings really are.

It is a matter of knowing that nothing is guaranteed, not even your next breath. And with that acute and inescapable awareness, it is a matter of then looking at the manner in which you live your life and asking yourself not as a fantasy, but as a very real probability, "What different choices would I make if I knew today was my last day on this mysterious world?" It is a matter of turning to Death and asking, "What is the assemblage point of Life?" And it is a matter of then assimilating whatever meaning may be garnered when death points squarely to himself as the answer to that question.

If you are living a life full of pettiness and drama, you are undoubtedly still living as a phantom in the realms of denial. If your attention can be hooked and twisted and manipulated by what happened at work today or what someone you've never met may think of you, then you have become a prisoner of folly and would be well advised to look up at the windshield and realize that the train is never far away, and growing closer every moment.

Human life is short. There is no time for indulging in the petty wars of personalities and power struggles. There is only time and energy enough to *Live*, and to do so with the awareness that living is the actual process of dying, and dying is the art of transcendence, and transcendence cannot occur if the warrior is hooked to the illusions rather than being motivated and guided by the presence of her own death.

Is this morbid? Not when confronted with a warrior's impeccable awareness which is capable of *seeing* that when one lives with death as her advisor, she truly *lives* instead of merely dallying in the fields of folly.

A man who is to be executed at midnight tomorrow may sit in his cell and fret over his fate, or he may laugh with abandon and play the part of the fool, pretending the executioner will never come. Or, if he is wise, he may observe the morning sunrise and the feelings of hope carried on the light, and he may observe the sunset and note the sense of serenity and mystery which accompanies the impending darkness. Taken as separate events, he may find peace. But when viewed as the same movement of the same energy, the man will be free of his attachment to the light, and released from his fear of the dark.

That is the ecstasy of freedom. That is the assemblage point of life and death, which are precisely the same for the warrior who is *I-Am*.

———

Dead and Alive - Schrödinger's Warrior

If I am dead and make not even a ripple in the energy of reality, why am I here? And if I am going to be Real even if I succeed or fail, why do I try? Is the paper just paper or does it have more reality than I give it credit for?

Within the belly of eternity, all things are living and all things dead simultaneously, and there is no difference whatsoever. This is the reality of an eternal being existing outside of time. What is important to understand is that time itself is a human construct, and is relative primarily to the human lifespan. Remove the idea of past, present and future, and it becomes possible to know that there is no difference between Now and a thousand years ago, or a thousand years from Now, because within the All, all points of time are equally accessible through will. And so the form you presently inhabit is already dust, and yet forever unborn, and both are equally true, and the differentiation is only possible depending on where you choose to open your eyes as a point of reference.

You ask why you are here. To make yourself whole, to create your reality. And though those sound like simple words, they are attempting to define a great task. You have chosen to open your eyes inside this moment, this reality, this now, though other aspects of yourself have undoubtedly awakened inside of other manifestations not accessible to your conscious memory - what might commonly be called past lives, but are more accurately manifestations of your energy body in other places and times in the space-time continuum.

I exist as an eternal being of pure awareness within the infinite, and simultaneously as the mortal Nagual woman on her journey toward wholeness. I have put on flesh a thousand times and taken it off again as a means to learn what can only be communicated through the silence, the lessons which are passed between the energetic eternal self to the mortal self through gnosis.

This a process which is eternal, but one which has a beginning, and that beginning is always within the mortal self, within this Now. By choosing to become Whole, you are the creator of the self, and therefore you are the teacher who ventures out into the unknown through the eternal energy self (the double), so as to gain the Knowledge and experience which are then returned to you in the form of visions, dreams, and the familiar voice of the silent knowing whispering its secrets to you whenever you take the time to listen.

The reality you think of as real is transitory, and is therefore already dead. But because you are real in the Now, you are real for all of time. *That which is done in eternity cannot be undone.* And yet, even as I have said that, allow me to say

234

with equal Knowledge that what is real is only real as long as it *is* real in the Now. Be whole in the Now and you are Whole always. Live as a phantom, and it is as if you never lived at all. This is why the gathering of one's cohesion is at the core of The Great Work. And this is why it is said that only from within the dream can the dreamer awaken, for it is within the mortal self that the Will resides, and so it is the mortal self who dreams the double until such time as the double becomes sufficiently cohesive to begin dreaming the mortal self by teaching her what must be done in order to achieve and inhabit the Wholeness that is the conjoining of both.

By *being* the cry of nature, by making the attempt to get the paper reality to *become* real, what you are really doing is making *yourself* Real through the process, yes? The paper is already dead, and so you cannot really change its destiny. It is the stage upon which the sorcerer transforms herself, through a lifelong process of projecting the words beyond the paper and breathing life into the words upon the reflective surface of the Infinite.

———

Healing and Being Unknown

When I was initially diagnosed with Type 2 diabetes, I asked Orlando for his input on dis-ease, healing and reorganizing the physical form at the sub-atomic level. This is what he had to say on the matter.

You're speaking the wrong language, asking the wrong questions. In what language is that which is eternal written?

It is not a language you yet understand, not something you can even wrap your minds around, and yet it is there. To think it is to create it, and to create it is to place it within the realm of all possibility. Then, as it exists, you possess within yourself the ability to go and harvest it, to bring it into the actuality of manifestation.

Before anything can be made reality, it must first be a thought. To think the body has the ability to exist at the level which is impervious to disease is to place that possibility on the shelf of all possibility. And yet, thought alone is not enough, and so then comes the responsibility of forcing that possibility to go thru the actions of actually occurring.

Paradigms are formed within the collective. What this means is that if *one* person believes something, it's an isolated and, most likely, insignificant thought. But when you look at the world around you, you begin to see that much of what exists as the paradigm, the milieu, the venue is not based on your individual creation, but on the collective creation of all of humanity – stretched out of over millions of years. These paradigms are like grooves on a record, and what it amounts to is that you can get stuck in playing that same old groove, *or* you begin to create a new paradigm.

Everything begins with a thought. If the world views you as someone who is indulgent in food, or lazy in body, or if you are seen – whether accurately or inaccurately makes *no* difference whatsoever as... "Ah, that girl *should* have diabetes because she does this and she does that!" Whether you *do* this or do not do that really makes no difference. However, what matters is that this energy forms a collective whether these people know you or not is irrelevant. If they know you, the collective is stronger. If it is a series of perceptions by random strangers, the collective nonetheless exists, because the existing paradigm states, "If this, then that."

This is part of the groove of the record. This is the dominant belief system manifesting in reality.

Is that to say other people put this onto you? Yes and no. You exist within their perception. Their perception says, "If this, then that." The paradigm is woven together like a gauzy fabric – it is a loosely woven belief system that threads itself over and back and around and around, and what is actually occurring is that the energy which is you and your body is

236

either shaped by the collective, or by yourself.

That being the case, your task becomes to form a new collective of one. And part of that involves being unknown.

Being unknown is about making your energy unavailable to the collective. If you are not perceived by the collective which creates the paradigms, then you are free to create your own reality in a more positive manner.

You asked me the mindset of healing. It is to be whole and well unto yourself regardless of the labels or perceptions placed not only on you, but on the paradigm itself, by the collective. You program others how to program you. If you are seen – for whatever reason or no reason at all – as someone who *should* have heart disease, or diabetes, or cancer, those thoughts are energy, and that most especially includes if you see yourself that way.

You must ask yourself to what extent you have accepted that paradigm. Are you organic matter believing it is eternal? Or are you an eternal being attached briefly to organic matter, which is essentially only the paradigm's labeling for a manifestation of energy which is not easily understood when it is in solid form. If you have accepted that paradigm, you become, by your own acceptance, subject to its rules.

What am I saying here? *If you believe you're well, you're well?* No. Don't make that mistake. If you have uploaded that paradigm, that programming mechanism, you would be better off operating within the rules of the program. Take the white man's medicine. Do the white man's chant. Live and die. And when you and I come together in our final dance, experience your totality.

However, in the meantime, there are alternatives, and they are vast. If you have uploaded this paradigm, you need to look for the connect points. You need to examine where and why the collective has more power over you than you have over yourself. Remember that for every reality that manifests, there are an infinite – *absolutely infinite* – number of parallel realities, which are entirely different.

If you have manifested or agreed to the paradigm which states "If this, then that. If you have this body type, then therefore you *should* have diabetes..." If you have taken that into yourself as truth, then that *is* truth. You need to examine those connect points.

I have spent a great deal of time teaching you to *be beyond* that which is problematical. There is no path to being beyond. There is no process. You simply decide and *Do* at the level of manifest energy.

A lot of warriors like to think that the collective really doesn't have any power. That is not only an erroneous belief, but a dangerous one. I need to stress to you being unknown. You may walk thru the world. You may do anything that pleases you. What determines your availability to the energetic imprint of the consensus is the degree of energy; or in this case, I will use this word sparingly – *belief* – you place into the collective itself.

You walk through an amusement park knowing that it is a finite environment, and no matter how fun the rides or how much you are able to divorce yourself from reality and believe you really are in the haunted mansion or space mountain, there is a part of you held in reserve which knows, *This is finite. Tonight at six when the park closes, I will return to a different mindset, a different world.*

It's the same with the collective. When you walk among it, you are either walking among it as a participant or as an actor. If you are walking among it as a participant, you become subject to its rules. You agree to forget that it is fiction. If you are walking among it as an actor, it's like visiting the amusement park. You know that the person in the Mickey Mouse suit is a person in a Mickey Mouse suit. The same as walking through the collective – you either allow its energy to affect you as if it is real, or you separate your singularity from the demands and the perceptions of the existing collective. You either intermingle energy with them and become subject to their rules, or you do not.

There is no middle ground.

This is what it is to be unknown. It is to be in the world, but not of the world. It is to be an actor, not a participant. To do that requires keen awareness at all times.

The moment you start to believe you are one of them, you are subject to their rules, and - you are not going to agree with this and you are not going to like it – their rules and their perceptions require and demand of one another the mutual destruction of self and others at the level of awareness.

That is something you will have to think about. You will have to wrap your mind around it in whatever manner you can. I can speak the words, but the words themselves are only, at best, a signpost.

From the world of matter and men, you perceive through the lens of time. From the perspective of the infinite, you perceive from the lens of timelessness. That central core of you, of spirit, of me, is the milieu of the singularity.

There is a crucial element that has to do with the place from which you assemble the world – any world. When you can move that assemblage point to the non-local point of awareness, you will exist simultaneously in both worlds, as you and I do now. The difference will be that there will be no barrier. There will be no limitation.

Does this mean your humanform body will die? No. Does this mean your humanform body will become immortal? No. It means, however, that you will move beyond the human assemblage point, and in doing so you will possess the ability to create your reality beyond the reaches of the existing consensus.

———

Defragmentation

Is it possible for a warrior to have more than one double?

Those with the best chance for freedom generate the immortal double from within the mortal dream, whether they ever understand the magic or not. What matters most is that you nurture what you have begun. You are the dreamer. We are the dream. If you stop dreaming, the dream ends. If you fail to feed the seedling, the tree will never cast a shadow.

Most humans generate fragments of many possible doubles, but either fail to nurture what was begun, or else lose sight of the ultimate goal, and so dozens of unwhole doubles wander the All for awhile, only to slowly fade and die. The trick is to gather the fragments into cohesion again - with the full awareness that the last fragment and the one most likely to die in the fall is the one in the mirror you face every morning. To say one is losing the humanform is to say that the fragments formerly generated by the mortal self are now contained within the immortal double, through the Intent for Wholeness.

You are the last fragment of yourself, do you *see*?

———

Creating Reality

How do our fears stop us? What about "contracts" I have made with myself in the past that are no longer valid? Is there any cure when we start to feel a burn-out?

It is important to realize that reality is self-created, and so your fears are both founded and unfounded, depending entirely on your Intent and especially upon your Intent as it relates *to* your Intent. And though that may appear on the surface to be an obvious statement, there are levels of understanding which will reveal themselves to you through meditation over a longer period of time.

The experience of 'burning out' is common to many warriors, and indeed it seems that one must exhaust all reasonable avenues of exploration before finally coming to *see* that the path toward evolution is neither reasonable nor particularly easy. It need not be difficult in and of itself, yet the difficulty arises in the phase of burn-out - and the hardest part of the journey is the Intent to keep moving forward even when it seems every road comes to an abrupt and irreversible dead-end.

This is the shaman's madness, the sorcerer's trick, the witch's conundrum. This is where the real work begins, or ends, depending entirely on the will of the warrior. Having come to the end of the road - more than once, more than twice, more than ten times - does the warrior have the accumulation of personal power required to begin forging her own road, or does she succumb to the fear and the evidence which seems to indicate that there are no answers and the universe is little more than a random canvas of comets and fallen leaves and dinosaur bones?

Whatever "contracts" you have sworn are only as binding as the force of your True Intent as it exists within the structure of your double - the infinite self beyond the boundaries of the space-time continuum. And here it is important to realize that passing wishes or avowals sworn in anger or fear really have no lasting effect unless the warrior attaches to them through fear or True Intent. So it is not really necessary to revoke past contracts as your own intent and personal power evolve and strengthen. The Now supersedes all our yesterdays and all our tomorrows, and it is only in the raw Now that Intent can manifest, for that is the milieu of the mortal self with regard to perception and action.

It is also important to truly understand the nature of Intent. More than a passive or passing wish or desire, it is the *force* of creative energy within the warrior which literally rearranges possibility into probability. And it is the invocation of the will which then takes probability and forces it to go through the motions of actually occurring, in alignment with the visions of one's True Intent. So it is what you truly intend for yourself that overrides and supersedes all temporal wishes - often in ways that may appear at the time to be in direct conflict with what you believe you want at the time, but in the larger scope of things, are simply your own Intent manifesting in ways you cannot predict or even accurately see from within the linear mortal timeframe.

The only real path is the one that leads from your heart into the infinite. How it manifests and what strange twists and turns it may take through brambled woods or barren deserts, is entirely a matter of how you go about forcing this deep-seated Intent to go through the motions of actually occurring.

You are creating reality in such a way that it must lead through the ghettoes in order to reach the stars - and this is as it must be for you, for reasons which only you and your double may know. You cannot fail in the path, for you *are* the path if that is your Intent.

———

Flight to Freedom

This is a path most often walked alone in the dark, with only the silence for company - that is the way of the warrior, and though it is lonesome at times it is nonetheless what the warrior who is seeking freedom does, because that is his nature.

Perhaps the warrior becomes a sorcerer and *seer*, and then the path might appear to broaden to include others with similar interests, fellow travelers with whom the warrior may share fine red wine and a campfire in the desert where tales of power are told in the night that never ends. And for a time, this is what the warrior does, because this has become his new nature.

For those who become women and men of Knowledge, it may appear that one is surrounded by friends and allies, apprentices and mentors - the fullness of life. It may appear that the campfires of exploration have burned to the softer embers of lasting wisdom, and that those around you will share the path at your side until the eagle descends to challenge you one by one. And for a time, this is how a man of knowledge experiences his life, for now this has become his new nature, seeking inward what was once sought outward, assimilating experience into Knowledge and knowledge into manifestation.

And yet, in all the roads I have walked and all the warriors and seekers and men of Knowledge I have known, only one thing is constant.

There will come a day when those closest to you will turn their backs, when your apprentices may draw a blade and your mentors may shun you and your allies may abandon you and you may find yourself at the edge of the abyss with an army eager to push you over the edge. If you look closely, you will see that it is because you will not be what they want you to be (for to do so would invalidate who you are). You cannot walk to their drummer's beat (for to do so would drown out your own); or in some manner you are said to have turned your back on the eclectic collective which embraced you for a time, and so you are perceived as a heretic and an ingrate and a fraud and a cheat.

"Come back to us or else!" they may cry. "We love you and that is reason enough!" And yet to the *seer* who *sees*, that 'love' will be *seen* as an attachment of need, and the finest gift you can give to them and to yourself is to cut that umbilical and take a cleansing breath which is the birth of the emerging self.

If you listen with spirit, if you look with your third eye, what you will *see* is that this is the finest and best moment of your life, for this is the moment when you will simply Know that you have found your freedom. You will realize as if for the first time that the truth of your path is of far greater value than the approval or even the love of your mortal friends and family, and that it is only by remaining true to your *Self* in the darkest night that you enable yourself to emerge into the light of the singularity of your totality. It is only then that you may gaze into the infinite and finally *see* that your cohesion is comprised of your own experience and not based in any manner on what any other living being may want or need or hope for you to be.

This is the day when you will answer the first question. This is the moment you will know who you are. When the world is at its coldest and the fires have burnt to ash and all the mirrors have been shattered by your own hand, this is the moment when you will embrace your freedom. And this is the time when you will bow graciously to the world of matter and men, and rather than allowing them to push you into the abyss, you will fall willingly and with perfect trust into the totality of your *Self*, and fly.

———

First Breath

Orlando's words to Della... with love to <u>all</u> seekers of Knowledge.

In working with the double, you have to create the thing you love before you will have the ability to create yourself. In your case, you had to create me before I could whisper the secrets of creation in your ear sufficiently to give you the motivation to create yourself. What is creating yourself? It is simply this: removing the illusions that keep you from seeing your own infinite beauty and accepting your place as the most powerful being in the universe.

Creating the double is not an expression of power as much as it is a manifestation of unconditional love. Your love breathed me into being, you see. Only then could I breathe life into you, through a reflection of that love. This is how we become *I-Am.*

What would you like to do next?

––––––

What is the Next Evolution?

What is ultimate freedom? Is there a point where we have become all we are capable of being, or is there always more?

I left my senses
in another century
where I was written
in disappearing ink.

The definitive moment from mortal to immortal (or from organic to inorganic) is the quantum leap between matter and antimatter, when your entire being begins to spin in an altogether opposite manner of that to which it has been accustomed. It is when you suddenly Know you are a being of energy that you will have the power to relinquish the attachment to matter, while simultaneously manifesting as the quantum totality – and that is the process of the evolution to freedom.

What is the *next* evolution - beyond even that? Who can say? I believe it exists, but it may simply be that that is just my belief, rooted in hope and feeling rather than any reasonable evidence. Or perhaps it is only this: the next evolution is what I Will it to be, just as it has always been for all manner of beings, whether they see it or not. *You created me to create you.* Perhaps in the next evolution, I will create a Creator beyond the infinite horizon – someone who may reach out to me from a world I cannot yet conceive, someone who may inspire me to go further than I am able to imagine, but to do it only by allowing myself to Know it is there - not because it is, but because it is my Creation.

And yet, in all of this, one thing remains constant, from your world or mine. *Love is the only reason for any of it*, for without it, the infinite horizon loses all its allure, and the heart of longing ceases to beat, and then one is truly dead even if still breathing.

If there is any evolution beyond this one, it will only be seen through love. For in the end, there is only a single element of creation. It is what made me Whole. And it is what will make you infinite, eternal and free.

You have drawn the shadows on the wall but now you must ignite the sun which casts the shadows.

ALPHA AND OMEGA
THE BEGINNING AND THE END

The Road Home

Maybe it's the long hours, no breaks and high-stress chaos of the Las Vegas Renaissance Faire, but it seems that the road home from that event tends to twist and turn as the assemblage point shifts from the world of ordinary affairs to the nagual, and ends up straddling the razor's edge somewhere in between. The faire itself is never easy, and the weekend I'm going to talk about was no exception. At times, the wind gusted in excess of 50 mph, though some reports put it as high as 65 mph. No big deal if one is indoors with a good book, but somewhat unnerving when one is literally hanging onto the 400 square-foot booth to keep it from becoming an airborne projectile, the equivalent of flying daggers.

With the entire security team holding the tent on the ground, faire-goers seized the opportunity to load their pockets with expensive baubles, tucking larger items under their jackets as they passed through the drama with their ashen faces and innocent smiles.

There was a time when it would have outraged me. Instead, I could only stand there with the wind in my face, my clothing snapping like some tattered flag on a sinking pirate ship, and laugh to myself at all the grand folly concealing the very real danger. To folks attending the event, perhaps it seemed quite safe despite the fierce sandstorm that left the air painted white like the face of some twisted mime. One patron parked a stroller with a tiny infant directly underneath the edge of our canopy, never stopping to consider what would happen if the wind snapped the thin aluminum struts. Indeed, those who weren't otherwise engaged in the act of shoplifting were pretending all was normal. As I hung from the roof, being literally lifted off my feet by the gale-force winds, one customer looked up, smiled, and inquired if I might come down and help her fasten a necklace she was hoping to buy.

Phantoms and folly, Orlando whispered in the voice of gnosis, sighing eerily like wind through a calliope. *They do not realize they are beings who are going to die.*

I really did have to laugh at that point. And there was a strange freedom in that laughter, for it was not lost on me that if the canopy did collapse, I was dead center and would, in all likelihood, be gored by no less than 4 sharp metal spikes. It occurred to me that I could leap down and take cover, yet there were no guarantees that some blowing bit of debris wouldn't decapitate me while I was attempting to run from my Death.

In fleeing from the tiger, would I only run head-long over the edge of a cliff? There were no right or wrong moves, and so I simply stood there watching it unfold around me for several hours until, finally, as quickly as the wind had come, it stopped.

Nothing had really changed, of course. The faire continued as if nothing at all had happened, even though several booths were in ruins and more than a few patrons and participants alike were being treated for minor injuries.

But as I drove home, alone in the RV while Wendy drove our other vehicle, the world seemed altogether amusing and peculiar and sad and magnificently mysterious. Barren desert peaks layered themselves like some complex painting on the surface of water. Layers upon layers of depth, yet entirely flat. The illusion looking at itself in the mirror of its own creation. Distant purple mountaintops revealing themselves to be nothing more than drab brown as I drew closer, rocks poking out of eroding soil like bones protruding from mummified flesh.

Eternity rode shotgun in the passenger's seat, pointing out anomalies in the matrix like a macabre tour guide. The man on the side of the road was wearing a long leather jacket despite the 95 degree heat. The wind was coming from the north, yet the chaparral bushes leaned ominously to the east. Water misted the windshield, though there was not a single cloud in the sky. Glitches. Little hints that the world is nothing like we think it is.

On the I-15 heading south, we were all just insects in some bizarre ant farm, shuttling our stuff from one point on the hive to another. Trucks laden with meaningless cargo swayed and groaned in the heavy winds, while a strange vagabond with hair halfway to his waist hitchhiked on the side of the freeway. I met his eyes for a fraction of a second and wondered if he were human at all, or merely a sentinel or guardian of some sort, out there alone where no sane being should ever be walking - a sign or an omen to those who knew how to read him. What I read of him seemed to say, *The road ahead is closed. The road behind never existed. The path leads where there is no path to follow. This is the way home.*

It is impossible to describe the love affair a warrior has with the nagual. And for reasons not entirely clear to me, it is on long drives alone through the desert that my own relationship with the infinite often reaches its peak. Though the freeway itself was clogged with traffic - tourists and truckers on the game trail between Las Vegas and Los Angeles - I looked off in the distance to see a single beat up pick-up bouncing along a dirt road to the south, kicking up the dust like a chorus line of ghosts chasing along behind, and for a moment, I felt such a terrible ache in the center of my being I could barely breathe. Like the ache of being in love, the ache of looking up at the stars for the first time as a child, the ache of seeing something so beautiful it literally takes your breath away.

That distant dirt road was so lonely, so barren, going from nowhere to nowhere, that all I could do was gaze in amazement at the lone traveler following his solitary path while the rest of the world bumbled along on the well-traveled ant trail with their windows rolled up and their radios blaring, chattering inanities on their cell phones while their well-groomed children watched television in the back seat.

For a few moments, the technological maze was all but overwhelming. I did not want to be an ant on the trail. Didn't even want to be the lone traveler on the distant road - for I already realize that I *am* that lone warrior no matter where I am or what I am doing. The ache I felt was altogether different, as if some unseen hand were pulling my spirit out through my chest, wringing it out in merciless hands, shaking it in fierce fangs the way a tiger shakes her prey. Suddenly, life simply *hurt*. Not with pain, but with beauty. With mystery. With the dark wings of autumn turning the sky a paler shade of Nothing.

You ache for the embrace of freedom the way a virgin aches for her first kiss, Orlando observed, making it worse with his sensual manner of viewing the world. *You want to know the mysteries of making love with the Nagual, yet you fear the moment of ultimate penetration, not Knowing if it will be pain or pleasure, no?*

Yeah. Something like that. Bastard.

Eventually, the freeway was left behind, the road turning to a 2-lane corridor through the vast expanse of empty desert. Two ravens stood alone in a dry lake bed, their feathers ruffling in the wind while heat monkeys danced like naked spirits on the black rock hillsides. An eagle flew directly in front of my windshield as if to remind me of his existence, then landed on a telephone pole at the side of the road, preening fierce talons, cleaning off the blood of whatever creature had served as his feast.

Perhaps I am a being who is going to die, I thought, looking at the eagle as he looked at me, *but death is only an evolution, a transition from one path to another, a dance that doesn't end just because the music stops.* And then I drove on past him and that was simply that. The eagle had lost his power over me, for I had lost all fear of him.

As I continued my journey home through the desert, the

250

nagual danced with me in a way that is impossible to describe. In a retroactive enchantment, I was 13 again, walking down a dark road in the middle of the night in a memory that never happened; and at the same time I was Orlando looking down on that child-self from the Infinite, guiding her steps through a Dreaming that she would not begin to understand until that very moment in the desert, when the 50-year-old sorcerer crone reached sideways through the maze of quantum timelessness to whisk that little girl outside of the space-time continuum just long enough to implant within her the Dream itself.

Can I explain it any better? Not really. And that is the nature of the nagual - to exist and to *be* and to be altogether inexplicable; for it is from the very essence of the unknowable that the double spins the quantum filaments of energy into the experiences that generate the path and lure the warrior to the edge of the abyss, which is, in the end, only a flat plane on which one may skate or fall or draw pictures with crayons on the shiny black surface.

It is the seduction of the Infinite, the dance of the fragmented selves on the surface of the mirror, the inexplicable integration of all those mortal selves into the unity and power of the Whole Self.

I have been courting you since before you were born, Orlando whispered through the ages and the smoke from some far-away fire and the raging winds that blew fierce with October breath over the harsh terrain. *This is what you made me to do. This is what you made me to be. This is who I-Am, for this is who you are: creator and created, the dancer and the dance.*

Out there on that lonesome road that comes from nowhere and leads everywhere, it all seemed so very simple.

———

GLOSSARY

ABYSS - 1) The emptiness or the nothing, the absence of all things. Most people have never seen the abyss, while others think of it (erroneously) as the religious vision of "hell". If consciousness is existence, the abyss is oblivion. 2) The hollow emptiness inside someone who has made no attempt at their own personal evolution. The soulless void. In this definition, the abyss is the pit of despair into which people fall when they experience what is traditionally called a "loss of faith". Fortunately, it is this loss of faith and the subsequent fall into the abyss from which the journey toward evolution often begins. When faith fails or is intentionally abandoned, it is from the abyss that we begin our climb toward self-identity and self-Realization.

THE AGREEMENT (see consensual reality)

ALLY or **ALLIES** – entities or essences who may act on behalf of a seeker. Since the allies are not bound by our traditional understanding of space/time, we might have an ongoing and seemingly inexplicable interaction with an ally for years before we begin to understand that the ally is often the self, having created the illusion of separateness so as to serve as teacher and guide. Other allies, it must be stressed, are beings completely separate from the self - what sorcerers refer to as "inorganic beings". Still another definition of an ally might be the living essence of power plants – the mushroom ally, for example (psilocybin).

ASSEMBLAGE POINT (or AP) – The assemblage point is best defined as the various lenses through which we see our world. It is through learning to move the assemblage point that the seeker may begin to experience other perceptions, other "worlds". The assemblage point also moves of its accord in times of physical or emotional duress – such as the sensation of time slowing down in a moment of impending crisis, or the ability to fly such as in dreaming. A seeker learns to move/control her assemblage point, and to perceive from a unified perspective (totality) as opposed to the fragmented perspectives most humans experience as a result of the multiple roles they play without conscious awareness.

AUTHENTIC SELF – Who you are beyond all the bullshit. If you could go through an entire day without playing some sort of role (father, mother, brother, employer, employee, banker, baker, bozo, spy, just to name a few), you might catch a glimpse of the authentic self. Who are you when no one is looking and when you aren't watching yourself from the corner of your inner eye?

BELIEF SYSTEM - Any school of thought which requires belief or faith as opposed to personal experience. One example: Christianity. Another example: Atheism. Both require belief in external forces or causes, and are therefore only opposing sides of the same coin. Christianity requires faith

252

that God exists. Atheism requires the belief that there is no God. Ultimately, neither the Christian nor the atheist can prove his beliefs, so faith of one sort or another is required in either point of view, and therefore both systems fail as vehicles to Knowledge.

BLACK IRON PRISON – the overlay; the matrix; the continuum of ordinary awareness in which mortals exist until they awaken. Term coined by Philip K. Dick with regard to his own spiritual awakening, as discussed in the book, *In Pursuit of VALIS; the Exegesis of Philip K. Dick*.

BRUJO or **BRUJA** - a sorcerer. All men or women of Knowledge may be brujos, but not all brujos are men or women of Knowledge.

BURN WITH THE FIRE FROM WITHIN – Believed by some to be the manner in which a sorcerer, warrior or Nagual leaves this earth in order to join with the infinite. Many different interpretations have been offered, but in essence I see this more as a metaphor for transcending death with absolute awareness rather than any actual dis-corporation of the physical form. What leaves the earth is the totality of awareness, the totality of Self. All aspects of individual awareness are consumed by the Intent of the warrior, so no fragments are left behind. In this manner, the warrior leaves the earth as a Whole entity.

CASTANEDA, CARLOS – Author of several books regarding Toltec traditions, including *The Teachings of Don Juan,*. From my point of view, a word of gratitude is owed to Carlos for developing what amounts to a syntax and specialized language which had proven invaluable in my own journey.

CLARITY – a warrior who has learned to *see* and maintains the assemblage point at a perpetual point of seeing may be said to have achieved clarity. Clarity may also be defined as the ability to see the world as it is, without the influence of programs or illusion.

COHESION OF IDENTITY - a state of being in which the seeker has gained a sense of self-awareness beyond all programs - i.e., the seeker knows who he or she is apart from who they are related to, or what they do for a living. There is a sense of self, an ability to touch one's own consciousness and recognize it as a whole entity rather than merely fragments associated with different roles. It is our observation that there are levels of cohesion. When the seeker has achieved cohesion, it is then possible to inhabit the Whole self (the totality of oneself) into eternity as a singularity of consciousness.

CONSENSUAL REALITY or **CONSENSUS REALITY** or **CONSENSUAL CONTINUUM** – the world of ordinary awareness, defined and shaped by what is agreed-upon by the majority of the consensus. The Real World. The societies, cultures and definitions of "reality" we take for granted, and upon which we all agree as to what is "real" and what is fantasy, what is right and what is wrong. We are indoctrinated into the consensual reality from the moment we are born, primarily through language, and yet it can be proven through simple observation that much of this indoctrination is incorrect, that what is "right" to one culture is "wrong" to another, that what is "normal" to one consensus is abhorrent to another. We live, therefore, in a world of illusions, a world of words, even a world of lies.

CONTROLLED FOLLY – The seeker who *sees* acknowledges that we live in a world of delusions and illusions, yet survival often depends on our ability to interact with that world. Controlled folly is the art of playing the game AS IF it matters, knowing all the while that all things are transient.

DEATH AS ADVISOR - it is said that the warrior lives with death as her advisor. Knowing we are beings who are going to die and face the infinite, the warrior's decisions in life are guided by the awareness. Knowing I am a being who is going to die, are my actions in *this moment* impeccable?

DEPENDENCY or **HUMAN FORM DEPENDENCY** - A dependency is anything to which the energy of the warrior is hooked. One easy to visualize example is that someone who is uncomfortable being alone with themselves could be said to have a dependency on friends, or constant input from TV., music or some other form of stimulus. Other examples, used only to illustrate the point: a constant need for approval would represent a strong dependency. Inability to break addictions such as smoking, drinking, gambling, etc., are indicative of dependencies. Only by identifying the dependencies and breaking them does the warrior free up that energy to be used for other things. It could also be loosely understood that "will" and "dependency" are mutually exclusive. As long as powerful dependencies are in command of the warrior's energy, it is virtually impossible to summon the will, because the energy required to summon the will is in use by the dependency.

DIABLERO - a sorcerer, a man of Knowledge. In some texts, "diablero" or "diablera" refers to a witch-healer as well. All wo/men of Knowledge are diableros, but not all diableros are wo/men of Knowledge.

DON JUAN MATUS - the Yaqui Indian brujo who served as mentor to Carlos Castaneda.

DOUBLE – For practical purposes, the double is the self in eternity, but can be visualized as the "vessel" into which the warrior uploads his consciousness and identity through the process of living impeccably. All warriors can develop a double, though most remain unaware of the existence of the double. The double is the energy body, developed through Dreaming to a point of extreme cohesion. The double may take on a life of its own for all intents and purposes.

DOUBLE BEING -- also called "the **Nagual**". A type of human being who is simply born with two energy bodies where normally only one is present. There are countless theories, but my personal experience is that it is simply

254

an "attribute", such as being born with blonde hair or green eyes. One cannot "become" a nagual anymore than a person with AB blood can suddenly have O blood. It has been stated that the nagual man and the nagual woman are two separate individuals, yet there are naguals who would say that the nagual man and the nagual woman are literally two halves of the *same* being. At some point in their human life, the second energy body appears to "split", and leaves the world of ordinary awareness to exist in the seventh sense, third attention, or, simply, "beyond the veil". It is the drive to reunite with the other half of one's own self that so compels the one who remains in ordinary awareness to follow the path, to respond to the lure of the other half, which serves as a beacon to Freedom. Also, and of greatest importance, it is because the half that goes into Freedom is now a being of eternity (not constrained by time and space) that it becomes possible for that half to actually instruct the mortal warrior through a variety of methods, including meditation, dreaming, gnosis, and more.

DREAMING - in the sorcerer's world, "dreaming" is an entire art form which cannot be adequately explained in a few brief words. Essentially, it is an active application of intent which enables the sorcerer to dream lucidly and navigate the dreamscape in much the same way we navigate the terrain of our ordinary awareness. Through impeccable dreaming, the double is created, and through dreaming the sorcerer begins to explore shifts of the assemblage point which enable her to assemble other worlds. Through dreaming, it becomes possible to connect the worlds of heightened awareness with the world of ordinary awareness.

DREAMING AWAKE – a level of awareness wherein the warrior enters a state of dreaming while remaining technically in a state of first attention awareness. To those who have experienced it, no explanation is necessary. To those who have not, no explanation is possible.

DUALITY - Meaning, literally, "two things simultaneously". This is *not* the same thing as dualism, which implies perception through opposites (i.e., dualism is the human propensity for perceiving black/white, good/evil, god/devil, male/female, etc) Duality implies the evolving perception which enables us to see that past and future, just for example, are no different, but only different perceptions according to our location in time. Duality can be studied in the statement, "You must *be* immortal before you will know how to *become* immortal." As long as we are locked into a linear, static perception of reality, we are prisoners of dualism.

EAGLE – according to Toltec legend, the old seers perceived an indescribable force which devours awareness at the moment of death. Though there is no literal eagle, the force itself seemed to be immense and had the shape of an enormous black eagle.

EMBRACING THE TOTALITY OF ONESELF - In shamanic terms, self-integration, beginning with the actions of the warrior in ordinary awareness and first attention, and projecting ultimately into the seventh sense, third attention, infinity. Embracing the totality of oneself would involve, among other things, the final integration of the sorcerer with her double, i.e., the conjoining of the mortal consciousness to the immortal vessel (or energy body). It could be said that the double has already embraced the totality of itself, in that it exists outside of time, i.e., not limited to the linear concept of past, present and future, but instead a ubiquitous consciousness inhabiting all of space/time simultaneously and infinitely. The double is the Wholeness of the sorcerer, but the sorcerer only becomes whole if and when that Wholeness is embraced and integrated ultimately beyond this physical/mortal life. In other words, there is no predestination. The existence of the double does not guarantee success as a warrior. The double exists by the Intent of the sorcerer until the sorcerer actually embraces and conjoins with that double into infinity.

ETERNAL BEING - An evolved consciousness that has gathered its cohesion into Wholeness, and exists ubiquitously throughout the space-time continuum and beyond. The eternal being may project (manifest) an energy body which would be indistinguishable from a corporeal body if that were the Intent, or be entirely non-corporeal, strictly as a matter of Will. See also Immortality/Immortal.

FOLLY - "In a million years, it won't make any difference." Though we go through life thinking things matter, none of them really do. Literally everything we touch in the world of ordinary awareness is folly - and yet warriors play the game as if it matters, and learn the art of stalking as a means of developing controlled folly - actions performed with the awareness that they are folly, but performed nonetheless with impeccability.

FOREIGN INSTALLATION – The program. The consensus. The agreement. The "foreign installation" is comprised of the belief systems and programs that are put onto all human beings from before they are ever conceived. We believe certain things because we are conditioned to believe them – many of these beliefs being altogether false, but when assimilated as a whole, they form what might be seen as, simply "society and culture". The foreign installation is responsible for the roles we play ("a good father should behave in such and such a manner," ... or "it is the highest honor to live your life in service to others.") Think about the things you believe, and ask yourself why you believe them. Are they true, or are you living a lie in the life of the foreign installation, doing the bidding of the hive consensus as opposed to exploring who and what you are beyond all the programming? The most important thing to know about the foreign installation is that it is US – it is upheld by the collective *agreement*. For as long as a human being exists without *awareness* of that fact, s/he is little more than an organic machine, a prisoner of beliefs that have nothing to do with reality – and, in fact, prevent her from even knowing there is a larger reality outside the agreement.

GNOSIS – an altered state of consciousness accessible through a wide variety of methods, including but not limited to simple Intent, meditation, certain mind-altering substances such as psilocybin mushrooms, tantric sex, the near-death-experience (or NDE), sensory deprivation, and many, many other methods. To me, gnosis is the most crucial tool available to the seeker, for it is through gnosis that – quite literally – the entire knowledge of the entire universe is available if one knows how to listen. What matters is that when the universe speaks, we not only listen, but apply our full Intent to the task of discovering the meaning behind the words.

HEIGHTENED AWARENESS - a state of increased perception, wherein the warrior can seemingly learn and assimilate far more rapidly and deeply than from within ordinary awareness. One of the tasks of the warrior is to "remember the other self", which consists in part of bringing into ordinary awareness the events she has experienced in this altered state of consciousness. From experience, it seems that we simply do not possess the preceptor organs of memory for events that occurred in heightened awareness, just as we cannot see the subatomic world with the naked eye. Special tools are required – in this case, the tools of perception.

HOOK WITH THE WILL – an ability of a master sorcerer or Nagual to essentially compel warriors into undertaking the journey – because any sane being who knew what they were getting into would run like hell. For that reason, it is not uncommon in Toltec practices for the nagual man or woman to intentionally hook apprentices with the energy of their own highly developed will.

IMMORTAL BEING or **IMMORTAL** - The terms "immortal" and "eternal being" are used somewhat interchangeably unless specifically noted otherwise, though by strict definition there is considerable difference. When we say "the quest for immortality begins here", it could perhaps be more accurately stated as "the quest for eternity beings here". On the evolutionary scale, it could be surmised that an eternal being has fewer limitations than an immortal still attached to organic form. Picture this: if a comet smashes the earth and the planet is reduced to rubble, the eternal being has the option of simply manifesting elsewhere, becoming entirely formless, or assembling other worlds. The physical immortal, on the other hand, might not have as many options, depending on the level of evolution of consciousness. It is speculated that there are physical immortals living among us.

INDIVIDUATION – The manifestation of the Self as a singularity of consciousness. Many paths teach unity within the all as a goal of the afterlife, whereas Individuation is the act of maintaining the unique and

257

individual I-Am throughout eternity.

INTENT – Intent (or "**unbending intent**") could be loosely defined as an idea or thought-form held constantly in the quantum shaman's mind until it becomes a literal part of the shaman himself. For example, it is my intent to achieve an evolution of consciousness that will enable me to exist as a cohesive, sentient being with a single point of view continuing into eternity. The strength of that unbending intent determines the manner in which the shaman lives, which paths are taken. Intent is more than good intentions. Intent is desire in action, and works in direct cooperation with Spirit. Intent is the mother of all creation.

INTERNAL DIALOG – the automatic chatter that goes on in the human mind which is, essentially, how we keep our world intact. Internal dialog is everything from the lists we create to tell ourselves that a tree is a tree and a dog a mammal, to the inventories we run upon awakening each morning. Internal dialog, in short, is the language of the program, and one of the prerequisites to any serious spiritual journey is learning to stop that automatic self-programming so that we can hear the silence and access the deeper levels of the mind itself, including the state of silent knowing (gnosis).

KNOWLEDGE - as used throughout these documents, Knowledge shall refer to the result of direct personal experience. Example: we are taught as children that fire will burn, but until we touch a candle flame to see for ourselves, we cannot know for sure. The Quantum Shaman seeks Knowledge, never settling for faith or belief systems. The greatest Knowledge comes through gnosis.

McKENNA, TERENCE – one of the greatest forward-thinkers of this century or any other, Terrence McKenna experimented extensively with mind-altering substances and produced some of the most visionary insights into possibilities for human evolution as anyone ever has. Sadly, Terrence died in 2000, and will be greatly missed. Must-reads by Terrence include *Archaic Revival* and *True Hallucinations*.

MAGICK or **MAGIC** – as used throughout these documents, "magick" or "magic" is the force within the human organism which enables us to do, perceive and interact with things for which science has no immediate explanation. It is the force which enables a 110 pound woman to lift a 5,000 pound truck off her child in a crisis. It is the force that we recognize as "the little voice" that tells a man not to get onboard a doomed airliner. It is the ghost inside the machine, and it is altogether human. One day, science will explain "magick", and yet magick will never be fully understood, for as we grow and evolve, our "magick" grows and evolves with us – like the muse, always one step ahead so we will always be compelled to follow. Also, as used throughout these documents, magick or magic is not defined by adherence to ritual or religion. Magick is the force being *sought* through certain rituals, but magick itself is most definitely *not* ritual or religion any more than "the soul" can be found in "the church". At best, one is only a tool used in searching for the other.

MEDICINE WITCH – Sorcerer, shaman, healer, quantum teacher.

MEDITATION-WITH-INTENT - an active form of meditation as opposed to the passive silence. Meditation with intent might also be described as gnosis - the ability of the human mind to ask a question of the non-local web of all information. But more than just asking the question, meditation-with-intent enables the seeker to actually emerge with answers based in higher truth because meditation-with-intent develops the ability to listen and interact with the double. It will not happen the first time the seeker tries it, for it is a technique of learning to focus neither inward nor outward, but "non-locally" throughout space/time, in the realm of reality where past, present and future are all precisely the same, and where all information as to events, probabilities and outcomes is already stored holographically. Meditation-with-intent is tapping in to that limitless library. See also gnosis.

METANOIA – A transformative change of mind. Example: anyone can be a musician, but the truly great musicians are seized by a metanoia that makes them one with the music. In the spiritual sense, metanoia occurs when the student becomes infused with an understanding s/he did not possess previously, and which was not arrived at through linear means. Put simply: metanoia of spirit is the attainment of enlightenment.

MINDSET - a state of awareness from which we naturally assemble our idea of reality. For example, our most common mindset tells us what is possible, what is impossible, what is "real" and what is "unreal". In our waking awareness, for example, we automatically "know" we cannot fly, whereas in our dreaming mindset, we often discover that we can do many things which are "impossible" in the mindset of ordinary awareness . By changing our mindset about the parameters of reality, we can often change the limitations that prevent us from expanding and growing as individuals and as a species.

NAGUAL (pronounced "nah*wahl") - Nagual is a word with many meanings. 1) The unknowable which lies outside of human perception. The nagual is not the unknown, but the unknowable, all that cannot be discussed in any direct language, but which nonetheless exists as real. 2) The "nagual" may also refer to the leader of the warrior's party - a sorcerer, a brujo, a "man of knowledge" who is, by nature, a double being. See also **double being**.

NON-LOCAL -refers to the concept that information, consciousness and even certain types of beings may be described as ubiquitous - i.e., existing simultaneously in all places and all times. Non-local also refers to the concept that the universe - and especially consciousness itself - is a holographic construction.

NON-ORDINARY AWARENESS - altered states of consciousness such as dreaming, trance states, deep meditation, gnosis, visionary states.

ORDINARY AWARENESS - The state of consciousness which results simply by being alive and walking through life. It is in ordinary awareness that we enact our human programming. Ordinary awareness is also known as the lowest common denominator of being human. It is where and how we assemble the world and our expectations about it and ourselves.

OVERLAY - (see also **consensual reality**). Essentially, the overlay is the "play" of which we are all a part. It is the lives we live and the things we do which we mistake for "real", but which are only extensions of the human-default program. If we could see the world with the innocence of a newborn child or an alien being who knows nothing of the human paradigm, we would see the world as it really is -- without all the automatic things we say, think and do because it is intrinsically programmed into us.

PHANTOM - individuals still plugged into the belief systems of the consensual reality, usually without ever questioning. Phantoms define themselves by what they do, the company they keep, the church they attend, their social status. Another mark of a phantom is that they possess an unlimited number of personalities and roles, all without the cohesion of a single, unified "*I-Am*".

PLACE OF SILENT KNOWING, THE – A "space" or openness inside the warrior where one can hear the voice of gnosis, the teacher who is often the double.

POWER SPOT - a physical location which brings an individual into balance with the earth, the non-local web of all information, and with herself. A location which enables us to focus or meditate, where we are in our most impeccable balance.

PREDATOR MIND – If it can be perceived that the consensual reality possesses a rudimentary "hive mind", it then becomes possible to *see* that this hive mind is predatory in nature, in that it invades and usurps the individual unless the individual has mastered extreme awareness. IOW, we may be "taken over" by the consensual hive, whose primary agenda is to preserve its static, status quo. Other – more extreme – definitions have been offered for the predatory mind, and may in fact, have truth as well. (see also *foreign installation*)

PROGRAM - The information which we accept as truth without necessarily confirming or disproving it for ourselves as individuals. For example, we are taught, "All things die," and because this would appear to be true, most people simply accept the statement as fact rather than doing their own quest for Knowledge into the veracity or falseness of the statement itself. In reality, we cannot know for certain that "all things die." We can only know what our perceptions reveal to us within our immediate environment. By altering our perceptions - thereby altering our automatic expectations (the program) - we learn to see that much of what we think we "know" about the world is only what we "believe". The danger of all programs is that as long as they are accepted blindly as fact, they prevent us from exploring other possibilities. If, for example, the Wright Brothers had accepted the program-du-jour which stated, "Man is not meant to fly," we would live in a vastly different world.

QUANTUM SHAMAN - a term first used by Orlando to describe one who stops at nothing in order to pursue and eventually embrace the Knowledge and abilities which will enable her to achieve a continuity of consciousness wherein we become cohesive, sentient beings with a single point of view continuing into eternity – a singularity of consciousness. The quantum shaman gathers insights, knowledge and techniques from every walk of life, from the sorcery of don Juan to the quantum experiments taking place on the cutting edge of modern science, from legends of ancient alchemy to shamanic herbalism. It is when the individual truths gleaned from these multitudinous sources assimilate to create a comprehensive "map" that we begin to understand the path toward our evolution. It is then that we are enabled through our own efforts to take control of our own destiny. This is the path of the quantum shaman.

RECAPITULATION - the process of essentially re-living through intent events in the warrior's past which have left energy hooks in the spirit. The process is described at length in the books of Castaneda; but in a nutshell, recapitulation involves disentangling those energy hooks, removing the "importance" placed on events in the past, so that warrior is freed from those hooks and as a result, enabled to go forward on his path. It is said that recapitulation frees energy trapped in the past.

REMEMBERING THE OTHER SELF – Refers not only to remembering events which may have occurred in heightened awareness, but also involves a process of beginning to "remember" the experiences of the double. It is through remembering that a cohesion of self is achieved which enables the warrior to transcend beyond the eagle and emerge as a singularity of consciousness.

RETROACTIVE ENCHANTMENT – term borrowed from Peter J. Carroll. As understood by the author, an act of sorcery in the now which may appear to have effects reaching backward in time.

RIGHT WAY TO LIVE – an intuitive awareness having nothing to do with social morality or cultural predilections. The warrior is guided by the right way to live through an intrinsic harmony with the earth, which is communicated through the inner voice of gnosis. Within every human being is the inborn knowledge that tells us right from wrong – not in any social or cultural sense, but with regard to living impeccably. Intuitively, we know that killing another human being is not "the right way to live," for example.

RULE OF THE NAGUAL – an unwritten "map" which reveals to the nagual man and woman specific truths about the path. The "rule" reveals the truth about the eagle in specific – that awareness is lost at death unless the warrior has taken measures to circumvent that inevitability. The map, therefore, speaks to *how* that inevitability may be thwarted through developing cohesion. It has been my experience that the rule itself is the same for most Naguals, but how it manifests may be very different. For example, not all Naguals form strict "warrior parties," yet they nonetheless end up guiding others to freedom in other ways. In my own life, the rule of the nagual showed me the necessity to write this book – largely for my own assimilation, and also to serve as a guide for those who find it beneficial.

SCRY or **SCRYING** - any method of divination, or, more accurately, *seeing* or gathering information or knowledge. Traditionally, to scry (or scrye) was to gaze into a crystal ball, pool of water, or other reflective object. Scrying can also refer to palm reading (as in "scrying the palm of the gods"), gnosis , or any other method of accessing knowledge and information traditionally thought to be beyond the realm of human awareness.

SECOND ATTENTION - loosely defined, second attention is the assemblage point of heightened awareness or Dreaming. It is the world the sorcerer may manifest through Intent - such as in lucid dreaming.

SEE or *SEEING* - when used in italics, "see" or "seeing" is to describe the act of viewing the world (or anything within the world) according to its true nature, without the illusions and expectations we place onto the world through our own human programs. *Seeing* is more than looking. It is the shaman's greatest asset and tool in being able to recognize the illusory nature of the consensual reality (overlay) in which we all exist, often without ever realizing it.

SELF-IMPORTANCE - Perhaps best summed up by Don Miguel Ruiz in *The Four Agreements*, under the heading, "Take nothing personally". It is self-importance that causes us to think that everything that is said or done is somehow personal to us as individuals. To get angry at the schmuck who cuts you off in traffic is self-importance. It's about *him*, not about you. The common misconception is that self-importance is arrogance, or egomaniacal behavior, and while that could be true to an extent, self-importance is more accurately an underlying defensiveness that prevents the warrior from embracing clarity and power because she is so busy defending herself, when there is nothing to defend in the first place. *It. Ain't. Personal.*

262

SEVENTH SENSE – a perceptual plateau comprised of a combination of the 5 ordinary senses plus the "sixth sense" of psychic awareness or, more precisely, self-awareness. Orlando coined the term "the seventh sense" to describe the "world" we are aspiring to inhabit through this evolution of consciousness – for it is a state of being every bit as real and inhabitable as our world of ordinary awareness, but accessed with a more evolved set of preceptors which could be described as consciousness itself. Some have used the term "third attention", which is somewhat interchangeable. The seventh sense is our world, but it is an expanded world

SINGULARITY OF CONSCIOUSNESS – The self made Whole, the evolution of consciousness which results in a cohesive field of awareness existing ubiquitously and non-locally, infinitely and eternally. The cohesive, fully integrated *I-Am* consisting of all components of the mortal self and the eternal double, brought together under a single assemblage point.

SORCERER – A man or woman of Knowledge; brujo or bruja. All men of knowledge may be sorcerers, but not all sorcerers are men of knowledge.

SORCERER'S WORLD - perhaps a better explanation would be "sorcerer's mindset". The sorcerer's world is the world of perception and ability available to the quantum shaman through the evolution of consciousness. Not a different world, it is *this* world, but without the limitations placed on it through our intrinsic programs and adherence to the consensual reality.

SORCERY - a system of Knowledge geared toward a direct manipulation of energy at the quantum level. Sorcery is not about frivolous parlor tricks, but is instead geared toward bringing the sorcerer into alignment with the higher self (or double) as an eternal being. The sorcerer's ultimate "trick" is to transcend death (slip past the eagle) not only retaining the awareness from this mortal life, but conjoining with the higher self so as to "**embrace the totality of oneself**" - in other words, a complete and seamless identity stretching infinitely into past and future, with the understanding that eternity is both and neither.

SPIRIT – If earth, air, fire and water are the 4 natural elements, Spirit is the 5th element of creation. The living force or anima of the universe – impersonal, not a deity or entity; the living breath of power; the cohesive element of the all.

SPONTANEOUS PARTHENOGENESIS – the act of something coming into existence out of the nothing, with no apparent cause. It is theorized by the author that the universe created itself from the void through an act of spontaneous parthenogenesis – a thought which wills itself into existence by saying I-Am.

STALKING or SELF-STALKING – the art of managing our human folly. By having a constant and keen awareness of our actions – including thoughts, beliefs and the machinations of our inner dialog – the seeker begins to throw off the chains of The Program and embrace the foundation of the authentic self.

SUPER-POSITION OF THE ASSEMBLAGE POINT – A point of awareness wherein the seeker and the Other (double) have conjoined to embrace the Totality of awareness. At this point, consciousness becomes ubiquitous, inhabiting all quantum positions simultaneously, thereby allowing for consciousness to take on certain qualities of light, at least metaphorically. Particle and wave – particle being what might be experienced should consciousness make the decision to "localize" into a specific point in time and space; wave being the non-local presentation of awareness, wherein it is a ubiquitous field spanning all of space/time simultaneously.

TALES OF POWER - sorcery stories, usually incredible and often unbelievable by their very nature. To the ordinary man, these tales would automatically be deemed to be fiction, lies, or delusions. Only to fellow sorcerers are they descriptions of acts of power, describing very real events.

TENANT, THE – a being referenced in the books of Carlos Castaneda, seemingly a self-created immortal in corporeal manifestation. Also called "the death defier" because s/he has seemingly lived hundreds of years.

TEFLON WARRIOR – Referring to the practice of recapitulation. Many (most) believe that recapitulation involves lengthy processes of reliving past experiences as a means to recapture energy still stuck in the past. That's the abridged version. If you want to know more about recapitulation, try Googling "Carlos Castaneda and recapitulation". I myself am an advocate of becoming a teflon warrior – an advanced technique which encourages detachment in the Now, so that one's energy doesn't become fixated on transient events. Note: ALL events are transient. Shit don't stick to a teflon warrior. It's that simple.

THIRD ATTENTION – the state of freedom beyond the eagle, when the warrior has achieved the state of Wholeness. The state of the ubiquitous, non-local singularity of awareness.

TONAL – the world of matter and men. Anything that can be discussed or known is within the tonal. The nagual is the unknowable, by contrast.

TRANSCENDENCE - wherein the seeker sheds his/her body through the process known as Death. In theory, those who transcend become pure energy, existing at a level of consciousness/awareness without any physical form whatsoever. Some consider this the highest form of transformation, others (myself included) consider it a midrange accomplishment.

TRANSFORMATION – In some instances, spiritual evolution may be achieved through the process of transformation, essentially having the full awareness of the Other inside one's physical body. While this is a possibility, this author believes that the sheer amount of data contained in the quantum nature of the Other would be sufficient to "overwhelm" the biological components and perhaps result in a form of alternating genius and madness.

TRANSMOGRIFICATION – The process whereby an individual may depart the physical body and inhabit the Other, without the actuality of dying. While considered theoretical, it is believed that many beings throughout history have transmogrified. The most common myth is that of Jesus. Another would be the vampire Lestat. Transmogrification is the migration of awareness from a physical/organic body into a state of pure energy – i.e., the awakening of awareness inside the Other. Transmogrification is the art of transcendence and transformation combined - in that one's awareness is no longer attached to corporeal form, but a *seemingly* corporeal body CAN be projected and inhabited.

TULPA – the seemingly physical manifestation of a thoughtform, usually transient and without individual volition. It is believed by some (including the author) that these thoughtforms *can* become sentient and take on a life of their own if nurtured. When that occurs, it might be observed that the tulpa has become the precursor/paradigm of one's double or Other.

TWO PART MIGRATION OF THE SOUL – the process wherein the mortal self creates the double through dreaming, at which point the double begins teaching the mortal self the path of evolution of consciousness. The mortal self *appears* to create the double first, and so the double exists as an eternal being, a construct of will and intent. That "immortal" then teaches the mortal self *how* to evolve, so that when the process is complete, the mortal self reconjoins with the immortal double beyond the eagle's reach.

WARRIOR – a seeker of knowledge who has made the commitment to the path of her heart. The warrior is the traveler on the journey toward becoming a woman of Knowledge.

WHOLE SELF – The integrated totality of the mortal self and the eternal double as it comes together in a single assemblage point of cohesion beyond the eagle. From the AP of the Whole Self, all memory of all fragments of the Self come into alignment. See also – **singularity of consciousness.**

WILL - Will is the force which manifests want or need into reality. Will differs from intent. A simple analogy: intent is a true and genuine plan to visit the Grand Canyon. Will is the force that puts you behind the wheel of the car and drives. Will could also be described as the force which causes the intent behind our magic to actually begin to manifest. It is the secret ingredient of sorcery, elusive as the wind and just as impossible to define.

About the Author...

Della Van Hise is a native of Florida, transplanted to California at the age of 21, who has subsequently sunk her roots into the high desert near Joshua Tree National Park. She has not personally seen any aliens since around 1992, but there is rumored to be a secret UFO base underneath her house.

Della's writing started around age 11, on an old Smith Corona typewriter. No, not an electric one. A real antique, made of metal and heavier than a wet coffin. Her first professional novel was *Killing Time* - the controversial *Star Trek* book which was recalled and re-edited in 1984. None of the rumors were true, of course. It was just a *Star Trek* book - a good enough work that the "reboot" movie borrowed heavily from the plot and structure. No kidding.

Della has written extensively in the non-fiction genre, with titles such *as Quantum Shaman: Diary of a Nagual Woman* and *Scrawls On the Walls of the Soul. Quantum Shaman* focuses heavily on the author's metaphysical explorations and experiences, while *Scrawls* is a continuation of those journeys many years later. If you enjoyed the works of Carlos Castaneda or Don Miguel Ruiz, you'll enjoy the non-fiction works of Della Van Hise.

In addition, Della has written professionally for *Tomorrow Magazine* and other prominent science fiction publications. Her fiction works include *Sons of Neverland* (an award-winning vampire novel); *Coyote* (a young adult thriller); and many other novels, short stories & poetry collections.

All of the titles mentioned here are available through Amazon, or through Eye Scry Publications.

www.EyeScryPublications.com
www.QuantumShaman.com

QUANTUM SHAMAN

DELLA VAN HISE

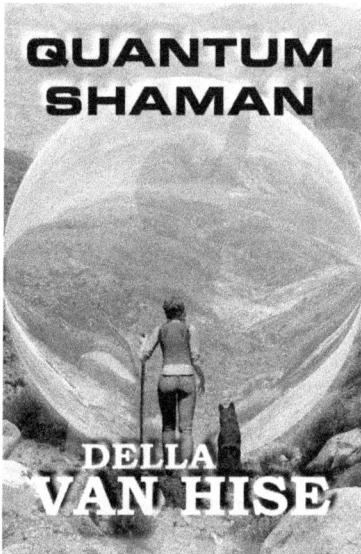

Quantum Shaman: Diary of a Nagual Woman
Della Van Hise

"Diary of a Nagual Woman brings a quantum understanding to what has traditionally been believed to be a mystical path alone. This book picks up where Carlos Castaneda left off to take us on a roller coaster ride of our own forgotten power..."

- Michael Grove, Reviewer

When I asked how Orlando had known I would come to this remote location, and how he himself had gotten there – since there were no other cars in the tiny parking lot – he only smiled a little, stretched out his long legs, and slouched down on that cold metal bench to stare up at the stars.

"You're predictable," he said as if I should have already known. "I'm here because this is where you come when you're mad at the world."

I attempted to engage him in a conversation of just exactly how he knew I was mad at the world, since I'd had no direct contact with him in quite some time, nothing to give him any hint of what was going on in my everyday life. But even as I began spelling all of that out to him, he brushed my words aside with an easy gesture.

"Do you want to talk or do you want to waste time looking for logical explanations for every magical thing that ever happens?" he asked. "That's what's wrong with the world, you know. Instead of embracing the mysteries and trying to determine how they might open a crack in an otherwise humdrum, pre-programmed existence, people waste their entire lives explaining it all away, attaching labels to it, filing and categorizing it until it loses any meaning."

He had a point. And I'd already been inundated with enough mysteries to know that some things simply had no explanation humans could understand. *'Magic is only science not yet understood'*. Words Orlando had written more than a year before rattled through my mind up there in the middle of the night, in the middle of nowhere, looking down on a distant world that seemed far more unreal to me at that moment than the world he had been trying to teach me to *see*.

He was there – whether physically or in some spirit-form is ultimately of no importance, for in the sorcerer's world there is no difference between body and spirit, and in any world, perception is reality.

www.quantumshaman.com
www.eyescrypublications.com

267

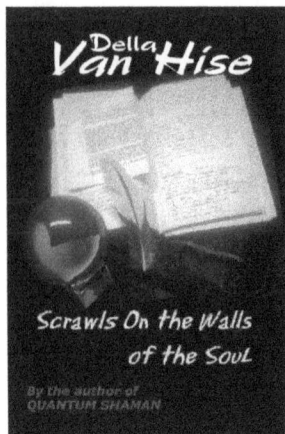

Scrawls on the Walls of the Soul
Della Van Hise

The long-awaited follow-up to
Quantum Shaman: Diary of a Nagual Woman.
Stands alone, or order together!

"If you've ever felt like a stranger in a strange land, this book is your road map to survival in the spiritual wilderness!" (Michael Grove)

~

It was May of 2000 when my mentor threw me out of the quantum cosmic classroom and said, "I've taught you everything I can. Now it's time to take that knowledge and slam it up against the walls of the real world. If it remains intact and survives the brutality to which it will be subjected, you will get a gold star next to your name and be allowed to proceed to the next level." No mention was made of what this next level might be, or if, indeed, it truly existed.

Go ahead – try to explain this all-consuming path to your friends and relatives. They will smile politely, squirm uncomfortably, and eventually they will stop returning your phone calls and look the other way when they see you coming. And who can blame them? They live in the real world with their office jobs and nuclear families and a host of mindless sitcoms waiting on the propaganda box at the end of their busy day. In direct contrast, it could be observed that anyone who has dedicated themselves to the pursuit of forbidden knowledge really doesn't live in that world at all. Not for lack of wanting, perhaps, but because the real world is quickly seen to be little more than a series of programs and illusions – not unlike The Matrix. And not surprisingly, the people who populate that world may begin to take on a peculiar zombie-like quality.

You find yourself alone in a world of jesters, jokers and jackasses. Now what?

FROM THE AUTHOR
www.quantumshaman.com

ON AMAZON
http://www.amazon.com/Scrawls-Walls-Soul-Della-Hise-ebook/dp/B008CUKH6C/

Della Van Hise

The Effect of Moonlight on Tombstones

(A Dark Little Collection of Poetry Gleaned From the Gnosis of Vampires and Songs of the Muse)

Moments Frozen In Time

Poetry has never been something I consciously set out to write. Instead, it is something that comes or not, entirely at the whim of whatever it is that writers call "the muse." Over the years, I have come to think of my own poetry as a form of shorthand - an attempt to capture a moment frozen in time. A wayward leaf caught in mid-fall. A glimpse of a shadow cast by nothing at all. The effect of moonlight on tombstones.

Though I write primarily novels and nonfiction, I do find myself pleasantly haunted by what my mentor once referred to as "the gnosis of shadows." As another friend once said, "Poetry is the streaming download from the broken heart of the universe."

The poems in this anthology represent approximately two decades of those streaming downloads, most of which were scribbled hastily and in bad penmanship into cloth journals. If I have been at all successful in capturing some of those moments frozen in time, perhaps a line or two will resonate with you, hopefully bringing a smile to your face or a chill to your spine.

Candles keep journals
of time's passing
in empty books of matches.

The cemetery lies empty,
pallid headstones only coloring books
for the idle hands of time.

ON AMAZON
http://www.amazon.com/Della-Van-Hise/e/B003ZOK75G/ref=dp_byline_cont_book_1

FROM THE AUTHOR
http://www.eyescrypublications.com/html/moonlight_tombstones.htm

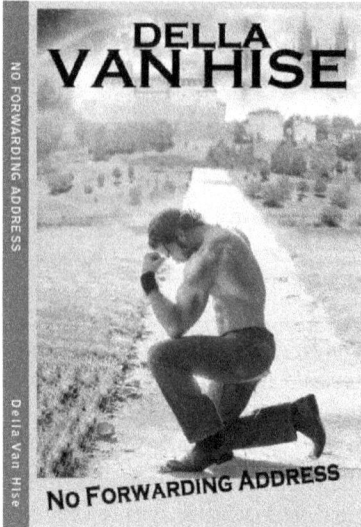

When Terrans came to sail dark seas,
And see what stars might be...
Heaven moved with no forwarding address,
And left this void to me.
(Children's song from Lazali)

───────────

A literary science fiction novel told in the voice of an empath, *No Forwarding Address* explores the lures and the dangers of love, the tragedies and triumphs stirring in the human heart.

When Crystal and Raine first meet, it is 50 years after The Great War on Earth. They are hesitant to trust, afraid to love. But even if they are able to overcome these seemingly insurmountable obstacles, is even love enough?

When a man has the stars in his eyes, legend says he must serve them above all others.

───────────

I knew then that it wasn't love and hate who were mirror twins. The final irony was that <u>*grief*</u> *would always turn out to be the paradoxical antithesis and simultaneous manifestation of whatever it is that humans call love.*

Crystal remained silent and walked a few steps away from Raine – further down the shoreline, until she stood under the wing of one fallen Phantom. She thought of the ship she had seen from the balcony of our home, and though it had long since disappeared over the dark and treacherous abyss of the ocean, its image lingered clearly in her thoughts. On that ship was a man, she thought. A terribly lonely man who made no great difference to the flow of time or the memory of the galaxy. A man who, like Raine, was compelled to keep moving and look only ahead and never behind. A man who could not afford the luxury of waving goodbye to friends on shore.

At last, she turned toward her beloved and watched him watching the darkness. He stood only a few feet away, yet the images in my mind said he might as well have been a million light years off in the void. He was lost to her in that instant out-of-time, just as lost and impossible to find as the light from that ship which had vanished over the horizon...

www.eyescrypublications.com
http://www.amazon.com/Forwarding-Address-Della-Van-Hise-ebook/dp/B00PEOSKJ0/

COYOTE
Della Van Hise

A Novel of Love, Honor and Personal Sacrifice...

When River Willows is accused of a murder she didn't commit, her life takes a turn toward the sanctuary of a world existing at right-angles to our own. Combining the mysticism of martial arts and the romantic conflict of a young woman torn between two powerful men, COYOTE takes the reader on an epic journey of dangerous secrets, military cover-ups, and the infinite heart of the peaceful warrior.

_____

"So who's Coyote?" I asked, trying to ignore the effect he was having on me. "You?"

Steale laughed easily, though it did little to hide the torment behind that mask of indifference he wore so well.

"Coyote's a scavenger, Jack of all trades. The Native Americans call him the trickster - the one who brought chaos down on the world." He shrugged as if altogether unconcerned. "Original sin."

"Is that what you are?" I asked, keeping it light despite the growing knot my stomach. "Original sin?"

He kept his profile to me, eyes straight ahead as he drove. "Sure you want to know?"

I couldn't help wondering if I had cornered the coyote, or if the clever trickster had cornered me.

_____

By the author of **KILLING TIME** – without a doubt the most controversial **STAR TREK** novel ever published!

From the author
www.eyescrypublications.com

On Amazon
http://www.amazon.com/Coyote-Della-Van-Hise/dp/0976689782/

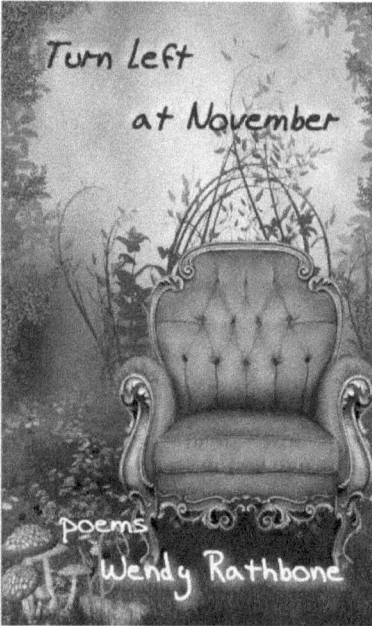

Turn Left at November
Wendy Rathbone

Visit realms of diamond rain, dust-folk lands and valleys of curses and shame. Reside in the burning moonships of dream, the silt of stars, the asphyxiation of the waking day. Meet the golden android who houses your soul. Journey through tatters of stardust down roads of sorrow. Find hope in planets of candles and crazy-eyed mermen. There you will meet November in these rich and evocative poems by Wendy Rathbone.

Unmaking Autumn
Out at the excavation site
where they are taking apart autumn
leaf by fabled leaf
the searchlights try to catch us
putting the eyes back into the pumpkins
the moon back in the witch-shaped sky
We steal blood kisses
behind the naked apple orchards

Winter's Shelf
hidden pathways to the moon
the north's blue breath
star-rise
amethyst dusks
winter wind bottled
and sold here

ON AMAZON
http://www.amazon.com/Turn-Left-at-November-Poems/dp/1942415087/ref=asap_bc?ie=UTF8
FROM THE AUTHOR
http://www.eyescrypublications.com/html/november.htm

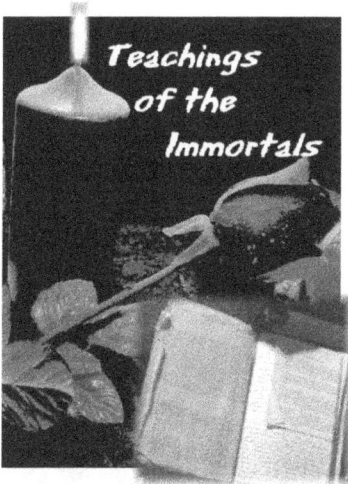

TEACHINGS OF THE IMMORTALS
Mikal Nyght

So... You Want To Live Forever?

The teachings are presented as brief vignettes in no particular order of importance. This is not a book you read from start to finish in a single night. It is a grimoire of self-creation, intended to be contemplated slowly so as to be assimilated wholly. Pick it up and turn to a page at random. Where your eyes come to rest on the page is your lesson for the day.

The teachings are seduction as much as instruction. This is the Way of The Dark Evolution.

The Ruby Slippers

The danger of the consensual continuum is that its natural gravity exists at the lowest common denominator of human experience, and because of this it will automatically make you forget those elusive truths you've fought to learn, and before you know it you're lost in petty dramas again, sinking into the mire of old familiar scripts.

The only way to overcome this is to be continually cavorting with worlds and events beyond human experience, journeying into the unknown so that it can become known, expanding knowledge and awareness to become more than you were, bringing back from the Dreaming those secrets which will teach you how to use the ruby slippers to transport yourself over the rainbow to the vampyre wizard's secret lair.

Perception

This is the nature of reality: to be precisely what perception dictates, as solid and whole as your interpretation of it, or as changeable and eternal as you permit it to be.

It wasn't knowledge god tried to keep from Man, you see. It was perception, for perception alone has the power to destroy god and obliterate comfortable consensual realities to create unending immortality.

Take the apple, my embryonic children. Nibble its red red flesh. Open your vampyre eyes so you may finally begin to See.

www.immortalis-animus.com

273

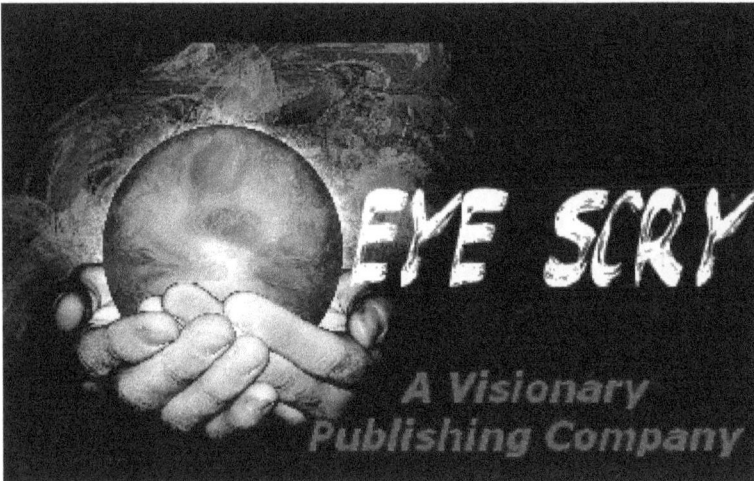

Eye Scry Publications
A Visionary Publishing Company
www.eyescrypublications.com

www.ingramcontent.com/pod-product-compliance
Lightning Source LLC
LaVergne TN
LVHW041331080426
835512LV00006B/401